The Enlightened CEO:

How to Succeed at the Toughest Job in Business

Bob Fifer
&
Gordon Quick

The Enlightened CEO - *How to Succeed at the Toughest Job in Business*

Copyright © 2007 by Robert Fifer and Gordon Quick

All rights reserved. No part of this book may be used or reproduced in any manner whatsoever without written permission from the authors, except for the inclusion of brief quotations embodied in critical articles and review. Although every precaution has been taken in the preparation of this book, the publisher and authors assume no responsibility for errors or omissions. Neither is any liability assumed for damages resulting from the use of information contained herein.

For information, address Franklin Hall Publishing at:
123 River Park Lane
Great Falls, VA 22066

THE ENLIGHTENED CEO is a registered trademark of Franklin Hall Publishing.

Printed in the United States of America.
First Edition

Library of Congress Cataloging-in-Publication Data
Fifer, Robert and Quick, Gordon.
The Enlightened CEO: How To Succeed at the Toughest Job in Business -- 1st ed.
p. cm.
Includes index

ISBN 978-1-934380-10-9

Cover design and internal artwork by Troy Bishop.

To Mom and Dad,

Nancy,

Danny, Becky, Jonathan and Amy

---

*To Jeanelle —
who has been my inspiration,*

&

*To My Late Parents —
who provided me with a world of opportunity*

Contents

Preface i

Part I: The Toughest Job in Business

Chapter 1
The Limits of Power 3

Chapter 2
Difficult, But Not Complex 7

Chapter 3
One-Dimensional Prescriptions are Not Enough 11

Part II: A Framework for Leadership

Chapter 4
Systematic vs. On-the-Fly Leadership 17

Chapter 5
The Complete CEO 19

Chapter 6
Enlightenment as the Core 23

Part III: Enlightenment

Chapter 7
The Nature of Enlightenment 29

Chapter 8
Self-Awareness: Strengths and Weaknesses, Likes and Dislikes 33

Chapter 9
Self-Awareness: Needs and Aspirations 37

Chapter 10
The Journey Toward Self-Awareness 43

Chapter 11
Principles of Purpose 47

Chapter 12
It's Not About You 49

Chapter 13
5 out of 6 Won't Work 53

Chapter 14
Principles of Thought 57

Chapter 15
Openness 59

Chapter 16
The Quest for Understanding 63

Chapter 17
Objectivity 67

Chapter 18
Principles of Conduct 71

Chapter 19
Calm 75

Chapter 20
Humility 81

Chapter 21
Equity 87

Chapter 22
Your Power as CEO 93

PART IV: CREATING THE INSPIRATION

Chapter 23
A Unifying Purpose 99

Chapter 24
The Problem with Vision Statements 103

Chapter 25
Why We are Unique 105

Chapter 26
How High? 109

Chapter 27
The Role of Rewards 113

Chapter 28
Spreading the Gospel 117

Chapter 29
Refining the Inspiration 121

PART V: CHARTING THE COURSE

Chapter 30
Why You Need a Strategy 129

Chapter 31
True Competitive Advantage 135

Chapter 32
The Path to Profitability 147

Chapter 33
Strategy Up and Down the Organization 151

Chapter 34
Strategic Growth 161

Chapter 35
A Living Strategy 169

PART VI: SHAPING THE TEAM

Chapter 36
Making the Investment 177

Chapter 37
What is a Team? 183

Chapter 38
The Enlightened Team 189

Chapter 39
Openness, Candor and Respect 193

Chapter 40
Selecting the Players 201

Chapter 41
Making Decisions 209

Chapter 42
Managing for Excellence 215

Chapter 43
Creating the Spark 223

PART VII: TRANSLATING INTO ACTION

Chapter 44
Your Fourth Role 229

Chapter 45
From Strategy to Operations 239

Chapter 46
Focus and Clarity 247

Chapter 47
Giving Them What it Takes 253

Chapter 48
You're Almost Home 259

Part VIII: Following Through

Chapter 49
Getting Results 263

Chapter 50
Monitoring Progress 269

Chapter 51
Staying on Course 277

Part IX: Communicating

Chapter 52
Squandering the Opportunity 285

Chapter 53
The Rewards of Communication 291

Chapter 54
Enlightened Communication 297

Chapter 55
Leveraging Your Board 303

Chapter 56
Swimming with the Tide 309

Part X: Your Future as CEO

Chapter 57
Your Power ... Over You 315

Acknowledgements 321

Preface

It has been fourteen years since I published my most recent book, entitled *Double Your Profits: 78 Ways to Cut Costs, Increase Sales and Dramatically Improve Your Bottom Line in Six Months or Less*. It obviously struck a chord, as CEOs including Jack Welch at General Electric, Larry Bossidy at Allied Signal and Jamie Dimon at Travelers/Citigroup bought copies by the hundreds and made it required reading for their people. Meanwhile, tens of thousands of CEOs of small and mid-sized enterprises were attracted to the book, and it was translated into everything from Chinese to Czech so that it could be shared by business leaders around the world. To this day, I receive a steady stream of calls and e-mails from CEOs expressing their appreciation for the focus on profits which the book provided for them and their companies.

Based on that feedback, it is clear that one source of the book's popularity is its simplicity. As the book makes clear, if one applies common sense and discipline it is not difficult to find opportunities for companies to cut costs, raise prices, and focus their selling efforts and strategies in ways that could in fact dramatically improve profitability. *Double Your Profits* lays out a straightforward path to improved financial results that is applicable to virtually any company.

Since the book was published, I have worked as a consultant and Board member at dozens of companies, in addition to running several of my own. In both settings, the identification of where results *could* be improved turned out to be the easy part: The greater challenge resided in inspiring management and employees to share the vision and to make it happen. In the frustrations expressed by my CEO clients and friends, a common pattern emerged: They know what needs to be done, but getting those around them to actually do it is a whole different matter. As a result, almost from the moment the book was published my advice to companies evolved to encompass not only profit enhancement, but the challenges of shaping the senior management team, motivating employees and achieving successful execution.

At the same time, one of my first clients from way back in 1982, Gordon Quick, was proceeding on a journey of his own. When the two of us met, Gordon was an executive for one of the largest companies in America, where he ran a number of divisions. Over the next twenty-five years, he proceeded to hold COO and CEO positions with a succession of venture-backed companies, both public and private. Gordon is not only a "doer" but he is a "thinker," and as he grappled with and mastered the challenges of business leadership, he accumulated a growing body of powerful insights about what distinguishes successful CEOs from less successful ones. Today, he has augmented his career as a CEO and serves as a consultant to other CEOs, helping them to implement far-reaching and lasting upgrades to their companies.

Finally, Paul Favaro, who has been a close friend and business associate of mine since 1981, was hard at work on the same problem. Paul has been a leader of one of the country's pre-eminent management consulting firms, an adjunct professor at Northwestern's Kellogg School of Management and a Fortune 500 executive, and in all of these roles he has reflected on what makes for an excellent CEO. For the past two years, Gordon, Paul and I have been comparing notes and merging our perspectives. In the process, we discovered that we had the makings of a comprehensive framework for what it takes for CEOs to overcome their feelings of powerlessness, and to inspire their organizations to move as one in the desired direction.

As we worked on that framework, another layer of the problem quickly came to the fore. All three of us grew to realize over the years that it is not enough for CEOs to know how to set their company's direction and then mobilize their resources towards that objective. All the CEOs we know are talented, ambitious and complicated individuals who are motivated by an array of factors, only some of which are readily apparent to the CEO. In both our work with CEOs and our reflection on our own careers, it became clear that only when CEOs take accurate stock of their own concerns and aspirations — and recognize the ways in which they unwittingly sabotage their own success — will their efforts to lead their companies to greatness proceed undiluted and on track. When CEOs are able to understand and get beyond their personal demons, then and only then are they ready to embrace more enlightened principles of leadership which will unlock the full potential of their companies.

So this book provides two fundamental offerings to the reader. In Parts IV through IX, we present a comprehensive and disciplined framework for CEOs to fulfill all of the roles required to turn their vision into reality and results — and to surmount the many frustrations of the job. We begin in Parts I through III with straight-talking advice about how best to understand your own performance as CEO, and more importantly how you can elevate that performance to another, more enlightened level. In both cases, the prescription we offer is straightforward, candid and based on common sense, as we know that the real key lies not in embracing excessive complexity, but in focusing with discipline and resolve on those factors which truly make the greatest difference.

As the concentrated work of writing the book began, Paul soon discovered that he could not devote as much time to the project as Gordon and me, and in the end he insisted that he had not earned the right to be listed as an author. As a result, you see only two names on the cover of the book. Yet Gordon and I know that when measured by the quality of thinking and not the amount of hours, this book has three authors and not two — and we are enormously grateful to Paul for helping make *The Enlightened CEO* a reality. All three of us will be *most* gratified if, as with my previous book, we learn that it has helped you achieve your objectives for your company — and for yourself as CEO.

— Bob Fifer

Part I: The Toughest Job in Business

Chapter 1

The Limits of Power

"We have a plan, but we can't seem to get it executed."

"My team isn't motivated and focused the way it should be. They spend too much time competing with each other."

"How many times do I need to communicate my vision before everybody 'gets it' and rallies behind it?"

"Why can't my people make better decisions when I'm not around?"

"I keep getting distracted from the most important parts of my job."

"I'm at the top of this pyramid, but I often feel so powerless."

The two of us have been CEOs, taught CEOs, consulted to CEOs and befriended CEOs. Over a period of thirty years we have worked with hundreds and met thousands, from scores of Fortune 500 leaders to myriad small business owners and leaders of venture capital-funded start-ups. Most have been bright, personable, and highly motivated, and — despite the bad apples reported in the popular press — fundamentally good, well-intentioned and ethical people. Looking from the outside in, one might suspect that the CEO has it all — power, money, respect, perks, fun and, within his own circle if not a broader one, a degree of fame. To those who aspire to power, being CEO may seem like the answer to all of their problems, for once there they can tell people what to do and finally make things happen the way that they choose.

Yet as anyone who has held the title knows, in reality it is much more of a mixed bag. They've spent their careers aspiring to the CEO position and, having reached it, they have no intention of trading it in. Yet the frustrations of the job are many, with just a small sampling of them included above. Yes, the CEO commands respect, but what does he then do with that respect? How does he get the three or three hundred or thirty thousand human beings in his organization to move as one towards the desired goal? In a 24-hour, seven-day week (or the portion of it dedicated to his job), how does he manage the hundreds of things he needs to get done? Faced all day long with decisions large and small, how does he stay focused on what is most important and maintain his judgment? And when the inevitable surprises and disappointments occur, sometimes seemingly a lot faster than the successes, how does he turn those around, keep the organization on track and motivated, and not lose his credibility as a leader? As CEOs we know what others find hard to understand: Despite the trappings and illusions of power, being CEO is the most difficult job in the organization, and success is far from a foregone conclusion.

Almost every CEO enjoys a degree of euphoria the first time she rises to the position — either by appointment or through her own initiative in starting a business — and that euphoria lasts for a while, perhaps even a long while. Yet ultimately that euphoria is tempered by frustration, confusion about the limits of power, battle fatigue, and disappointment about the organization's mixed results. In most cases, those concerns lead to even more fundamental questions the CEO asks herself from time to time:

"Am I really cut out for this job? Do I have what it takes?"

and:

"Is this what I really want to be doing? Am I having fun?"

Even the CEO who believes he is doing well asks himself:

"How do I take myself and the organization to the next level?"

We ourselves have lived this journey and witnessed it in countless others. We've experienced it all — we've made all the mistakes, and thought all the unhelpful thoughts. Yet the good news is that when one makes enough mistakes and is willing to be open-minded, observant and introspective, one ultimately understands the roots of the problem and finds the answers. So finally, somewhere towards the back end of our 30 years working this challenge, we've come out the other side and reached a hard-earned understanding of what it takes to succeed as CEO.

Having done so, we want others to get there faster than we did, and without as many wrong turns and blind alleys. We want them to enjoy and thrive in the CEO role from the outset, and to consistently improve their performance throughout their careers. And we want their organizations to see the results that come only when the CEO truly understands what his role is and what it takes to master the most difficult job in business.

This book is written for everyone who is a CEO, or who runs a part of an organization (for which the challenges are similar), or who aspires to be CEO some day. Master the principles in this book, and you'll get there faster, perform at a consistently higher level, and derive more satisfaction from the job. And in doing so, you will achieve something enjoyed by only a small minority of your peers.

Chapter 2

Difficult, But Not Complex

Your responsibility as CEO is nothing more nor less than helping shape the right future course for your company within an infinitely variable and ever-changing environment, and then aligning the efforts and motivations of those working for you — a set of human beings with an infinitely variable set of talents, limitations, needs and concerns — towards the pursuit of that desired future course. As long as that infinity of variables remains in the environment and among our fellow men and women, achieving excellence as CEO will always be difficult.

Yet that does not mean that the CEO should throw up his hands and walk away. Every important pursuit in life — whether oriented towards career, family, friendship, charity, public service or faith — is about aspiring to and making progress towards an unattainable ideal, and business leadership is no different. We've never met the perfect CEO, but we've met some who are a lot better at the job than others — and this book is about how each of us can move closer to that end of the spectrum.

Here is the good news — mastering the job of CEO is difficult, but what it takes to do so is *not* complex. To the contrary, what it takes is to see past the complexities that continually threaten to distract you and to clutter your mind. The great businesses, whether large or small, are led not by those who can design or comprehend the most complicated decision models, but rather by those who when presented with the seemingly complex can instead stay focused on the simple truths, and then act with clarity and consistency.

All CEOs live this struggle every day and all day long. When you suggest something that needs to be done, you're inevitably presented with additional variables which you're told you had neglected to consider — variables that present obstacles to the desired course. When you propose an organizational or personnel change, you're told all the reasons why it will cause problems, and why a more complicated, less direct approach is needed. When you go to an internal or outside expert to help solve a problem, you're presented with a new-fangled, complicated model designed in part to justify that expert's existence and fees. Not only would others have you believe that everything you have to do is complicated, but they further point out that it's even far more complicated than you realized when you first raised the issue. The way to do your job, it would seem, is to forever add greater levels of complexity to the model with which you run your company. It's as if there was some formula that the higher your pay, the more complicated your mental model needs to be — when in fact the exact opposite is closer to the truth.

• •

The great businesses are led by those who when presented with the seemingly complex can instead stay focused on the simple truths, and then act with clarity and consistency.

• •

As the person at the top of the pyramid, you inevitably will have to take into account more variables, more issues and more decision models than anyone else in the organization. The key, however, is to be aware of them without falling victim to them. *Your* role as CEO is to rise above them and not be unduly distracted by them, to maintain your focus on the simple principles and truths that are the key to your organization's success — principles that comprise the balance of this book. Once you've committed to these principles, you need to keep them close at hand and, when faced with a seemingly intractable problem, pull them out and read them again. In their simplicity, in the clarity with which they remind you of what matters and what doesn't, and in the direction they give you as to how to make decisions, the answer to the intractable problem will become clear, allowing you to move on to other seemingly "intractable" problems and to conquer them as well.

Not only do you need to maintain this clarity for yourself, but it is your job to promote it throughout your company. All day, month and year long members of your team bring you their problems as well as their attempts to solve them. The most valuable response you can offer is to help them cut through the clutter, see what is really important, and move forward with renewed focus and resolve. More pervasively, to the extent that you can build processes and a company culture which is dictated by the premise that the simplest and most direct answer is always the best, the more you will empower the organization and multiply your own effectiveness. Simpler answers are inherently easier to implement successfully than difficult ones, and since the goal is success, simplicity is its own reward. However, for you to clear unneeded complexity for others you must first unclutter your own mind as well as your approach to being CEO.

Again, *achieving mastery as CEO is difficult, but it is not complex.* Not only is this good news, but if you're willing to open your mind it is *very* good news. All that stands between you and greater mastery of and satisfaction from your job is introspection, focus and resolve — not an advanced degree in some management or technical discipline that you somehow missed along the way. If you are willing to honestly look inside yourself, set aside the time to think clearly, commit yourself to what it is that you discover, and then put in place reminders to keep you on that path consistently and forever, you will be the CEO you want to be. In doing so, you'll then know that you are exactly where you belong.

So what are the simple truths that should guide us as CEO? If the answer is simple and only requires consistent resolve, what is that answer? We'll get to that soon, but first let's look briefly at the answers from some of the usual suspects.

Chapter 3

One-Dimensional Prescriptions are Not Enough

Browse the business section of any book store, read the business press, or listen to the academics and management consultants, and you'll have no shortage of prescriptions for what it takes to be a good CEO. The prescriptions tend to come in waves. In the 1970's strategic planning was the rage, while succeeding decades saw a boom in process-oriented prescriptions such as Total Quality, Re-engineering, and Six Sigma. More recently the book stores and lecture circuits have been dominated by experts preaching the importance of interpersonal and organizational skills, spawning a succession of fun little books that teach business lessons by parable. The two of us read these books and keep abreast of the advice of the "experts," much of which is good and quite helpful. There is so much to learn as CEO, and a voracious appetite to devour the wisdom and experience of others is an important part of keeping fresh and staying on top of your game.

While many of these management prescriptions are helpful, they also can be dangerous if applied the wrong way. In order to get noticed and make their mark, management pundits tend to sing the praises and plumb the depths of a single piece of the CEO puzzle without due regard for the limits of that one piece and its inter-relationship with the others. A great CEO is balanced and is able to think at a variety of levels of abstraction, draw upon different tools, apply different solutions, and use different words and styles to communicate, all depending on the needs of a particular situation. The CEO who becomes overly enamored of the hottest management fad and who tries to apply it too universally to her organization usually makes a splash and achieves some surface changes — but fails to achieve lasting, sustainable improvement in her organization commensurate with the time and resources expended to propagate the particular technique.

Even when a management technique produces meaningful and lasting results, the usefulness of that technique as a change agent and motivator declines over time, and sooner or later the CEO comes to recognize that her imbalanced focus on that technique has brought with it a neglect of other equally important parts of what it takes for the CEO to lead her organization with excellence. As you continue to expose yourself to and adopt particular management processes, it's useful to think of them as akin to working to improve one aspect of your life, such as your health, your career, your family life, or your golf game: While it is a worthwhile endeavor, if pursued at the cost of imbalance and neglect of the others then you're likely to wind up worse off than when you started.

• •

> Despite the proliferation of business, leadership and self-help books, we are hard pressed to find any one that presents a balanced view of the CEO's role in its various elements, and which does so in simple, clear, uncluttered terms.

• •

The offering of management advice has been a high-growth and profitable industry. Yet the two of us knew 100 CEOs during the 1980's and we've known a different 100 during the current decade, and despite the proliferation of business thinking we'd be hard pressed to say that the profession as a whole is doing materially better on average than it was back then — as measured by the evaluations of the CEOs themselves, or those of Boards, shareholders, members of the executive team or employees. Part of that stagnation can be blamed on the increasing challenge presented by the external environment, including such factors as global competition, the increasingly short-term focus of investing professionals, and the rapid rate of change and competitive upheaval brought about by an explosion in technology.

However, another culprit is the overly impassioned devotion to one-dimensional, one-size-fits-all cure-alls, and the turning of the organization upside-down to devote too much of its attention to the latest and greatest catchy new process. As we stipulated in the previous chapter, the CEO's job can and must be defined in simple terms, but reducing too much of it to only one part of what needs to be a balanced set of roles is the wrong direction in which to look for that simplicity. The presentation of one narrow set of principles as the Holy Grail of leadership can be educational if absorbed selectively and proportionately. Yet if you rely on it too heavily, you will fail to embrace the full range of skills and disciplines which are required for the CEO to be successful.

The fulfilled CEO knows that the challenge and joy of the job derive from the wide range of talents required to do it right – in the realms of the intellectual, interpersonal, and ethical, among others. In order for your organization to realize its potential, and in order for you to feel satisfied with your own performance, you need to give every part of the job its full respect and attention. Despite the proliferation of business, leadership and self-help books, we are hard pressed to find any one that presents a balanced view of the CEO's role in its various elements, and which does so in simple, clear, uncluttered terms. *We'd like this book to fill that void.*

Part II: A Framework for Leadership

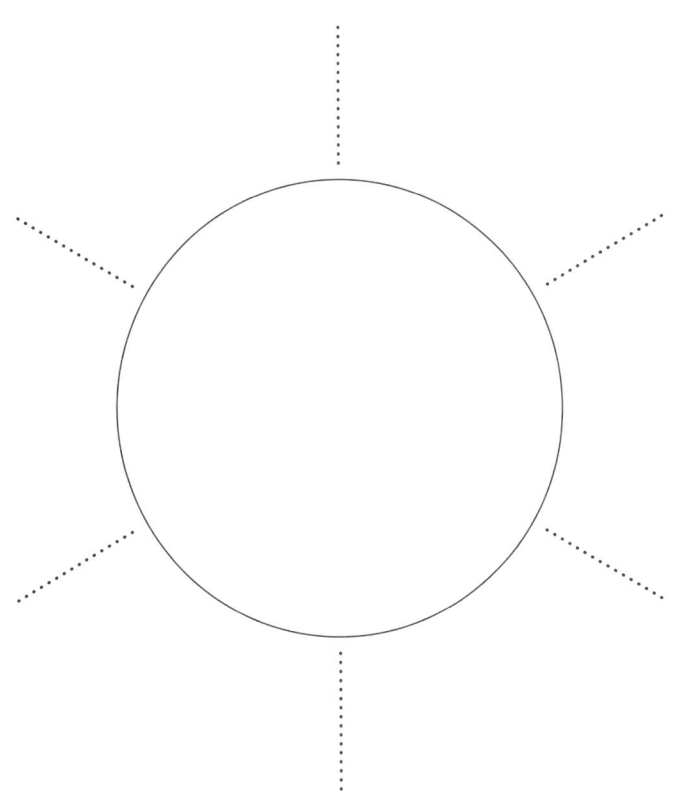

Chapter 4

Systematic vs. On-the-Fly Leadership

All CEOs have strong personalities. Whether at a Fortune 500 company or an enterprise starting from scratch, the CEO would not have his job without strong doses of at least some of the following traits: Ambition, decisiveness, extroversion, charm, guts and intellect. Most of all, virtually all CEOs have big egos, as it is the desire for the respect and admiration of others for a job well done that drives much of their ambition.

Not only is it inevitable that most CEOs have big egos, it is also desirable and not fundamentally in conflict with the humility which is also a requirement of the job. On the one hand, in order to be successful a CEO must have the self-confidence to take on the most difficult job in business, and must consistently project that confidence to an observant organization. At the same time, she needs to maintain the humility to realize that the organization is bigger than she is — that her success derives from that of the organization, and that it is created primarily by the accomplishments of others and not just her own. Ego by itself is not a problem, but the challenge is for it to manifest itself in only the appropriate ways.

Similarly, all of the traits listed in the first paragraph are helpful for the job and some may even be requirements. Without them, the CEO would not be CEO. Yet those very strengths can also be weaknesses unless they are put to work in the service of a disciplined approach to leadership. The CEO who tries to do her job "on the fly," relying solely on her natural talents (however strong they may be), will get herself and her company in trouble sooner or later. We have known CEOs (and been them ourselves) with talents strong enough to get by for years with on-the-fly leadership styles. Yet beneath the surface, problems had begun to fester and grow, and with time the problems overran the successes. Talent and personality alone are not enough for the CEO to stay out of trouble and to achieve success — a more systematic approach to her job is needed.

As suggested earlier, the required systematic approach is straightforward and based on common sense, and it is not complex. What prevents many CEOs from seeing it and sticking to it is not a lack of intellect but rather their strength of personality. Having risen to the top based on intellect, charm, decisiveness, guts or the like, CEOs tend to manage the same way. Then when trouble hits because some part of the necessary systematic approach has been neglected, CEOs do exactly the wrong thing: Rather than fill in the gap, they fall back even more heavily on those traits that they may already be overemphasizing. *To be a complete CEO, to do the job up to your own high standards as well as the standards of others, there is no escape from this simple truth: You must give each of the major roles inherent in being CEO it's proper due, and you must keep them in balance.* Anything less than a systematic approach is likely to prove insufficient in the face of the inherent difficulty of the job.

Chapter 5

The Complete CEO

A systematic approach to the job of CEO includes six fundamental roles. To be fully successful, the CEO must not only take on each of these roles, he must fulfill them diligently, with skill and based on a series of critical underlying principles specific to each role. The six include:

1) **<u>Creating the Inspiration:</u>** If the CEO is to lead, he must first define a direction for the company which is inspirational for his organization. Choosing the right vision and expressing it with sufficient eloquence and clarity is the first challenge of true leadership.

2) **<u>Charting the Course:</u>** Far too often, CEOs assume that any worthy vision can be achieved with enough determination and hard work. The reality is that there are fundamental rules of markets and competition, and inherent capabilities and limitations of any organization, which make some visions attainable while others are not. To ensure that the CEO has created the right inspiration for his organization, he must carefully chart the course by which the inspiration will be pursued and achieved, and while doing so he must test that course with sufficient rigor relative to both external and internal realities.

When presented with mixed or disappointing results, too many CEOs jump to the conclusion that the problem lies in the implementation, and turn to personnel or process moves to try to fix the problem. While that is sometimes the right corrective course, other times it is not. Instead there may be something fundamentally flawed in the vision or the strategy chosen to execute it. Mastery as CEO requires a logical, clear understanding of the environment and the organization's role within it, in order to continually address the question of where the mid-course correction needs to be made: in the internal workings of the company, or by better aligning the organization's course with the business realities with which it is presented. This process — realistic analysis of the strategic truths and imperatives so as to chart the right course for the company — is the second key role of the CEO.

3) **Shaping the Team:** A great CEO must have the humility to understand that he is only as good as the people with whom he surrounds himself. However, choosing the right people is only one part of the much larger job of shaping an excellent management team. The very same ambition and self-confidence that enable people to become CEOs often lead to destructive results when it comes to leading a team in a way that fuels their ambition and self-confidence and which drives optimal decision-making. Great CEOs understand what must be done to strike the balance required to be an inspirational leader while simultaneously encouraging, rather than drowning out, the independent thinking and leadership capabilities of the other members of the management team.

4) **Translating Into Action:** It is easy for the CEO to fall into the trap of assuming that an inspirational vision plus a well-charted course plus a strong team will automatically yield results. When the returns that come back are inadequate, the CEO often scratches her head. In these situations what is inevitably missing is a detailed, carefully defined plan of action which translates the charted course into a much finer level of detail: Who is going to do what, when, in order to get us where we intend to be.

Some CEOs instinctively view action plans as an unglamorous part of the job, and as a result they neglect them. Alternatively, they may view this as the role of the COO or senior managers, and not their own. That may be the case in significant part, but what *is* the CEO's job is to make sure that action plans of sufficient detail and quality are continually in place. Regardless of the size of the organization and the depth of management talent, there are critical steps which the CEO must go through to ensure that this happens, as we'll explore in depth in the section of the book (Part VII) dedicated to this role. The CEO who abdicates responsibility for the company's action plans runs a serious risk that he will be disappointed in the company's results.

5) **Following Through:** It is also not enough to create a plan for who will do what — the CEO must also ensure that the plan is implemented. Go back to the questions at the very beginning of the first chapter: Lack of execution is one of the most common frustrations expressed by CEOs. Yet it is an entirely avoidable frustration if the CEO commits himself to the fundamental principles of follow-through and has the discipline to practice them consistently.

6) **Communicating:** Frequent, high-quality communication underlies every one of the five roles identified above, but it is so critical that it merits a sixth role all its own. Every business is ultimately a people business, and every CEO communicates to her organization every minute of every day: either consciously or unconsciously, by commission or omission, and well or poorly – in meetings, one-on-one, in writing, and by phone. Great leaders understand that as one person leading many it is almost impossible to communicate too much, as there are always people who need more encouragement, more guidance or a sympathetic ear, and there are always ideas which need more reinforcement or refinement. Yet communicating with sufficient frequency is only part of the answer, as it is easy to fall into any of a variety of traps of bad communication: micro-management, over-promising, and many others. Figuring out how to communicate constantly but excellently is one of the critical challenges for the CEO. The payoff is the ability to influence not only the senior management team, but also all the other of the CEO's constituencies — including employees, the Board, key investors, customers, and suppliers.

Furthermore, the CEO will succeed only when communications work equally well in both directions, which means the CEO must maintain the processes necessary to listen as well as to speak. The great CEO knows that not only does she not have all the answers, but she has relatively few of them, and that listening to others will provide her with the ones she needs. She knows that she is at least as dependent on the wisdom of the organization as the other way around.

This two-way nature of the communicating role means that the six roles don't occur as a one-way sequential "line" but rather as a circle, for in the process of communicating the CEO learns what is required to continually upgrade the inspiration, the course, the team, the action plan, and the follow-through. The six roles take place continuously and simultaneously, mutually reinforcing and upgrading each other in a never-ending circle:

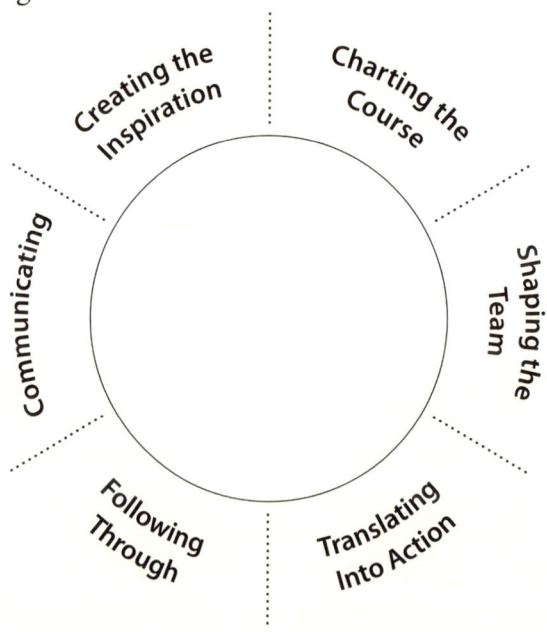

All of these six roles contain challenges and pitfalls, and for each there are core principles and proven techniques to serve as your guide. Parts IV through IX of this book are devoted to exploring each of the roles in detail. However, before diving into those details we turn first to what must reside at the center of those six roles if one is to join the ranks of outstanding CEOs.

Chapter 6

Enlightenment as the Core

Virtually without exception, the CEOs we have known believe the following:

- My company can and should be performing better.

- It is my job as CEO to figure out how.

- No matter how many people I've turned to in search of the answer, no matter how many issues I've addressed, and no matter how many techniques I've tried, there is still something missing. The challenge remains.

Since you picked up this book and have read this far, our guess is that you may already suspect what that missing piece is. It is not enough to intellectualize the six roles of the CEO. You can study them, dive into the detail, and remind yourself of their ongoing importance. Yet if that's all you do then your sense of frustration and something lacking will remain, because by itself the six-role framework will be just one more academic management prescription. The true missing piece — the key to what we call *enlightenment* as CEO — lies not in those six roles alone, not in strategy and action plans, not in management teams and employees, and not in issues of markets, technology, operations, product or customer service. The true answer lies not in those things "out there" — outside of you — but rather those *inside* of you.

CEOs don't lack great talent and in truth they don't lack great power — in fact, most CEOs have an abundance of both. However, they are also faced with a never-ending parade of crucial and difficult issues to which they have to apply that talent and power, and they must do so under pressure and seemingly never with enough time. They are also burdened (and blessed) with powerful personalities which can limit their openness and objectivity to apply the right solution to the right problem — as well as a loneliness that comes from controlling other peoples' fate and therefore never being able to know for sure when they're being told the truth.

Add into all of this the CEO's own personal objectives, needs and concerns, both professional and personal, and you're left with a dangerous mixture of ingredients that can produce an unpredictable concoction, one which can result in success, mediocrity, or disaster. Yet your job as CEO, swimming in the middle of that stew, is to ensure success, and when cast in this context it's no wonder that you're not always fully pleased with your own performance.

• •

> To be CEO in the frenetic world of ever-changing variables and personalities, what is needed is not ever-increasing complexity, but rather the perspective to consistently see things simply, clearly and objectively.

• •

No CEO can optimize her company while caught up in that concoction: Instead she must rise above it to gain the needed perspective. She must train herself to avoid her instinctive over-reliance on the strengths that got her the job in the first place, and instead lead with balance and objectivity. She must maintain the calm and perspective necessary to put the interests of the organization first, instead of whatever inner demons are plaguing her at the moment. She must have the sense of humor to be intrigued rather than frustrated by the limitations of those around her and to see the glass as half full and not half empty. She must also have the humility to listen to others and to capture the full power of all the people capable of contributing to the organization's success.

And there is one more crucial task to which that humility must be applied. It is true that virtually all CEOs need to do a better job of at least one of the six roles, and that educating oneself about the requirements and methodologies which comprise those roles is part of the path to improved performance. However, that education is helpful only in dealing with the parts of the challenge which are external to the CEO; the other half of that challenge resides within the CEO himself. And unless that internal half is analyzed and managed equally well, the toughest job in business will not yet be mastered.

The CEO must have the humility to search inside himself with the same critical eye and rigor with which he evaluates external personalities and problems, and must develop the self-awareness to understand himself as accurately. Only when he drives towards that self-awareness will he shed sufficient light on himself to achieve the perspective, calm, sense of humor and humility needed to go beyond intellectualizing the six roles and to truly make them his own.

It is the CEO who is as enlightened in his understanding of himself and his own behavior as he is about the external world who will maintain excellence at all six roles, and by doing so, maintain excellence at his company.

To be CEO in the frenetic world of ever-changing variables and personalities, what is needed is not ever-increasing complexity, but rather the perspective to consistently see things simply, clearly and objectively — a perspective that can come only when you have tended to your own mind, personality and spirit. So before proceeding to the six roles we turn first to the search for that enlightenment in Part III.

Part III:
Enlightenment

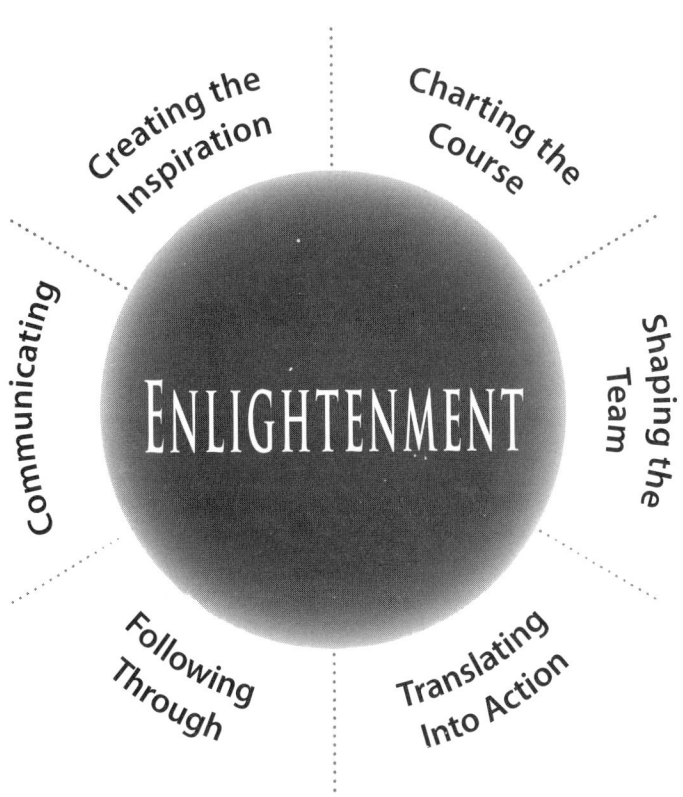

Chapter 7

The Nature of Enlightenment

So how does one bring clarity to a job that is constantly pulling you towards complexity? How does one consistently illuminate rather than obscure, align rather than divide, focus rather than distract, and inspire rather than de-motivate? Surely the answer cannot lie in Machiavellian intrigue, frenetic motion, or excessively nimble mental or moral gymnastics — too many of which you've probably tried already without the desired results. The challenges that surround you are complicated enough on their own: To illuminate them with clarity requires not more layers of movement and complexity, but instead a fixed point of reference, accurate tools of observation and a clear understanding of the rules of perspective. The more constant you can keep your base and modes of observation, the easier it will be to see the paths to success amidst all the extraneous or misleading information that surrounds you.

In fact, the only way to cut through the complexity is to base your leadership on a set of fundamental *principles* that bring order to the potential chaos and that guide you towards the right decisions made for the right reasons. Furthermore, your commitment to those principles must be unfailing and non-negotiable: They become your North Star as you navigate the often murky and perilous waters that can surround and permeate both you and your company.

As an enlightened CEO you will lead based on principles which govern the **purpose** which guides your efforts, the **thought** process you apply to the world around you, and your **conduct** when you interact with that world.

The first set of these, **Principles of Purpose**, enable the Enlightened CEO to remain clear and steadfast in his motivation and responsibilities:

- He recognizes that the company's agenda is different in important respects from his own, and makes sure that the former takes precedence.
- He accepts the full range of responsibilities incumbent on the CEO and fulfills all of those roles.

The second group, **Principles of Thought**, ensure that the Enlightened CEO sees the world as fully and accurately as possible:

- He practices openness, not only accepting but actively encouraging input from a wide range of sources from both within and outside of the company.
- He invests sufficient time and energy in the quest for understanding of the wide range of subjects and disciplines required to do the job well.
- He maintains objectivity, helping him to see the facts as they are, without bias, and to make decisions based on the merits.

Third, **Principles of Conduct** enable the Enlightened CEO to carry himself and to treat others in a way that maximizes his positive impact on the organization:

- He keeps extreme emotions in check and, no matter how productive and fast-paced his day may be, maintains the calm necessary for accurate observation and dispassionate decision-making.
- He has genuine humility, recognizing how dependent he is on the knowledge and talents of others.
- He treats all around him with equity, appreciating the strengths and empathizing with the needs and struggles of others. He makes hard-nosed decisions regarding personnel and other issues in order to advance the interests of the

company, but does so with balance and understanding and not out of frustration.

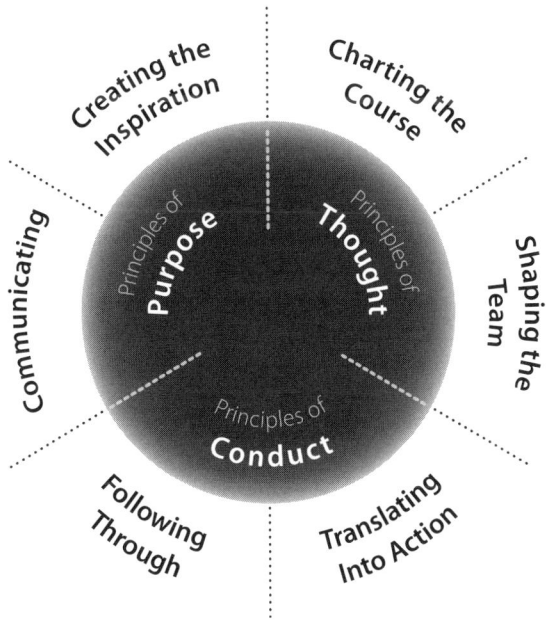

We will explore each of these principles in more depth in the remainder of Part III, but as you look at this list now you will agree that it is a straightforward and largely intuitive one. And that is precisely the point: To become an enlightened CEO, the direction in which you need to look is back towards basics, not out to some wild and unexplored unknown. The distractions, temptations and pitfalls that have influenced you and become part of who you are and how you lead need to be stripped away, so that you can connect with the principles of enlightened leadership and, once you have done so, stay connected to them forever.

Yet there is no way that those temptations and pitfalls can be stripped away unless you are first able to see and acknowledge them. To proceed towards enlightenment, you must first understand the complicated entity that you yourself have become — your strengths and weaknesses, your likes and dislikes, and your needs and aspirations — and how all of those both help and hinder you as you seek to excel as CEO. Enlightenment is at the core of the six roles of the CEO, but what lies in turn at the core of enlightenment is *self-aware-*

ness — for without a truly accurate understanding of yourself, you will have nothing fixed upon which to dock the principles of purpose, thought and conduct. Before we discuss those principles further, let's first explore in more depth the journey toward self-awareness.

Chapter 8

Self-Awareness: Strengths and Weaknesses, Likes and Dislikes

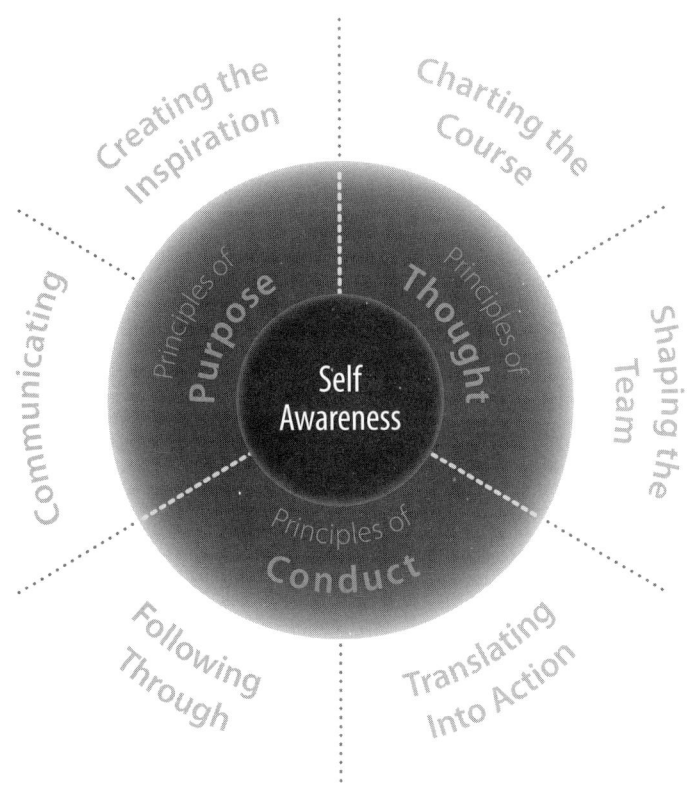

In Chapter 5 we introduced the six roles which together comprise the job of CEO. However, being strong of personality, virtually all CEOs have pronounced tendencies towards some of the six roles while giving short shrift to others. We've met CEOs who display many varieties of this syndrome and so probably have you.

Some love to dream, and are constantly conjuring up exotic futures for the company characterized by dramatic growth and unlimited horizons. When faced with a disappointing jolt of reality, they wax eloquent and repeat the call to arms in ever more lofty terms. These CEOs are in their element when executing Role 1: Creating the Inspiration.

Others are cerebral, dissecting all problems in detail and searching for the answer in ever-increasing quantities of data and analysis. These CEOs tend to be logically inclined, and when others don't respond as the analysis says they should they painstakingly lay out the logic in even more detail, in the hope that the recipients' level of analytical proficiency and understanding will increase. These CEOs thrive in Role 2: Charting the Course.

> Strengths and weaknesses and likes and dislikes together comprise a common reason why CEOs fail to lead their companies with excellence.

A third group of CEOs have convinced themselves of the centrality of people to the problem. They add new members to the management group only after extraordinarily deep research into their backgrounds. Once that group is assembled, they stop at nothing to encourage open communication, build consensus, provide feedback and tend to bruised egos. In many cases these CEOs are also diligent communicators, and naturally dedicate themselves to Role 3 (Shaping the Team) and Role 6 (Communicating).

Then there are the "doers," who love to roll up their sleeves and get their hands dirty. They are uncomfortable leaving anything to chance, and go to great lengths to make sure that the team knows exactly what is to be done and then actually gets it done. These CEOs are in their comfort zone in Role 4 (Translating into Action) and Role 5 (Following Through).

While most of you won't precisely fit any of these extremes, you nonetheless are likely to favor some of the six roles at the expense of others. You probably find some of them easy and may in fact over-indulge in them, have to work harder at others, and spend not nearly enough time on the remaining ones. It is truly the rare CEO who devotes himself appropriately to all six roles, and who conducts all six well.

The reason that CEOs are disproportionate in their focus on the six roles could not be any more natural. CEOs are human, and humans tend to allocate their time based on two decision rules.

First, they prefer to spend their time on things they do well. The skills required for each of the six roles are truly varied, requiring different types of thinking and different kinds of interpersonal skills. A quick run through the six roles, regardless of stylistic differences among CEOs, reveals a need for cerebral traits including creativity, analytical skill, organization, and logic, and personal characteristics such as eloquence, empathy, patience and trust, among others. No one is equally proficient at such a wide range of attributes, and when faced with a difficult challenge under pressure, CEOs naturally fall back on their strengths, which in turns drives them towards some of the six roles more than others.

Second, CEOs prefer to spend their time on activities that they enjoy. Likes and dislikes often correlate with strengths and weaknesses, but not always. Sometimes a CEO is quite competent at a role but simply finds it drudgery, and therefore tends to neglect it. Of all the perks of being CEO, none is greater than being one's own boss. Liberated from the dictates of others, on either a conscious or sub-conscious level CEOs naturally structure their time around that which they enjoy, which in turn leads to imbalanced performance with regard to the six roles.

We are not saying that the CEO has to be inherently and equally skilled at all six roles, because that is unrealistic. We also recognize that there is and should be a wide range of different management styles for CEOs to fit both the circumstances of the company and their own personalities and strengths. However, what we *are* saying is that regardless of the CEO's strengths and style, the six roles must be attended to with sufficient focus and skill, and that if any are neglected the company and CEO will not succeed. In other words, the differences among management styles can be wide but not so wide as to give short shrift to any of the six roles. Hence, the CEO's weaknesses and dislikes must be compensated for in some fashion so that no role is neglected.

Strengths and weaknesses and likes and dislikes together comprise a common reason why CEOs fail to lead their companies with excellence. The problem is avoidable, but only for CEOs who are willing to be introspective and honest with themselves about their skills and preferences — and then to find a way to compensate for them. The CEO who fails to seek that self-awareness will remain stuck in his historical behavior — and will increase the likelihood that his company will be stuck with its historical results.

Chapter 9

Self-Awareness: Needs and Aspirations

Everyone in your organization is human, and with that humanity comes a unique list of personal needs and aspirations, only some of which align with the company's objectives. Yet when the individual's needs and aspirations are allowed to have too much sway over the company's agenda, any number of problems can result. Unfortunately, this risk exists for well-intentioned executives who are not fully conscious that it is taking place, and not just for the less well-intentioned.

Despite your position as head of the company, you are just as susceptible to this phenomenon as anyone else. However, given your position, the cost to the organization when your personal concerns take precedence is even greater than when a senior or mid-level manager exhibits the same behavior. Not only do you have the most power to make things happen, but your words and actions are watched more closely than those of anyone else in the organization. When you display behavior driven by your personal needs more than the company's, many will emulate you and others will be de-motivated. It is difficult to get others to fully devote themselves to your vision of what is best for the company when you yourself are clearly less than fully committed to that cause.

Although CEOs sometimes lead with their personal agenda consciously, in order to meet some important personal need, it is more common for it to happen subtly, without the CEO being fully aware of what it is he is doing. As a result, if the CEO is to come to grips with this problem he must first strive for enhanced self-awareness. He needs to understand what is driving him at a very deep and fundamental level, and to make sure that those motivations are not taking precedence over what is best for the company.

The potentially dysfunctional needs and concerns of the CEO come in a huge variety of forms, including:

- The CEO's personal objectives for his own financial well-being. For public companies, it has been well analyzed (by Warren Buffett among others) how stock options can drive executives to manipulate the stock price in ways that actually hurt the company. Similarly, bonus targets can lead to dysfunctional behavior (such as sacrificing the company's long-term health for short-term results) unless they are chosen, crafted and managed with extreme care. In the most extreme cases some CEOs' pursuit of personal wealth actually places the company in legal jeopardy, as is documented with regularity in the business press.

    For privately-held companies, the structure may be different but the temptations remain. In companies where there is more than one shareholder, the CEO may be distracted by the implicit competition among partners and his need to maintain or increase his share of the pie — which may cause him to employ financial tactics or structures which are good for him but not for the company. Even sole owners frequently allow their personal risk profiles or cash needs to produce decisions which run counter to the best interests of their companies. While this is their right as owners, they often fail to see that there are better approaches which will reconcile both sets of needs, as we will explore in Chapter 12. Public or private, large company or small, the desire for greater wealth is high on the list of concerns for most CEOs, and it is often a barrier to doing what is best for their companies.

- The CEO's desire to build his resume. When CEOs see their current job as a stepping stone to the next one, then once again there is potential for a disconnect. For example, such a CEO might under-invest in the future in order to dress up short-term results for the benefit of his resume — leaving his successor to deal with the problems resulting from that under-investment. Another form of resume-fixation may be evidenced by how the CEO relates to his Board — avoiding discussion of tough issues or conflict when it is needed, and choosing instead to maintain more superficial but amiable Board relationships which will serve him well in securing his next posting.

> There are many potential pitfalls lurking in the needs and aspirations of the CEO.

- The CEO's need to feed his ego and remain king of the hill. Most CEOs have invested considerable energy in developing their vision for the company and in selling it to the organization. Yet if the CEO surrounds himself with strong individuals, then there will be many times when elements of his roadmap are appropriately questioned by team members. Since the CEO is human, he usually reacts to that feedback on two levels: (1) Based on the merits of the argument; (2) As a personal challenge to his credibility and leadership. The latter is a natural, almost reflexive reaction, but the enlightened CEO has trained himself to keep that reaction fleeting and internal, quick to pass and not to be observed by others. Instead, he makes his decisions based on the merits, and by doing so trains the other members of the team to do so as well. This basic trait of leadership is as critical for CEO excellence as any, and with self-control and discipline is achievable by virtually anyone. Yet practicing it consistently it is one of the rarest of leadership traits.

- The CEO's insecurities. Most successful people have a strong desire for the respect and admiration of others, and there is nothing wrong with using that as a core motivator, particularly if it works. However, this insecurity must be kept, as the journalists say, in "deep background" — and not be allowed to manifest itself in ways which lead to dysfunctional behavior. Too many CEOs waste valuable time with their team explaining away their limitations and holding themselves up (usually by implication and not explicitly) as models of near-perfection. They dwell on stories about their past successes as a counter-balance to the problems of the present — problems which are obvious to all around them. They may also choose to spend their time in ways which play to their strengths while avoiding activities in which they don't thrive, even if the latter is exactly where they are most needed.

  The irony, of course, is that the vast majority of people see right through these behaviors, as the CEO's insecurities are usually much more obvious to those around her than they are to the CEO herself. As a result, by leading with her insecurities the CEO experiences exactly the opposite of what she intends: She lowers herself in the estimation of others. The reality is that everyone knows that all humans are highly imperfect, whether they're the most junior person in the lowest-profile organization or the President of the United States. The surest way to win respect is to exhibit the confidence that you're comfortable within your own skin and that you are unapologetic about the overall package you offer to others. Trying to paper over your weaknesses only exposes them even more.

- Spillover from the CEO's personal life. Our companies and careers share our attention with the other pillars of our lives: marriage or romance, family, friendship, avocations and community or philanthropic causes. As driven people, CEOs hold themselves to high standards in virtually all of their endeavors, and wind up grappling with non-work issues which are as challenging as any at the office, sometimes with higher personal stakes. Work can be a helpful counter-balance to and refuge from those personal challenges, but it also can play the role of punching bag if we let it. The enlightened CEO works hard to ensure that his judgment at work is not clouded by important but unrelated issues outside of the office.

There are many potential pitfalls lurking in the needs and aspirations of the CEO. Yet the good news is that they are all avoidable — because in truth what is best for the company and for the CEO are disconnected only in the CEO's mind, and not in reality. In fact, the two sets of needs almost always point towards the same answer — as we will explore further in Chapter 12.

Whether the challenge is the CEO's strengths and weaknesses, likes and dislikes, or needs and aspirations, the first step towards enlightened leadership is self-awareness — *for until the CEO takes accurate stock of his attributes and inner demons he stands no chance of conquering or containing them.* Let's look next at how successful CEOs cultivate that self-awareness.

Chapter 10

The Journey Toward Self-Awareness

Self-awareness is for the most part a matter of commitment and discipline, and is achievable only to the extent that you are as rigorous in reflecting upon your own behaviors as you are in analyzing external variables. When you hit bumps in the road, rather than reflexively laying the blame on others or on outside events, look first for what you can control and how changes to your own profile can fix the problem. Most CEOs we know have a burning and never-ending desire to improve, and the starting point for that improvement is maintaining an accurate sense of self at all times.

Because self-awareness is such a critical element of executive performance, we include it on the list of key factors in any hiring decision in which we are involved. We get nervous when a potential member of the senior management team appears not to have a good handle on his own skills and motivations — as that is often a sign that there are important unresolved issues which will get in the way of performance once he is hired. Indeed, professional recruiters are coming to the same conclusion: In <u>The Globe and Mail</u>, Wallace Immen paraphrases recruiter John Tanton and reports that "Search committees are placing heavier emphasis on 'soft skills', like self-awareness, empathy, a sense of purpose, teambuilding and communication skills."

Most successful CEOs we know go beyond grappling with issues of self-awareness on their own, and also talk out their strengths and weaknesses, likes and dislikes, and needs and aspirations with trusted friends, family members, or business associates. Many of the internal issues that can be detrimental to the CEO's performance are hard to pin down, and the process of articulating them can help enormously. If you find yourself struggling to resolve one of these issues in your own mind, then you are probably onto something important that needs to be figured out, and articulating your thoughts to someone you trust is often a good way to do so.

Enlightened CEOs also listen carefully for feedback from others. CEOs receive a steady stream of such feedback all day long, either overt, or more often subtly through an offhand remark or non-verbal signal. Although your first reaction to negative feedback may be defensive, more often than not those around you are accurate observers and are doing you a service — if you are willing to listen for it. This doesn't mean that you should respond to every pushback or implied criticism that you receive, as many may be unhelpful — but that instead you should look for the consistent trends. If an aspect of how you lead your organization regularly meets with resistance or some other negative reaction, you are receiving important clues about something in your management style which needs to be changed if you are to lead with excellence. For this reason, confident leaders not only listen carefully for feedback, but also actively solicit it from people at all levels of the organization.

It is inherently difficult to hear criticism, whether justified or unjustified, and it takes discipline and self-control to hear it constructively. The key is to remind yourself to suppress your own ego, and to be confident in who you are and the job you are doing. If you allow your insecurity to drown out important feedback from others, you are forfeiting valuable input which can raise the performance of both you and your company.

You also have to be willing to acknowledge your mistakes. Like athletes, all CEOs suffer through many mistakes in order to enjoy their successes, and those mistakes can be highly instructive when you focus on them as opportunities to learn and grow in the job. On the other hand, when you deny them or rationalize them away you will have learned nothing, and are likely to repeat them.

Some CEOs may find it helpful or even necessary to go beyond the feedback of co-workers and trusted friends, and to seek the assistance of a professional coach or advisor. As CEOs ourselves, a critical step in our professional development was to find highly skilled advisors who told us the truth about our strengths and weaknesses and helped us sort out ways in which we were inadvertently acting contrary to our own and our company's best interests. If you do retain professional help, the critical ingredients for your advisor are: (1) Someone with the intellect or experience to relate to the problems with which you are dealing; (2) Someone with whom you have good chemistry — if it takes much more than the first interaction for you to feel like you are being well understood, you probably have the wrong person; and (3) Someone who understands the foundation of effective coaching, which means that he, unlike anyone else in your world, must be unequivocally in your corner with no agenda of his own — and must help you find the unvarnished truth while not letting you get away with believing only what you choose.

• •

> Although your first reaction to negative feedback
> may be defensive, more often than not those around
> you are accurate observers and are doing you a
> service — if you are willing to listen for it.

• •

In addition to examining your own behavior, much can be learned by observing the leadership styles of others, whether in person or by reading the business press, and also by reading about leaders in other walks of life. It can be particularly helpful to study their mistakes, as it is much easier to recognize and be objective about the mistakes that others commit than your own. Often, when you reflect upon the cost of the mistakes of other leaders, it is easier for you to accept how analogous behavior on your part is costing you and your organization. Similarly, when you observe successful leadership by others it can inspire and motivate you to round out your skills and raise your game to another level. We are surrounded by countless examples of effective and ineffective leadership, and it is to your advantage to make the conscious effort to study them and then be introspective about how those examples relate to your own performance as CEO.

Regardless of which of the above mirrors you use to become more self-aware, you should be able to actually put on paper an accurate accounting of your own strengths and weaknesses, likes and dislikes, and needs and aspirations. In addition, you should be able to write down how each of those is helping or impeding your performance on the job. Finally, you should identify what you intend to do to eliminate the ones that are impeding you, although simply identifying them honestly and openly often gets you a long way towards home in that regard.

Once identified and transcribed, these are good lists to keep close by and to review regularly. If you keep these issues at the top of your mind, then when you find yourself falling back on dysfunctional behaviors you can recognize them quickly and reverse them before they spiral downward. That is as close to perfection as any of us will ever get — and is likely to constitute a significant step forward in your quest to be a better CEO.

Chapter 11

Principles of Purpose

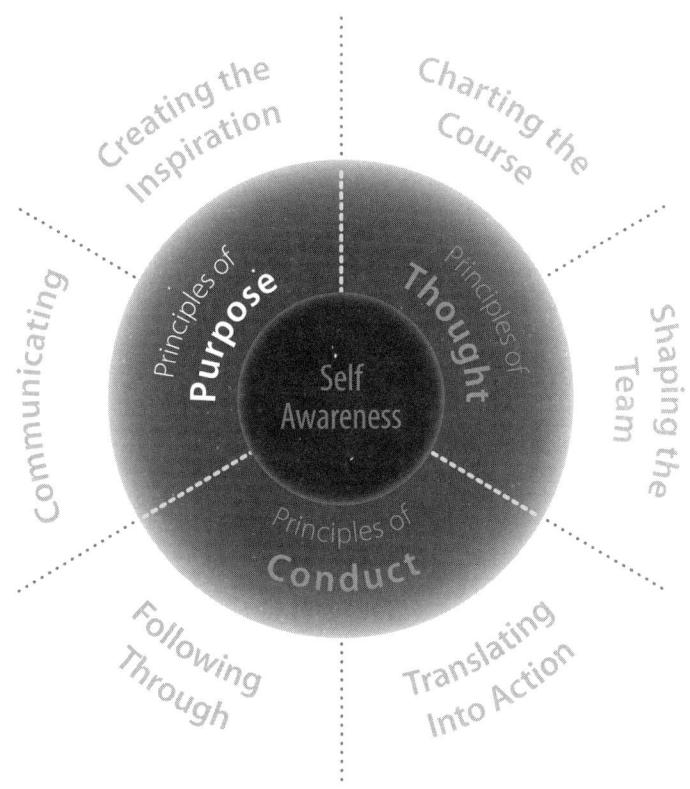

Having accepted the importance of self-awareness, the enlightened CEO has an accurate handle on her strengths and weaknesses, likes and dislikes, and needs and aspirations. She remains vigilant about their potential to distort her field of vision and to impede her performance. Employing the techniques outlined in Chapter 10, she is able to head off those distractions and to remain focused on what she is here to do as CEO.

Yet what should serve as the most fundamental tenets of her true function as the company's leader? The enlightened CEO is guided by two overarching *Principles of Purpose* — as we'll explore in Chapters 12 and 13.

Chapter 12

It's Not About You

In Chapter 9 we offered five illustrations of how the agenda of the company can be compromised by the CEO's needs and aspirations: Pursuit of personal wealth, resume-building, ego gratification, mollification of insecurities, and as an outlet for redressing frustrations in the CEO's personal life. Yet the irony underlying this list of supposedly disconnected objectives is that the disconnection exists primarily in the CEO's mind and not in reality. In truth, in almost all cases what works best for the company also works best for the CEO, and the more the CEO pursues his personal agenda as an end in itself the less likely he is to get what he wants.

For example, when the CEO competes with his own team, putting his need to outshine them ahead of the merits of the issue on the table, not only does he make the wrong decision but he loses the respect of those he leads. When he works too hard to paper over his weaknesses, he only draws attention to them and further lowers himself in the eyes of others. You are the most-watched person in your organization, and your employees have the collective intelligence to see you accurately for who you are and to grade your actions and behaviors on their true merits. The only sustainable way to win more respect is to become a CEO they *should* admire rather than trying to fool them into thinking you are something that you are not. Furthermore, the only way to *earn* that admiration is to put aside the psychological gamesmanship, and instead focus on being right a lot more than you are wrong. No one ever became a great CEO by under-estimating the intelligence of those around him.

Similarly, when the CEO puts his need for greater financial rewards ahead of the agenda of the company, he often acts counter to both the company's objectives and his own. One example we see frequently is the CEO/owner of the private company who has two over-riding personal objectives: First, to build his personal wealth, and second, to not be so all-consumed by work that he rarely gets to spend time with his family. We often see a pattern in which this CEO works hard for years to build the company, puts some money away (although not as much as he'd like to provide for the family in the future), and then does a gut-check when he realizes he's missing his children growing up. He decides to scale back his work-week, and then concludes — often incorrectly — that the best way to do so is to make his job easier by lowering his company's growth objectives.

The motivations behind this pattern are understandable and admirable, but the conclusion is misguided. There is an optimal path for the CEO as an individual which needs to be determined; in this case, it is to remain CEO but to work less frenetically. There is also an optimal growth target for the company — a target which should be based on variables such as the market opportunity and the company's distinctive competencies — and not on how much the CEO wants to see his children.

Faced with the competing pressures of work and personal life, and with a strong ego that falsely equates himself with the company, this CEO fails to see that the gap between his personal objectives and those of the company can be bridged without sacrificing either. If more growth is achievable than the CEO can drive personally, he can hire or promote from within a person or team to bridge the gap. The unenlightened CEO may see this as a threat, with increased power and credit accruing to a newly promoted person. The enlightened CEO, on the other hand, will understand that not only is that the best way for him and his company to succeed, but that doing anything less will lead to negative unintended consequences — such as a squandered opportunity for enhanced growth and profits, or the exit of talented managers who don't yet share his readiness to dial back the company's growth objectives. Truly internalizing that the company is an entity independent of the CEO and his ego, as difficult as that may be for some CEOs, expands his options in ways that are beneficial to everyone, including himself.

Another example is the CEO who identifies too strongly at a personal level with a particular growth path for the company. Globalization has put international expansion on the agenda of most companies of any appreciable size, but we are struck by how many CEOs let their own agenda about how much and where they like to travel influence their decision-making. Too often, a poorly chosen geographic expansion leads to aggravation and wasted time for the CEO which is far greater than any pleasure she may derive from passing through the chosen locale. As trivial as it may sound, we have successfully helped a number of CEOs recognize that they have the means and can find the time to travel anywhere they'd like on their own nickel. Not only will their company be better off but so will they — if they remember that the company's objectives and their own are two different things, and that co-mingling the two usually leads to both parties being worse off.

• •

The only sustainable way to win more respect is to become a CEO they *should* admire rather than trying to fool them into thinking you are something that you are not.

• •

Still other CEOs become overly enamored at a personal level with particular technologies, new products or markets, or perceived opportunities for the company to help society and make money at the same time. These paths may track with the CEO's own areas of expertise, his interests, or his charitable desires. Again, those are all understandable and sometimes admirable motivations, but more often than not the CEO does himself and his company more harm than good when he allows his personal objectives to muddy those of the company.

Achieving success for companies in a highly competitive world is tough enough when its motivations are defined purely by business logic. The level of difficulty may get prohibitive when the CEO further complicates matters with his own agenda and its inevitable cost to the organization. More often than not, there are ways for the CEO to separate the two sets of objectives without sacrificing either, by finding structural ways to pursue what motivates him outside of the legal constructs of the company. For the private company, that may mean separation into a for-profit concern and a not-for-profit foundation, while for the Fortune 500 CEO it may be a question of dedicating part of his own accumulated wealth or personal time in the direction of his own interests and ambitions.

The common theme in all of these examples is that there is a best path for you and a best path for the company, and it is essential that you stay clear about the difference between the two. The enlightened CEO — the one who will be most successful on both fronts — is the one who does not try to merge the two, but who recognizes that they are different, keeps both on the optimal path, and then finds creative ways to bridge the gap. Not only is there invariably a way to pull this off, but in most cases the alternative — sub-optimizing the company to meet the CEO's personal objectives — winds up hurting not only the company but the CEO as well.

Bill Ford of Ford Motor Company said it best when he stepped aside and asked Alan Mullaly of Boeing to come in as the new CEO: "I have a lot of myself invested in this company, but not my ego. I just want the company to do well. *It's not about me.*" (emphasis added)

We've met few CEOs, ourselves included, who wouldn't be well served to keep that quote posted on their office wall. Bill Ford had as much invested, in terms of financial interest, family and personal history, and emotional attachment, as any CEO does in any company large or small — yet he had the self-awareness and clarity of purpose to see that the best bet to maximize that investment was to lower his own profile in the company. Regardless of the ultimate outcome, this is a striking example of enlightenment, and one that should inspire us all.

Chapter 13

5 out of 6 Won't Work

Once the CEO accepts the furthering of the company's agenda as his true objective, he then must decide how to spend his time so as to achieve it. In Chapter 5 we presented the six fundamental roles the CEO must skillfully fulfill in order to optimally advance the company's interests: Creating the Inspiration, Charting the Course, Shaping the Team, Translating into Action, Following Through, and Communicating. In Parts IV through IX we will explore each of these roles in depth. Before doing so, however, we focus first on a critical overarching rule which spans all six of the roles:

Doing a good job of only five of the six roles is a prescription for failure.

Create an inspirational vision but fail to chart a rigorous strategic course, and your vision is merely a whimsical dream. Chart that vision and course without building an excellent management team, and who will make it a reality? Lead with an excellent inspiration, course and team but neglect to create detailed action plans, and performance will fall far short of expectations. Do the first four without following through to ensure that the action plans are consistently implemented, and guess what — they *won't* be implemented. And be brilliant in conceiving the first five but fail to communicate them over and over again to all the necessary constituencies, or neglect to listen carefully for the feedback, and watch the plan fade in effectiveness with the passage of time. All six of these roles are basic requirements for succeeding as CEO, no less so than breathing, eating, drinking, and sleeping are basic requirements for life, and the CEO can thrive without one of the six no more successfully than he could while neglecting one of those biological functions.

We have known many CEOs at companies large and small who have tried to do their jobs while paying only inadequate attention to one or more of these six roles. They may believe that their company is at a juncture when operating issues are the key, and that therefore a focus on strategy (Role 2) is not important. They may decide that ensuring high-quality action plans (Role 4) or follow-through (Role 5) is someone else's job, but not theirs. Yet others may be cerebral and introverted, and may prefer to lead without frequent communication (Role 6) to a wide range of others. It is our experience that these

• •

> Our bet is that you'll see a direct correlation between those of the six roles which need more of your attention and skill and the obstacles to your company's greater progress.

• •

assumptions stem from a fundamental misunderstanding of what the role in question truly entails as well as why it is so important. In detailing each role in Parts IV through IX our goal is for each of you to believe what we have learned the hard way — that complete and skilled attention to *all* six roles is necessary for *every* CEO.

When the CEO assumes that he can skip over one of the six roles for an extended period of time, he is assuming that his world is static — when to the contrary it is constantly changing. Your "answer" to a given role may have been fine when you drew it up based on the information you had at the time, but subsequently competitors made moves, customer behavior changed, technology progressed and internal personnel or politics took an important turn.

Furthermore, these changes are taking place far more rapidly today than in previous eras. In the 21st century the half-life of "static" strategic or action plans has become very short, and good CEOs know that they can never stop re-testing and re-crafting them as needed. And if the CEO is not continually communicating, he is not getting the feedback which is necessary to know what has changed, what is working and what isn't. Finally, members of the senior team are continually evolving themselves as they take on new challenges — they face new issues affecting their performance, they may need new skills, or members of the team may change as the company progresses.

All six roles have many moving parts, and no CEO can afford to take his eye off any of them for any significant period of time. It is essential to continually reaffirm the inspiration, the charted course, the action plan and the capability of the management team, and to stay abreast of all of those through regular two-way communication — because more often than not, continual refinements will be needed. The best CEOs drive execution based on currently in-place plans, while at the same time continually re-testing them and making the necessary real-time improvements.

Many a CEO has shared her frustrations with us, and in each case it's not hard to refer to the list of six roles and find the ones which have been neglected. It is equally straightforward to see the direct link between that neglect and the unsatisfactory performance of the company. Try this exercise yourself, right now, although you'll be able to do a much more comprehensive evaluation by the end of the book: Which of the six roles do you do very well, fairly well, or not so well? How much time and attention do you dedicate to each? Which do you enjoy and which do you instinctively avoid? Now think about what is holding back your organization from performing at a higher level. Our bet is that you'll see a direct correlation between those of the six roles which need more of your attention and skill and the obstacles to your company's greater progress. To succeed as the CEO, all six roles have to be fulfilled with consistent quality, and the roles where you are failing to do so will create the greatest problems for your organization.

Just as success at each role will be wasted unless you complete the roles "later" in the chain, there is inter-dependence in the other direction as well. What we mean is this: If you find yourself unable to construct an effective approach to one of the six roles, it is often because your approach to one of the *preceding* roles has missed the mark. For example, if you've been unable to craft a winning strategy to chart your company's course (Role 2), it's often because the chosen vision

(Role 1) is fundamentally unattainable and there is simply no strategy that will get you there. (One of us has always dreamed of playing in the National Basketball Association. That's fine as a dream but misguided as an inspiration for how to live his life, as it's simply not going to happen. CEOs make this mistake on behalf of their companies all the time, perhaps with more subtlety but equally destructively.) If the organization repeatedly fails to implement its action plans (Role 5), it's probably because you've not built and nurtured a sufficiently effective management team (Role 3). Similarly, if your employees or your Board members aren't reacting to your communications as you've intended (Role 6), the problem may lie in fundamental illogic somewhere in the first five roles which no amount of communicating, no matter how skillfully delivered, can paper over.

The six roles are inextricably linked to each other in both directions: Each one of the six is useless without the ones that follow it, and each one is impossible to craft unless the preceding ones are completed successfully. No CEO can succeed on a sustainable basis by attending to just five (much less fewer) of the six roles.

Chapter 14

Principles of Thought

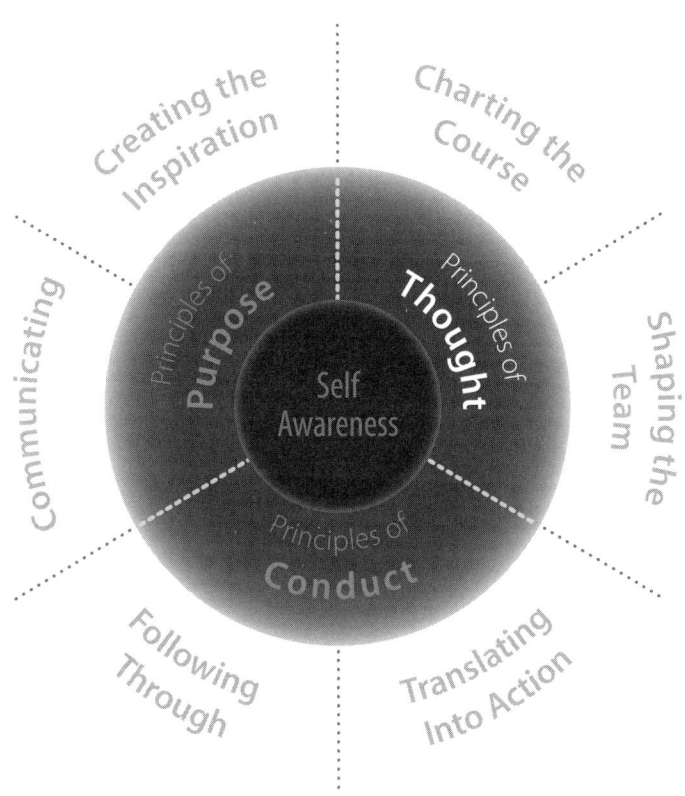

As we've explored in the previous two chapters, the Enlightened CEO is crystal clear about the agenda she is pursuing (the company's, not her own), and about what her job is to achieve that agenda (the six roles). Armed with that clarity of purpose, she then needs to make sense of the complex, noisy world around her so as to consistently make the right decisions as she fulfills her roles. The more clearly she can see that world, the better the decisions she'll make, and the better the chances that the company's objectives will be achieved.

To achieve that clarity, the Enlightened CEO stays true to three Principles of Thought: She is actively *open* to new input from a wide variety of sources; she invests her energy and time in a broad *quest for understanding*; and she evaluates issues on the merits, with *objectivity*. We address each of these three in turn in Chapters 15, 16 and 17.

Chapter 15

Openness

As CEO, you lead an organization which includes thinking, well-intentioned people who are in most cases a lot closer to the action — customers, market trends, operations and other personnel — than you are. As such, they can be a tremendous source of information and guidance if you keep yourself open to their input. Yet against all logic, most of us as CEOs squander a good portion of that opportunity by closing our mind to much that they have to offer.

The first step in maintaining openness is to recognize that you can learn from anybody. Someone's title may be modest, his IQ may be lower than yours, and even his intentions may be questionable, but he nonetheless understands some part of your company better than you do, and therefore has something to teach you if you give him the chance. All of us have two fundamental choices when we listen to others: to remind ourselves why we think we're smarter or better informed than they are and to spend our effort finding what's wrong with what they have to say; or to ignore whatever's wrong and instead focus on that portion of the input that is accurate and helpful. As long as you're spending time with someone else, why not focus on the latter?

Beyond being passively open — willing to listen when someone takes the initiative to offer us information — enlightened CEOs are actively open. They build formal structures in the organization, such as town meetings, site visits and one-on-one feedback sessions to encourage all throughout the organization to offer ideas and feedback. Procter & Gamble CEO A.G. Lafley was recently cited for his unusual willingness to receive continual feedback from employees as to how he can improve his own performance — including the use of 360-degree reviews. Wal-Mart has done this brilliantly throughout the whole company, deriving some of its best innovations from "associates" (its word for employees) who are constantly asked to share new ideas for products, intelligence on competitors' stores or suggestions to improve service with their managers.

• •

Poor listeners often answer even before the speaker has finished his thought, and before the real point has been made.

• •

To maximize the quantity of valuable information which you receive, it is important that you pay attention to the subtle, almost imperceptible ways in which you either encourage or discourage input. Do you express appreciation for all ideas offered, whether or not you believe they have merit, and hold up the person who has volunteered feedback as an example for others to follow? When you think an idea is baseless do you simply reject it, or do you help the offerer evaluate it herself in light of additional information which you can bring to bear so that she can get to the right answer along with you? The more you make the offering of input a positive experience for those in your organization the more of it you will receive.

In order to remain truly open to input, you have to avoid the common and all-too-human traps which we all fall prey to from time to time. One such trap is to be too locked into your own mental model of a situation to be open to views that challenge that model. We all need mental frameworks to structure our thoughts, but when we become overly committed to them with too much rigidity we are unable to upgrade those frameworks as new or contradictory information is offered. The enlightened CEO understands that he almost never finds the final, right answer to a challenge, but instead has in his head the best working hypothesis available at that moment in time. He then continually refines his hypothesis as new input is provided or as the situation evolves.

Another common mistake is for the CEO to respond too quickly to new information. Poor or mediocre listeners often answer even before the speaker has finished his thought, and before the real point has been made. As a result, they never receive the intended input, and have no chance to decide objectively whether it has merit. This overly hasty cut-off of information is a particular risk because you are the CEO. Often, people will bury their true message a level or two below what they initially say, because they are wary of your lofty title and uncertain about how you will react. Rather than quickly "docking" the new information into your existing framework, you would be well served to spend more time listening and exploring the speaker's frame of reference. There will be plenty of time soon enough to integrate that information into what you already know.

One can also lose an enormous amount of valuable input by being too judgmental. This adage has applicability to life in general, but is particularly true for someone with as much authority as a CEO. The person providing you feedback is almost never a threat to you, and even when she may be (such as a Board member or senior manager), CEOs often greatly exaggerate the severity or imminence of the threat. There is nothing to be gained by subtly or even silently "rating" the messenger or by trying to discredit them to save face. You have the power to act or not act on whatever input is provided, so take it at face value and don't distract yourself from the message by judging the person who offered it. Ironically, when we judge others we are giving them power over us, because we wind up expending our energy worrying about them.

The enlightened CEO knows that the key to openness is to listen, and then when she's done listening, to listen some more. She listens actively, probing deeply and engaging the speaker to help her understand the input. There is no rush to rate the input or to make a decision based upon it; invariably, those both happen fast enough without too much effort. The listening part of the process is the one that is more likely to be given short shrift, and where most CEOs need to increase their focus.

Being truly open requires considerable effort, discipline and patience, but the enlightened CEO understands that the ROI of that expended energy will be huge — as she expands her view of the world based on the knowledge and suggestions of everyone she encounters.

Chapter 16

The Quest for Understanding

Beyond remaining as open as possible, the enlightened CEO ensures that he exposes himself to information that is diverse along a variety of different dimensions. By expanding his knowledge in a range of different ways, the CEO stays abreast of the full range of issues which influence his organization's performance, and also increases the likelihood that he will recognize potential breakthrough ideas for his company.

First of all, the enlightened CEO maintains a sufficiently in-depth understanding of all parts of his own company. At Allied Signal/Honeywell, Larry Bossidy presided as CEO over a huge organization, yet in his book <u>Execution</u> (co-authored by Charan and Burke) he describes how he kept in touch by hitting the road and conducting in-depth multi-day reviews with management of far-flung divisions. At the other end of the spectrum, we have worked with CEOs of companies as small as ten million dollars who have not visited a division 200 miles down the road in almost a year, and who have only a superficial understanding of the true challenges faced by that part of the organization.

With the continued shrinking of the world, companies more than ever are expanding their geographic scope. As CEO you need to commit to the principle that if you aren't willing to develop a sufficient understanding of a part of your organization then perhaps your company is over-extended and should not be there in the first place. It is not enough to say "but I'm a delegator and I have good lieutenants." No matter how big the company and how good your team, ultimately the key decisions rise to your level, and you will not consistently make those decisions correctly unless you have a fundamental base of knowledge which extends to the entire company.

Of course, much of that understanding can take place remotely, enabled by the wide range of communications technologies that are available today. Much of it also happens by requesting information and reading it. Yet in our experience none of the new communications technologies is an adequate substitute for face-to-face interaction. In the end, physically showing up is an important part of the puzzle, because the most subtle and important "ground truths" are often those which don't show up in the more everyday forms of communication.

• •

> Many CEOs know their own companies in excruciating detail, yet forgo much of the available understanding of markets, customers and competitors.

• •

Obviously you can't know all there is to know about all corners of your organization. However, we have witnessed too many CEOs who extend that observation to an illogical next step; they simply forgo understanding an important part of their company at any substantive level. More often than not, that is a mistake that often proves costly, when the CEO recognizes too late that a problem in that part of the organization has spiraled out of control.

The way to conquer this challenge is to master the art of asking the right questions. While it may be impossible for you to be intimately familiar with all parts of your company, you should be able to ask tough questions of those responsible for a division or function and to recognize by the nature of their answers whether *they* have the in-depth understanding which they should. *When it is impractical for you to have an in-depth understanding, it is your responsibility to make sure that those around you do.*

It is equally incumbent on the CEO to stay intimately in touch with the external environment, including developments in the marketplace and the actions and profiles of competitors. No company can succeed in a vacuum, and many business failures can be traced to missing important market and competitive trends. Yet we know many CEOs who know their own companies in excruciating detail, yet forgo much of the available understanding of markets, customers and competitors. In today's world of powerful search engines, informal networks and skilled research resources, the enlightened CEO needs to commit herself to know as much as possible about the outside world as it relates to her company — no less so than she endeavors to know her own organization.

Both the internally and externally-oriented knowledge that the CEO maintains needs to be focused on the future far more than the present. Many CEOs can eloquently describe the needs of their current customer base, but are lax in forecasting how those needs are likely to change in the future. Most CEOs can describe the capabilities and limitations of the current management team, but are they equally focused on anticipating what will be needed from the management team in just one or two years as the business grows? Can the CEO relate succinctly the future outlooks for competition, technology, capacity, distribution channels and R&D? Too often, the answer to this question is "no," but the enlightened CEO understands that she is not as knowledgeable as she needs to be until she can answer them affirmatively.

Finally, the truly enlightened CEO extends his quest for understanding beyond the obvious boundaries of his company and its marketplace, to broader disciplines such as the extended business world, geopolitics, psychology, and others which can inform his job as CEO. In <u>The World is Flat</u>, author Thomas Friedman describes how McDonald's has experimented with drive-through orders taken by a person in a remote call center which instantly relays the order to the cook a few feet from where your car is sitting. The remote order-taker costs less, can spread his time more efficiently among multiple stores, and has access to technology that reduces errors. We have found that this simple story relayed to the right CEO can open her eyes to the opportunity that globalization presents for her company — even after direct suggestions as to how to capitalize on globalization were initially dismissed out of hand. Sometimes it is the examples furthest afield that best help us understand that which is right in front of us

— which is why it is important for the enlightened CEO to be well-read and to maintain broad knowledge outside of her own domain.

The range of knowledge needed to lead with excellence is diverse, but that is only because the responsibilities of the job are equally diverse. There is no getting around this tautology. Yet we often observe CEOs who work hard to stay informed about certain key areas while leaving gaping holes in others which are equally if not more important.

Why does this happen? It is true that the CEO is a busy person and that there are myriad competing demands on his time. Yet in our experience, that is not the true cause of the gaps in understanding. Most CEOs we know who work long hours, do so because they like to, and inevitably manage to find the time to understand the things that they choose to understand. The gaps in understanding occur instead because of an intellectual sloppiness, or stated a little more charitably, a lack of discipline. It is easy to acquire the knowledge in our comfort zones but harder to do so in the areas where more effort is required. The latter may include the company's IT challenges for the technologically inexperienced CEO, market and competitive knowledge for the CEO more comfortable with internal operations, or foreign operations for the CEO who spends the vast majority of his time at home.

Yet in accepting the CEO role you also are assuming the responsibility to relentlessly pursue understanding outside your comfort zone as well as inside; in fact, to spend more time on the former because that's where the greater effort is needed. The enlightened CEO recognizes where he has historically been intellectually lazy, and then goes out and fills those gaps with determined resolve. He understands that if the gaps are allowed to persist, then more often than not they will come back to haunt him in important ways.

It is impossible to succeed for very long as CEO unless you maintain a broad base of knowledge and continually upgrade it to keep pace with the rapid changes taking place all around you. Teachers at all levels are fond of saying that their most fundamental objective is to foster in their students a love of learning, and they've got that exactly right: The quest for ever-broader understanding is a key ingredient for success at the toughest job in business.

Chapter 17

Objectivity

The objective CEO:

1) Sees things as they are.

2) Makes decisions based on the merits.

Nothing is more obviously in the CEO's and the company's best interests, yet every CEO faces an ongoing struggle to remain consistently objective. There are a variety of factors and temptations which lead her astray.

First, the CEO must overcome the strong pre-conceived notions that she brings to the table. All of us have myriad assumptions which we've accumulated from a lifetime of experience. This process is necessary for survival, as we can't tackle every new problem we face with a completely blank sheet of paper. Yet too often we carry our assumptions from experience too far by assuming that the current challenge can be addressed neatly by a solution that has worked for us in the past. The enlightened CEO needs to be disciplined in drawing upon her experience up to the point that it is useful — without falling into the trap of conveniently assuming that a previous answer will work once again.

The keys to that discipline are the subjects of the preceding two chapters: openness and the quest for understanding. Working hard to be open to new ideas from a wide range of sources helps us test and challenge our pre-existing assumptions. When there is disagreement in the room, it is essential to spend the time necessary to give a full hearing to those views which differ from what you initially believe to be the right answer. Often, the quicker you try to cut off an opposing view the more it's a sign that there may be something to it. In the interest of efficiency and of protecting your assumptions, a part of you may not want that view fully aired; for once acknowledged there may be hard work needed to re-work your assumptions and find the correct answer. The CEO who builds objectivity into her organization trains herself to listen a second and third time for opposing views and to evaluate them independently of her own preconceived notions.

Similarly, the more energy the CEO devotes to assimilating new knowledge from both within and outside of her company, the more she will expose herself to a diversity of approaches. Armed with that diversity, she is more likely to evaluate ideas on their merits and not based on how long she has held them. Openness and knowledge are the antidotes to pre-conceived notions, and are thus the breeding ground of objectivity.

> Optimism can be an important ingredient of leadership, but as a basis to evaluate facts and make decisions it can be extraordinarily dangerous.

A second factor that limits our objectivity is the tendency to engage in wishful thinking. Naturally, we want things to go well for our company. CEOs work hard to achieve that outcome in the face of sometimes long odds, and that causes many CEOs to be optimists. Optimism can be an important ingredient of leadership, but as a basis to evaluate facts and make decisions it can be extraordinarily dangerous. Yet unrealistically optimistic CEOs are all around us. Many of the CEOs of the old-line, once-great Fortune 500 industrial companies, when faced with perilous competitive and market trends, seriously underestimated the implications of those trends. The leadership of these companies seemed to assume that history alone would be enough to ensure future success — but instead their companies became object lessons of short-sightedness and large-scale business failure.

We also know far too many CEOs who try to distract their employees from the fact that no good answers have been found to the obvious challenges facing the company — by simply reiterating eloquently that the day will come when the company will magically ascend to the upper ranks of its industry. Finally, there is the CEO who jeopardizes his company's strategy by wishfully assuming with certainty that a key action, hire, or technology change will work, rather than make a realistic assessment of the odds of success and then build in the necessary margin of error.

Rather than cling to these varieties of wishful thinking, a far more likely path to success is one of tough, reasoned skepticism. Ask yourself what can go wrong, and then build strategic and action plans that are robust enough for the company to prosper — even if those negative eventualities occur. Between optimism, realism, and pessimism, the most direct route to objectivity is realism — but if you're not sure exactly where those lines lie, you're much better off erring on the side of skepticism rather than naively assuming a rosy future.

· ·

> The less enlightened thought processes — pre-conceived notions, wishful thinking, resistance to change and corporate politics — are all around us, all day long.

· ·

Organizations and CEOs also can lose objectivity because they are afraid of change. There is a natural tendency to want the world of tomorrow to look like the one of today, and that can blind us to facts that suggest that it will be otherwise. As the CEO, when you are presented with an argument that some cherished aspect of the status quo is threatened by new realities, that is the moment for you to work doubly hard to probe and explore the view being offered, and to fight any natural tendencies to turn a blind eye to reality.

One of the biggest enemies of all to objectivity is corporate politics. Every member of your team has at least two agendas — the company's and her own — and virtually every argument or recommendation you receive is colored by both. Many CEOs get caught up in these politics, worrying inordinately about the moods of the different players and allowing that concern to influence which argument carries the day. This behavior is self-reinforcing: When team members observe that politics influences decisions, they will dramatically increase their politicking.

Conversely, the CEO who consistently exhibits that he makes decisions based on the merits of the issues forces his people to do the necessary work to perfect their recommendations — as they learn that it is the strength of their arguments and not of their politicking that gets them the desired results. In companies led by enlightened CEOs the best idea wins — rather than the convenient idea or that espoused by the most powerful or politically skillful person in the room.

In the face of these challenges, one way to reinforce objective decision-making is to build a culture which insists that decisions be justified to as broad an audience as possible. When a decision-maker, whether you or a member of your team, knows that he will have to articulate his reasoning to a broad audience, he will be more diligent in ensuring that it is based on sound reasoning. Conversely, a company culture which dictates that the person in power gets to make decisions — and then others simply do what he says without understanding why — opens the door to poor decision-making devoid of objectivity. For this reason, we have always believed that secrecy in corporations is over-rated. Obviously, there are times when it is not appropriate to share information or the rationale behind a decision with certain audiences, but all too often people in power, including CEOs, fall back on secrecy when they're not sure that they can justify their reasoning. Transparency improves the quality of decision-making, and excessive secrecy has exactly the opposite effect.

Maintaining objectivity as CEO requires enormous discipline, and it is an ideal you will never fully achieve. The less enlightened thought processes which we've described — pre-conceived notions, wishful thinking, resistance to change and corporate politics — are all around us, all day long. Yet the best CEOs are vigilant in weeding them out wherever they can — in the way they themselves make decisions, and in the culture they instill in the entire organization. When you have made the commitment to do the hard work of promoting objectivity throughout your company, you will have taken a huge step towards realizing your potential as an enlightened CEO.

Chapter 18

Principles of Conduct

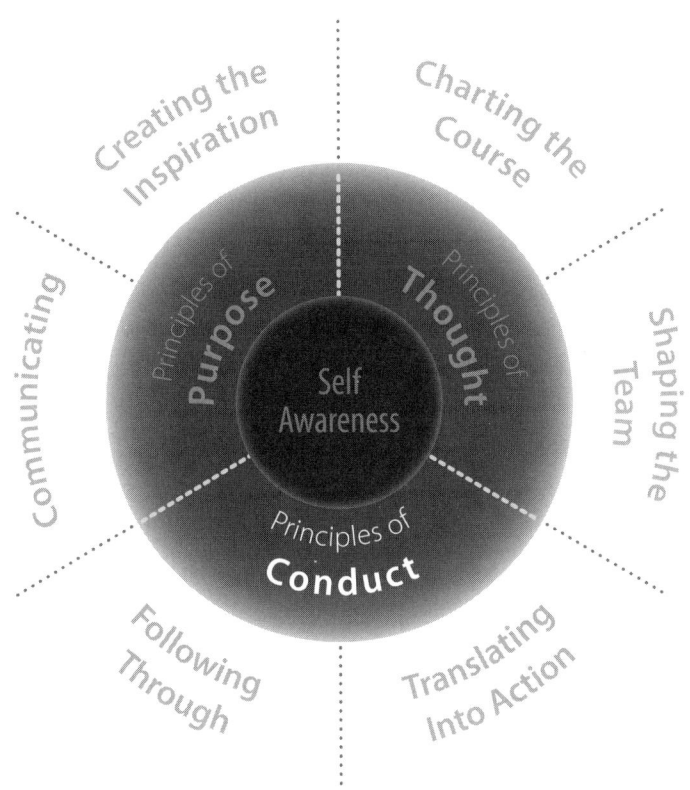

We began this book by speaking of the challenges faced by the CEO as he tries to inspire a large number of people to move as a cohesive unit in the direction of the company's long-term objectives — challenges that can at times make the CEO feel relatively powerless. Those challenges are real, and the prescription for conquering them comprises Parts IV through IX of the book.

Yet paradoxically, at the same time that most CEOs find it difficult to get management and employees to move as one over the long term, they discover that they have extraordinary and often unintended power to cause individuals to move almost instantaneously in lots of different directions. One of the most daunting realities that comes with being CEO is that within your own domain you are a celebrity — in fact *the* celebrity — and therefore people will react, and often overact, to everything that you do and say, whether logical or illogical, consistent or all over the map. For this reason (among others), your conduct will have a critical and multiplying effect, and to achieve excellence as CEO you have to apply the same principled approach to your conduct as to your purpose and thought.

So far we have described the Enlightened CEO as having a clear understanding of:

- His own strengths and weaknesses, likes and dislikes, and needs and aspirations, as well as how those have the potential to both help and hinder his performance (Self-Awareness);

- Why he is here and what he is trying to achieve (Principles of Purpose); and,

- The optimal way to internalize the information around him in order to maximize the quality of his decision-making (Principles of Thought).

With his purpose clear and his mind focused appropriately, the final step in the CEO's pursuit of enlightened leadership is to conduct himself in an optimal way towards those around him. How does he carry himself throughout the day? What sort of example does he set? What reactions does he engender? To what extent does the way in which he conducts himself: Motivate or de-motivate? Focus on the key paths forward or distract? Unify and align, or divide? Build trust or suspicion? Inspire lofty ambition, or engender cynicism?

As with "purpose" and "thought," it is quite common for the CEO to stray too often to the wrong side of those dichotomies. And as with those other domains, the key to staying on the right side is to remain true to a short list of critical tenets. We call these Principles of Conduct, and they include:

- *Calm:* The CEO must stay cool under pressure, remaining consistent in the face of the wide variety of distractions which have the potential to throw him off his game;
- *Humility:* In his interactions with others he is genuine in accepting the limits of his knowledge and power, and in his appreciation of the wisdom and skills of those around him;
- *Equity:* He understands at a very fundamental level that long-term gain will not be achieved by treating others unfairly.

By focusing on these standards of conduct we are not preaching ethics or advocating a particular brand of morality. Instead, our point is that the degree to which you master the Principles of Conduct will have huge implications for your ability to get the organization to follow your lead and achieve its objectives. To explore this notion in more depth, let's begin with the first of the three principles — "Calm."

Chapter 19

Calm

The first component of an enlightened approach to one's conduct is "calm," for if the goal of any organization is a consistency of purpose among the many members of the team, then your celebrity as CEO means that in the end that purpose will be only as consistent as your own behavior. Unless you as CEO can maintain a calm and steadiness under pressure you'll wind up spending at least as much time correcting previous directives, whether intended or unintended, as you will moving the organization forward towards its long-term objectives.

Before exploring in more detail what we mean by "calm," let's first be clear about what we *don't* mean: We are not prescribing a particular personality type for the successful CEO. The personalities of successful CEOs (and unsuccessful ones) range from highly animated to understated. Inspiration for the team can come from an extremely high-energy CEO who can light up a room with his optimism and insights. Yet it can also be generated by the CEO who is less excitable and speaks in more measured tones, but who invariably has something to say which is worth hearing.

Where the CEO's personality can get her in trouble is when she instinctively follows it too far, absent some internal checks and balances. For the more animated CEO, wowing an audience or impressing a listener with the speed and insight with which you can answer a question can indeed inspire, but many a CEO has found herself months later picking up the pieces when she realizes after the fact that she came to a conclusion and expressed her view too quickly. Similarly, the understated CEO, while less likely to speak precipitously, must continually remain conscious of where and when inspiration, insight, and emotional support is required, recognizing that others may be more in need of human interaction and affirmation than she is herself. For both of these personality types and a wide variety of others, we believe that staying calm, as we define it below, is necessary to ensure that one's personality remains a strength and not a liability.

The first element of calm is consistency of direction. A highly successful CEO once told us that in his experience the first 999 times he articulates an important element of his vision nothing sustainable happens, but on the thousandth the organization "gets it" and long-term movement in the desired direction begins to take place. Obviously he is speaking metaphorically, but his point is a critical one: It is the cumulative effect of the CEO's actions and communications over a long period of time, and not a single communication, which influences and moves the organization over the long term. Yet what is the manager or employee (or customer, partner, supplier, or Board mem-

· ·

There is a big difference between intentional, carefully-thought-out change and the inadvertent or destructive change which comes from undisciplined behavior, words or decision-making.

· ·

ber) to do if that cumulative effect includes frequent changes of direction or "flavors of the month"? His choice is to drop what he's doing and change gears every time the CEO says something different, or instead to be de-motivated and paralyzed into inaction. Neither option is a prescription for organizational success.

Obviously, consistency of direction shouldn't manifest itself as close-mindedness, inflexibility, or insensitivity to new information. As the cliché goes, change is a constant of corporate life. However, there is a big difference between intentional, carefully-thought-out change and the inadvertent or destructive change which comes from undisciplined behavior, words or decision-making. The CEO who maintains a calmness in his perspective and demeanor is able to implement changes, large or small, that are truly needed while avoiding those that are mere distractions or worse.

Beyond consistency of direction, the organization very much needs from you a consistency in the way that you display your emotions. If you as CEO operate with unpredictable emotions, people don't know how to accurately calibrate your reactions: Are you truly excited about the idea which I just offered and will you back it up over the long term, or will I go do the work and rally support for the idea only to have you ignore my efforts or pull the rug out from under me at a later point in time? Conversely, is your obvious displeasure with something I've said or done a signal that I truly need to make a change, or are you just having a bad day? When your emotional reactions are inconsistent and therefore can't be interpreted in predictable ways, people will interpret them based on any of a variety of truly dysfunctional decision rules: They will either do what best suits their own purposes, or what most easily avoids conflict, or they'll be paralyzed by their confusion and do nothing worthwhile at all. Again, both a high-energy and more measured CEO can inspire the troops, but both will be more successful when they display emotional consistency so that their intentions can be interpreted accurately.

In addition, all of your constituents, both within and outside of the company, are looking to you for anchoring and stability. When you display fear or concern the effect of that display is magnified, both because of the number of people who will notice it and because those people will exaggerate the concern in their own minds because of who you are. As CEO you will of course regularly have concerns and there will be many situations in which you will need to articulate them, but in doing so you must project calm, a sense of proportion and a control over the situation so as not to unduly disrupt the focus and productivity of your constituents.

This does not mean that you should sweep tough issues under the rug, because those around you can sense the true reality of the situation: When you display false optimism or appear not to grasp the seriousness of the situation, you undermine your credibility and effectiveness as a leader. What is needed is the appropriate balance, grounded both in reality and a vision for how the challenges faced by the organization will be conquered. The CEO who can simultaneously display his command and unflappability while rigorously and objectively dealing with sometimes harsh realities is far more likely to inspire his company towards success. Yet that dichotomy is very difficult to maintain unless the CEO is able at all times to draw upon an inner calm.

Finally, beyond your influence over others calm is a critical ingredient for maintaining your own objectivity and logic in solving problems. CEOs who lack calm are erratic in the quality of their decision-making — they have knee-jerk reactions and let their emotions rule. In times of conflict, they let others get inside their head and therefore lose objectivity while yielding the advantage to the other party. Conversely, the CEO who in the face of threats large or small is able to keep her cool, maintain a steady perspective and not overreact is much more likely to come out on top. There are always more than enough difficult components in the challenges you face: You are much more likely to work through them successfully if you don't add into the mix your own erratic perspective or emotional state as yet an additional variable.

• •

The philosophy behind this training, it was explained, is that the time one gains by hurrying is less valuable than the perspective one gains by moving at a more consistent and measured speed.

• •

As with so many of the principles of enlightened leadership, recognition and acceptance of the importance of calm is a critical first step. However, calm is a state of mind which must be continually re-nourished — it does not happen just because we want it to. Our professional and personal lives are full of potential upsets which threaten our ability to stay consistent in our words and emotions. What then are we to do to maintain that consistency?

The calm CEO is usually one who builds into her daily, weekly and annual routines the opportunity for reflection and emotional stabilization, whether through physical exercise, hobbies, vacation or simply regular mental temperature-taking and reminders to herself to stay the type of CEO she truly wants to be. Some CEOs can thrive with only limited time away while others need much more — but we've yet to meet the CEO who succeeds over the long term without consciously determining how much he needs and then building a professional and personal lifestyle to ensure that he gets it, even when times are tough. Working yourself towards mental exhaustion or emotional fragility, because you think the extra hours are called for by the challenges your company is facing, will never yield the same return as the perspective and consistency you will achieve when you walk out of your office and re-connect with an inner sense of calm.

The combination of the CEO's drive to get things done, the high level of energy he is likely to possess, and the myriad of stimuli he is exposed to all day long make it very hard to consistently maintain a true sense of calm. In seeking a means to do so, we are inspired by something we heard in the interview of a fireman who was at the World Trade Center on 9/11. He was asked why, in films of the tragedy, firemen are seen walking to the building from their trucks a block away and not running; and he responded that they are trained to walk and not run. The philosophy behind this training, it was explained, is that the time one gains by hurrying is less valuable than the perspective one gains by moving at a more consistent and measured speed. By moving too quickly, one loses one's solid foundation of perspective, and the poor decision-making which can result is usually more costly than any benefit gained from getting to the desired location a little more quickly.

Ever since we heard that interview we've tried to keep it in mind as we act as and advise CEOs ourselves. In effect, we've installed a check-and-balance on our personality, ambition and drive: Are we sure enough about our conclusion to act and speak now, or would a little more time be more valuable than a quick decision? The critical extra time may be a few seconds, a few minutes, a couple of days, or a month or longer, and sometimes no extra time is needed at all, but maintaining the discipline to ask and answer this question can make a measurable difference in the consistency of the CEO's direction to the organization and therefore in his effectiveness.

For the CEO, calm means a consistency of the direction you give to others, of the emotions you display, and of your own perspective as you address problems and make decisions. The leader who develops the discipline to remain calm in the face of the constant pressures of the job will have taken another large step towards becoming an Enlightened CEO.

Chapter 20

Humility

No one (or almost no one) ascends to the position of CEO without first experiencing a long series of successes earlier in life. As the CEO-to-be progresses through these successes, her self-confidence steadily grows, and that confidence breeds further success as it both encourages her to reach for the next rung and inspires others to look to her as a leader.

Success and self-confidence are of course both good things — unless they completely take over one's persona and crowd out something which is just as important: humility. For the CEO, humility means understanding and acknowledging the limits of one's own capabilities, however strong, and fully appreciating the value of the other members of the team. As simple and inarguably worthwhile as that definition sounds, it is an ongoing challenge for all CEOs to allow humility to take its rightful place alongside self-confidence as a guide for their conduct.

The reason that genuine humility is so important is because without it you will find it very difficult to stay true to most of the other principles of enlightenment. For example:

• The CEO who is overly egotistical will intimidate those around him. They will be less likely to share important information with the CEO for fear of being labeled "wrong" or made to feel "dumb." This is just common sense: The more you act as if you have all the answers already, the less new information you will receive. The cut-off of important information will compromise one of the Principles of Thought: the quest for understanding. Even to the extent that the CEO without humility continues to receive information, the truthfulness of it will be less consistent, as members of the team will color what they say in order to feed rather than offend the CEO's ego. Conversely, the truly humble CEO communicates to his team that he doesn't believe he is fundamentally smarter or "righter" than those around him, and simply wants to hear from them the unvarnished truth.

- Not only will the CEO who lacks humility receive a reduced flow of important information, he will also be less open to it, resulting in a further loss of information before it can be processed into his mental model of the situation. The all-important thing for the CEO who lacks humility is preservation of ego, which causes him to discard those parts of the message that may jeopardize his own self-confidence. The genuinely humble CEO, on the other hand, possesses a proportionate sense of self-confidence and is accepting of his own limitations. He therefore knows that nothing he hears can shake his basic belief in himself, and is able to hear and accept a wider range of input.

- When it is time to evaluate information and make a decision, the humble CEO is able to remove himself from the equation and maintain his *objectivity*. Conversely, the CEO who truly believes he's the smartest person in the room will find it difficult to avoid making decisions in a way that gives disproportionate emphasis to his own biases.

Without a successful quest for understanding, and without openness and objectivity, the CEO is unlikely to consistently arrive at the right answers and make the best decisions. The ego-compromised decisions of the CEO who lacks humility are therefore likely to exact a significant toll on the performance of the company.

Yet there is another argument for the CEO to be genuinely humble which is at least as important as any we've discussed thus far: Without humility, you are unlikely to ever build a team and an organization that is cohesive, loyal and sustainable over the long term. There are several reasons behind this truism.

First, as we described earlier in the book, employees and management tend to be very accurate observers of human nature, and especially the motivation of the CEO. Any charismatic or successful leader can temporarily inspire others, but when the leader is driven by his own ego and doesn't combine it with a genuine appreciation for the contribution of others, that inspiration will be short-lived. At the first sign that the power of the CEO is waning, or that the company under her leadership has hit a rough spot, or that a leader elsewhere in the organization is marshalling resources for an unproductive political confrontation, the support of her people can turn rapidly to something approaching organizational anarchy. In the end, people will remain fully committed to your vision and the company only to the extent that you truly care about what they have to offer, and to the extent that it isn't simply all about you. And who can blame them: Isn't that exactly what you would do in their shoes?

> The ego-compromised decisions of the CEO
> who lacks humility are likely to exact a significant
> toll on the performance of the company.

Second, as CEO you set an example for everyone in the company. If you carry yourself as the smartest person in the room and demonstrate that it really is all about you, then other leaders up and down the organization will follow your lead and do the same. For an organization to be successful its various parts have to be moving cohesively in the same direction, and that cohesion is enabled not by excessive egoism but by a sincere appreciation of the value of others — a perspective which comes from genuine humility.

Third, one of the CEO's most fundamental responsibilities is to build a company that would continue to be successful even if he were to disappear tomorrow. Companies led by overly ego-driven CEOs tend to become CEO cults, thriving to a great extent based on who he is rather than on strong principles and processes which are infused consistently throughout the organization. This can be a prescription for success in the short- and perhaps even the medium-term, but over the longer term the company will reach its full potential only when the broader organization, its culture and its people are what drive its success.

A lack of CEO humility can have another, sometimes disastrous cost to the company — one that can be seen on the front page of the Wall Street Journal more days than not — namely ethical violations which may undermine or destroy both the CEO and the company. Although unethical or law-breaking CEOs comprise a small minority of the profession, their experience is instructional for the rest of us. When one studies the highly publicized cases, what is striking is either the pettiness of the violations or, in other cases, the immense wealth of the violator who, in the pursuit of even greater riches, wound up unemployed or in prison. What drives such illogical behavior, where the payoff clearly isn't worth the risk, even aside from ethical considerations? We believe that the culprit is excessive ego, and that a dose of genuine humility could have prevented the downward spiral.

• •

Failure may be the seed from which humility grows, but it takes an open, reflective, and willing CEO to see the promise of that seed.

• •

The vast majority of CEOs grow up with reasonable values, yet the rogue CEO later compromises those values as his success and stature grows. For this CEO, success has gone to his head and inflated his sense of his own individual worth. He believes he is superior to others, knows better than others the difference between right and wrong, and is convinced that the rules that apply to others don't apply to him. This CEO thinks he is responsible for creating all of the value of the company (rather than being just one small part of that value creation) and that therefore he is owed more than he is getting. He then goes out on his own to redress the imbalance and grab more for himself by straying outside of accepted rules of behavior. If he's caught, he winds up with his company discredited and with himself in deep trouble. It is the inflated ego of this CEO which has instigated the corruption of his values and the loss of his and his company's integrity. Conversely, the CEO who works hard to connect with a genuine humility will be more appreciative of his role within a larger whole, and will be much less likely to cause that whole to come crashing down in his pursuit of personal aggrandizement.

Humility can be a difficult attribute to develop, particularly for successful people such as CEOs. Some CEOs are fortunate to be naturally humble or to develop humility early in their careers, while others never get there. However, perhaps the most common pattern is the CEO who as a young "Turk" didn't have a lot of time or patience to conduct himself humbly, but who increasingly appreciates the value of humility as he reaches middle age. Part of the reason for this phenomenon is that one of the greatest teachers of humility is failure, and until one has fallen on one's face a few times it is difficult to lose the sense of being bullet-proof and smarter than everyone else in the room. To the extent that it takes time to accumulate an impressive list of failures, it will also take time for some CEOs to conduct themselves with the humility that enlightened leadership requires.

Yet CEOs young or old do have some control over the rate at which they develop humility. Failure may be the seed from which humility grows, but it takes an open, reflective, and willing CEO to see the promise in that seed, give it the care and nurturing it needs, and turn it into a harvest of humility. We encourage all readers to study in depth not only your successes, so as to further breed the self-confidence which your job requires, but also the instances where things didn't go as planned, so as to connect with the inner humility which is equally important to becoming a great CEO.

Finally, the reader may ask, "How do I conduct myself with humility if I'm not truly *feeling* humble? Can humility be faked?" The answer is no — genuine humility, like any core human attribute, cannot be faked successfully over an extended period of time. The true "you" will come out, and others will see you accurately for who you are.

However, just as practicing a tennis stroke or speaking a foreign language will improve your game or increase your fluency, many learned behaviors become more natural with practice. If reading this book has increased your sensitivity to the value of humility but you believe that you're not yet there, then go out and start practicing humility one meeting or interaction at a time. Do so even if you have to make a special effort to be humble when it doesn't come naturally — just as you'd practice a new tennis stroke or foreign language that you've not yet completely mastered. Practice as many times a day as you can, and when you find yourself acting in an overly ego-driven way make a mental note that you'll try to do better next time.

As time goes by, you'll increasingly find that the humility which required conscious effort in the past will increasingly come to the fore naturally — while the ego-driven behaviors decline in frequency. In all likelihood none of us will ever reach the humility of a Mother Theresa, as ego is a pretty deeply ingrained element of the psyche of the CEO (and of all humans). However, if you believe in the value of humility and are willing to practice it in a disciplined way on a day-to-day basis, you'll be surprised how quickly people around you notice the change and begin to think of you as a genuinely humble person. And when that happens, you'll have taken yet another large step towards becoming an enlightened CEO.

Chapter 21

Equity

In the previous chapter we described how humility is a critical ingredient if the CEO is to build a team that is motivated to do what is best for the organization. Yet there is one more ingredient that must be in the mix in order for her to achieve that end. For management and employees to truly give their all and follow your lead, they must know that as part of the deal they themselves will be treated equitably.

Although equity can be measured by tangible rewards, the first step towards instilling a sense of fairness is to treat all with whom you come in contact with the respect that they deserve as fellow human beings. As CEO, you are likely more accomplished and more highly paid than everyone else in your company. Yet the enlightened CEO recognizes that that does not make her a superior person. If your conduct towards all is respectful, then you will be demonstrating your belief that even the most junior person in the organization is every bit as worthy as you. In doing so, you will have taken the first step towards building a culture of equity.

On the other hand, the CEO who bullies people in the name of improving performance — or publicly denigrates them at a personal level for not delivering results — is poisoning his organization by communicating that this is a company which uncaringly tramples over people in order to create profits for shareholders and rewards for the select few. A disrespectful approach is not a winning formula for building long-term strength and success for your organization, much less a fun place to work.

Beyond conducting yourself with respect for others, it is critical that you build a company which provides fair rewards for all. First of all, to retain and motivate employees over the long term your organization must compensate fairly relative to other companies and to societal norms. That means avoiding the temptation to pay as little as absolutely possible in order to squeeze every last ounce of profitability out of employees as if they were machines, but instead to share rewards in a way that communicates that we are all going to win or lose together. Rewarding fairly also means not *overpaying* by dramatic amounts, for as attractive as that may sound to some in the short-term, it inevitably creates imbalances that are unsustainable and that come back to haunt the company at some point in its future evolution. The excesses in some quarters of the late 1990's — and the reverberations which continue to this day — provide one example of how overcompensation can create problems down the road.

• •

> Employees need to know that the vision includes fair treatment for all — including respect, fair rewards and compassion where appropriate, at the same time that the company drives hard for ever-greater performance and results.

• •

Secondly, for rewards to be fair, whether in the form of salary, benefits, time off, promotion or attractive assignments, they must be distributed based on merit. Employees will watch closely and know exactly who in the company is being rewarded and who is not — as well as what behaviors and accomplishments are being rewarded. They will then connect the dots and ascertain whether or not you are in fact distributing rewards based on merit.

Their conclusions about fairness will have a huge and powerful multiplying effect on the success of your company. If you have built a system of fair rewards for the right behaviors, then you will encourage more of the desirable behavior, compounding your company's success. On the other hand, if employees observe that your company's rewards are often based on political connections, seniority or other non-merit-based criteria, they will conclude that working hard in the right ways has a diluted payoff, and they will be less motivated to do so. For this reason, it is well worth your effort as CEO to spend a good chunk of your time ensuring that you and those who work for you are very deliberate in fairly dividing the spoils of success to those who deserve them — and then in making those decisions as public as reasonably possible to serve as an example for all employees. By doing so, you will be building a culture of equity which encourages the right behaviors.

In sharing the rationale behind equitable decisions with others in the organization, it is important to remember that they will bring to those issues different levels of information and pre-conceived notions than you will. The burden is on you as the leader to carefully communicate your rationale so that others can understand the fairness of your decision. Too often, human resources or legal advisors recommend that you say as little as possible, and they have understandable reasons to issue such advice. Yet in doing so they usually weigh the downside risks more than the upside benefits, and it is your job as CEO to push the envelope as much as possible in the direction of openness and sharing of information in order to make it clear to all that you are running the company in an equitable way.

In sum, equity means treating people with respect, and it means rewarding fairly. Yet there is one more element which, if part of your arsenal, will truly convince your organization that you are all in this together. The last element of equity for the CEO is a genuine sense of *compassion* that goes beyond a purely mathematical sense of fairness. Because employees are human they inevitably come with a unique set of personal pressures, limitations and failings. The compassionate CEO accepts their humanity, and therefore knows that there are times when it is important to be understanding, and not just provide feedback and rewards in unthinking, reflexive ways.

Sometimes the role of a leader is to temper the rules and help the employee in need — whether in the form of extra time off to deal with an important personal problem; a second or third chance to save his job, complete with extra coaching to help him do so; or forgiveness rather than punishment when the employee under pressure has said or done something that is out of line. In the case of the latter, we've found that one of your most powerful "teaching moments" comes when the employee has "screwed up" and knows that he has done so. Rather than tell the employee the obvious and come down on him, let him acknowledge his own mistake. If you then respond by compassionately helping him sort out the problem to prevent it from recurring, you will have inspired loyalty both in that employee and in others who will observe the humanity with which even problematic behavior is handled.

Conducting yourself as CEO with equity does not mean running a company based on charity, tolerance of mediocrity or equal rewards for all regardless of performance. To the contrary, in the intense and often globally competitive environment in which all companies operate, the rules of capitalism must prevail if the company is to survive and prosper — rules that include hard work, excellence, meritocracy and a willingness to make tough choices. However, the CEO who takes those rules to a cut-throat extreme may see short-term gain but will not build success over the longer term. For employees and management to go the extra mile required to build a truly great organization, they need to know that the vision for the company's success includes fair treatment for all — including respect, fair rewards, and compassion where appropriate, at the same time that the company drives hard for ever-greater performance and results.

The enlightened CEO further understands that the concept of equity must extend beyond those on the company's payroll. She recognizes that customers are not a constituency to be "maximized" as if they were inanimate, but instead human beings who must be served not only with excellence but with respect, fairness and understanding. Like employees, customers keep very good scorecards of which competitors merely "sell to" them and which treat them fairly, and the latter will get their business over the long term.

Similarly, the quality and service you receive from suppliers over the long term, particularly when you get in a jam and most need it, will be proportional to the degree that you treat them fairly, and don't take undue advantage of them when you have them over a barrel. Furthermore, to the extent that you rely on partnerships or joint ventures, you'll be attractive to the most desirable partners only to the extent that you develop and maintain a reputation for treating them fairly. The adage "never do a deal that isn't good for both sides" sums up all of these corporate relationships, and is an important one for the enlightened CEO to keep top of mind.

One particularly enlightened executive whom we know takes this notion one step further — he maintains that it is even wise to treat your *competitors* fairly. That concept may sound like it contradicts the tenets of capitalism, but not if you understand his meaning. Of course he knows that the goal is to outperform the competition. His point, however, is that *how* you do so is important as well. When you succeed through the rules of fair competition, you are building a company that wins over the long term. On the other hand, if you win through questionable ethics or tactics then the short-term benefit will be gained at the expense of long-term corruption of your own organization. As counterintuitive as it may sound, for us the notion that even competitors should be treated fairly is a powerful reminder that the CEO who truly internalizes and applies the concept of equity to all constituencies will build a company with which all — employees, customers, suppliers, and partners — will want to do business.

• •

Conducting yourself as CEO with equity does not mean running a company based on charity, tolerance of mediocrity or equal rewards for all regardless of performance.

• •

In previous chapters, we've described the enlightened CEO as one who lives by the following principles: self-awareness, adoption of the company's agenda, fulfillment of all CEO roles, openness, quest for understanding, objectivity, calm and humility. All of these are important predicates for successful stewardship of your company, but where the rubber ultimately hits the road is in how you actually *treat* the people around you. Absent this last Principle of Conduct — equity — others will see the previous eight principles as mere thought exercises which do not actually benefit them. On the other hand, the CEO who conducts himself at all times based on the principle of equity will inspire others to rally around all of his principles of leadership, and to devote themselves to his vision for the company.

Chapter 22

Your Power as CEO

In Chapter 1 we described the impotence felt by all CEOs at one time or another, as they struggle to get others to move consistently in the direction they have prescribed for the organization. What CEO hasn't said to herself at one time or another, "Why can't I just describe what needs to be done and then have them go do it? Why is that so hard?"

This limit on the CEO's power is real but its characterization as such stems in part from a misunderstanding of the nature of the CEO's true power: It lies not in getting others to automatically do what we say, but rather in setting an example that educates and inspires others. In so doing, the CEO *teaches* them to do whatever is required by the challenges of the day rather than simply *orders* them to.

Because the CEO is the most-watched person in the company, he has enormous power to set the company's tone — for good, for bad, or somewhere in between. Just as many CEOs discover over time that they have overestimated their ability to *make* someone do something, observant CEOs also discover that they have *underestimated* their power to inspire — or corrupt — by their example. And that is perhaps the most powerful reason why it is worth your effort to embrace the principles of enlightenment: Because the degree to which you do so — whether it is objectivity in making decisions, merit in distributing rewards, or openness in encouraging input — will have a huge multiplying effect on the degree to which all within your organization follow your lead.

Not only are these principles important, their merit is indisputable. Yet the vast majority of CEOs we know — if they are honest with themselves — will give themselves only mixed grades for adherence to them. What is going on here? *Why do we actively compromise principles which are valuable and indisputable, and in so doing subvert our own success and that of our companies?*

The answer lies in the fundamental complexity of human beings — a complexity even more characteristic of individuals as talented and driven as CEOs than of the average person. Included in this complexity are a closet-full of personal concerns, temptations and hidden demons — which often work to *sabotage* our own success, at the very same time that we are striving to be successful.

• •

CEOs overestimate their ability to make someone
do something, yet underestimate their power to
inspire — or corrupt — by their example.

• •

This phenomenon is much easier to observe in others. If you've ever taken the time to ask a friend or business associate to describe in detail his career ambition, as well as what he is doing to realize that ambition, it is often easy to identify key steps that he is omitting or crucial missteps which are preventing him from getting to the next level. What is easy to see in others is more difficult to see in ourselves — yet it is quite likely that, as with your friends, there are unintentional yet destructive behaviors which are undermining your success as CEO.

Some of the most powerful steps that CEOs can take to propel their career and their company's success forward reside not in the outside world — but rather in recognizing the things they are doing which sabotage their own success, and then in eliminating and moving beyond them.

The framework we have described throughout Part III is intended to be a prophylactic against such self-sabotage. A more accurate self-awareness will help you recognize how you are getting in the way of your own success. And the principles of purpose, thought and conduct will help you align who you are as CEO with the best interests of your company, and therefore with your own ambition as well.

The thoughtful reader also may have recognized that the principles of enlightenment which we have described are all mutually reinforcing. For example, it is the genuine embrace of *humility* and the corollary valuing of others which enables the CEO to maintain *openness* to input and to treat others *equitably*. Likewise, the CEO with *humility* is much more likely to remember that it is not all about him, and to put *the company's objectives* ahead of his own. The steady point of reference which comes with *calm* enables the CEO to remain *objective* as he makes decisions. *Humility* itself stems from *self-awareness*, as one takes accurate stock of one's own strengths and weaknesses — and so on and so on. The elements of enlightenment which we've explored are intricately interlaced in many different ways — and as such provide a solid underpinning for the CEO, both to prevent him from falling into the depths of sabotage as well as to support him as he reaches to raise himself and his company to new heights.

So which is it going to be for you? With all that you've worked for over the years, and with all the hours you devote to your career today, will you continue to sabotage your own success in a few critical, debilitating ways — or will you invest in your future and that of your company by embracing the principles of enlightenment? We hope that by now your commitment to the latter is firm — so let's turn next to how enlightenment serves as the core of your six non-negotiable roles as CEO.

Part IV: Creating the Inspiration

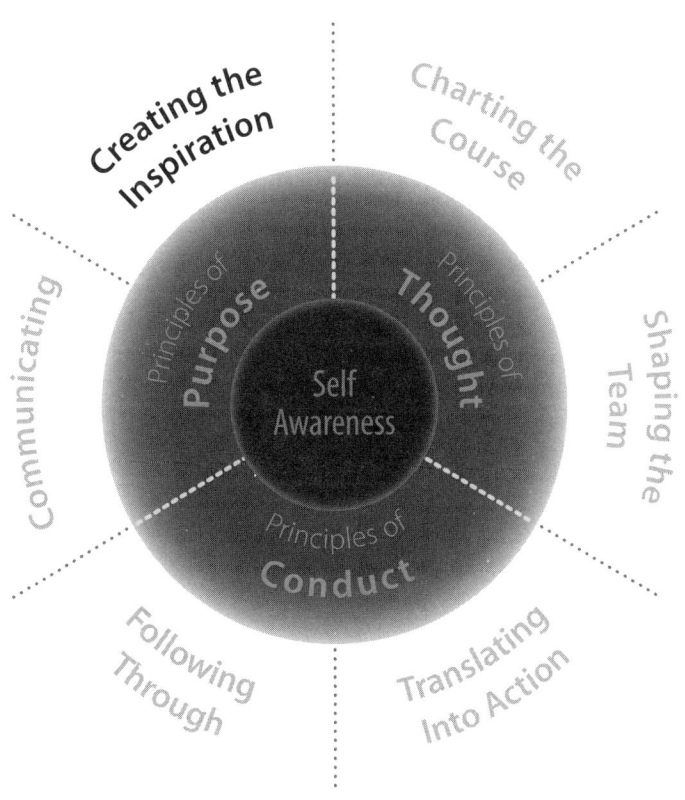

Chapter 23

A Unifying Purpose

All CEOs face the challenge of inspiring the members of the organization to move as one in a common direction. For that challenge to be conquered, the first step is to articulate a unifying vision for the company: Why are we all here? What broad objective are we all trying to achieve? As we each go about our jobs, what is it that bonds us together so that we are in fact working as a team? The presence or absence of an inspiring and clearly articulated vision for the company is one of the most fundamental tests of the stewardship of the CEO.

A strong vision statement serves three critical purposes. First, the very crafting of the statement forces the CEO and his team to become clear in their own minds as to the overarching direction of the company. Some companies have no vision statement, and many others have ones that say very little, as we will discuss in the next chapter. Often an absent or inadequate vision statement is a symptom of a much more important underlying disease: The CEO's and management's lack of decisiveness and clarity in choosing among competing alternatives for the company's future direction. Forcing yourself and your team to craft a clear and unambiguous statement of why we are here and where we are going ensures that you and your team will realistically assess your situation and make the tough choices which you may have avoided in the past.

Second, the vision statement is the starting point and core of your communication with all of your employees. Crafted properly, it is the unifying purpose that enables all to understand their jobs in a broader context, so that they can align their efforts with the overall mission of the company. Achieving that alignment is one of the CEO's most difficult challenges, and it becomes that much more difficult — if not impossible — in the absence of a clear statement of corporate purpose that is understandable by all. In fact, many companies also choose to broadcast their vision to other constituencies, such as customers, potential hires, corporate partners and investors. A strong vision statement then becomes a vehicle for aligning the thought processes and efforts of not only employees, but all members of the extended corporate family.

The third rationale for a strong statement of purpose is to give employees a reason to be excited to come to work on behalf of the company. While many employees out of necessity will be willing to do their jobs for the paycheck alone, they also crave to be part of something larger and more important. To the extent that that larger purpose is well articulated and shared by all, the company will do a far better job of retaining the most skilled and marketable employees while also maximizing the motivation and productivity of all on the company payroll.

• •

> Often an inadequate vision statement is a symptom of a much more important underlying disease: The CEO's and management's lack of decisiveness and clarity.

• •

To meet the first two rationales for the vision statement — helping the CEO and management to sort out their own thinking, and aligning the efforts of all employees — it must be clear and unambiguous. However, to meet the third — motivating employees — it must also be inspiring. The best vision statements inspire by describing how the company, through application of its unique capabilities, intends to advance some aspect of society for the better. Depending upon your industry, that societal benefit may be improving health care for a certain segment of the population, connecting people to global opportunities by bringing new telecommunications technology to an underserved market, or lowering distribution costs to make products more affordable to more people.

The inclusion of societal benefit in the vision statement need not be unique to leading-edge companies, and need not serve a purpose which could qualify for a Nobel Peace Prize. Home-builder CPMorgan specializes in first or second homes for those just working their way up the economic ladder, and employs rigorous production techniques to raise home quality while lowering cost. The company has embraced a powerful and elegantly communicated vision statement: "To provide more people with more home than they ever dreamed possible." (We particularly like their use of the word "dreamed," as it conjures up inspiration.)

CPMorgan then makes this vision statement the core of other corporate communications. The first five words on its website, after the company name, are "More Square Feet. Less Money®." The cover of one of their marketing brochures states simply "The inside story of More Square Feet. Less Money®. How we do it better," and the contents inside include "More Square Feet. Less Money®. is the result of a more efficient building system" — a system which is then explained in depth in the rest of the brochure and which, more importantly, guides all of the company's internal processes and relationships with suppliers. Here is a company in what some might characterize as an unexciting industry which has nonetheless crafted a unifying purpose which guides the efforts of all of its employees, suppliers and partners and which connects them to an inspiring and worthwhile mission, at the same time that it serves as a marketing message to customers. The point is that any company has the potential to benefit society by striving to serve its market in new and improved ways, and if it can weave that service to society into its vision statement then that statement is more likely to be inspirational.

In sum, a strong vision statement crystallizes CEO and management thought processes, aligns the efforts of all of the organization's constituencies, and inspires employees and others to apply themselves for the benefit of the company. Yet these benefits do not accrue from just any vision statement — only from strong ones. So what exactly does — or does not — constitute an effective vision statement? Read on.

Chapter 24

The Problem with Vision Statements

In the bull market of business buzzwords that characterizes this day and age, many organizations do in fact have a "vision statement." However, relatively few of these meet the test of being specific enough in setting a direction for the company. To meet that test, the first requirement is that the vision should actually *say* something meaningful. We'd like a dollar for every vision statement we've read that is some variant of the following:

> *"We will exceed the expectations of our customers, maintain a rewarding work environment for our employees, maximize returns for shareholders, and be responsible corporate citizens, while infusing excellence in all that we do."*

This statement is so broad as to be meaningless: It could apply to any company, and therefore says nothing about what *our* company seeks to do given our unique environment and capabilities. The statement reads as if a committee had been assigned to write it and its members wanted to offend nobody and to leave all options open. In the end, this hypothetical committee was able to "check the box" indicating that the vision statement was indeed completed, yet in doing so accomplished essentially nothing.

If your company's vision statement sounds anything like the example above, ask yourself whether it serves the three purposes which we outlined in the previous chapter. Does the content of your vision statement:

- Force you as CEO and your top management to make tough choices in setting a specific direction for the company?

- Guide your managers and employees so that they are able to align their efforts in a common direction?

- Inspire your people as well as others to come to work for your company?

The example above does none of these three. Yet too many companies have vision statements of this variety, or they have no vision statement at all — which is essentially the same thing.

Here's one more test to help you decide whether your inspiration for the company is well crafted. At many companies, the CEO and management team have agreed to the vision statement, and it is written at the beginning of various company documents. It may also be hanging on the wall in the lobby and in conference rooms. However, ask yourself the following questions:

How many of your mid-level managers actually refer to the vision statement as a guide when they need to make a difficult decision? And how many of your employees quote it to their friends and relatives when they explain to them what they do for a living?

If the vision statement hasn't infused both decision-making and corporate identity at those lower levels, then you are kidding yourself as to its effectiveness in communicating to a wider audience, and to a significant extent it has been a waste of time. More importantly, you have missed one of your most fundamental opportunities as CEO to set the tone and direction for your company, and you have not fulfilled your first critical role as CEO.

To fulfill this role, the CEO must be bold enough in his leadership and rigorous enough in his thinking to create an inspiration for his company which actually says something substantive about where the company is heading. Let's turn next to what such an inspiration should include.

Chapter 25

Why We are Unique

Simply stated, a well crafted inspiration should declare what your company is going to do better than other companies. This mission is defined by the intersection of three groups of factors:

- The markets you will target;
- The unique profile of strengths and weaknesses which your company will bring to bear;
- The competition you face, and how you intend to differentiate your offering.

The inspiration need not answer each of these questions in detail, and it may focus on one or two of these three dimensions more than the others, but it must provide enough specificity to identify what makes your company different and how you will succeed in the face of competition.

Sam Walton's vision for Wal-Mart was to offer a broader selection of products at lower cost to rural America. Google grew to prominence organized around one vision — to create the world's best search engine. Your company's inspiration might be to become the highest-quality gourmet food store chain in the Washington D.C. area, the broadest-line supplier of financial management software to small business and professionals, or the lowest cost provider of quality call center services to English-speaking markets — but it must in some way identify what you are going to do better than other companies, and for which groups of customers.

The question of how your company will be superior provides a straightforward and simple definition of what makes a strong vision statement. Yet answering that question for your company is an enormously important and challenging undertaking, which, if completed correctly, should have huge implications for all else your company does. Specifically, a vision statement is not sufficient unless it provides guidance for decisions, allowing managers to make choices and to allocate resources among competing opportunities and strategies. The vision statement should be broad enough to encompass all you want to achieve yet narrow enough to exclude many other projects which may be advocated in your company from time to time but which fall outside the scope of where your distinctive competence lies.

• •

A well crafted inspiration should declare what your company is going to do better than other companies.

• •

The starting point for all key decisions should be a check for consistency with the vision statement, and then, to hone in further, a check against your company's strategy (as we'll discuss in Part V) and operating plans (Part VII). Indeed, your vision should be the bounds within which your company's strategies are conceived, and your strategy should similarly bound the design of your operating plans. The inspiration you choose for your company is the first and most fundamental step in this process, and therefore the first of your six key roles as CEO.

As a further test of your company's inspiration, it should be one that would *not* be the right vision for many of your competitors. Of course, it is difficult to be absolutely unique. However, your company does bring to the market its own profile of strengths, weaknesses and capabilities. Until you can craft a vision statement that is more likely to be a path towards success for your company than any other, you are implicitly admitting that you have not yet identified how your company is going to differentiate itself and succeed in the face of its competition.

Choosing the inspiration for your company cannot be delegated by the CEO. If the vision statement is going to be substantive, as it should, then the challenge of crafting it is considerable and the perils of choosing the wrong path (or no discernible path at all) are great. You will no doubt need the partnership of your team to conquer this challenge, but in the end the decision will be yours. No challenge you take on as CEO will be more important, and if you are struggling to conquer it then start with this simple question: In what way is our company unique, or most likely to become so?

Chapter 26

How High?

All good CEOs stretch their people to reach as high as they can, and the vision statement is a logical place to express that aspiration. The vision you craft for your company should inspire your people to give their all so that the company can achieve absolutely as much as reasonably possible. To create that inspiration, vision statements are often expressed in lofty terms, as all people want to be part of a truly challenging and far-reaching endeavor.

Yet there is a limit to just how high the inspiration should reach, and here is where a good number of CEOs get it wrong. If the objective stated in the vision is so lofty as to be unrealistic or wildly improbable, your management and employees will figure that out, certainly over time and quite possibly on day one. Such a vision statement will be so lofty as to be meaningless, and consequently will serve no useful purpose. It may be quoted in a ritualistic way, but will be ignored in the day-to-day operation of the company — as it provides no guidance to your management in making decisions and no alignment for your employees. Even to the extent that it does provide *some* guidance, it is towards an objective that has no reasonable chance of being achieved, so it will likely lead to poor allocation of resources and bad decision-making.

A wish is not a vision. Having seen the profound and rapid impact that Google's founders have had on the world (and on their own net worth), the authors would love to take the time we're spending writing this book and instead start a company which is dedicated to one-upping Google with a better search engine so that we can take away their market. But guess what: Given our starting point, the odds of our company pulling that off would be infinitesimal. There are many worthwhile objectives which a company we started might reasonably be able to achieve, but that is not one of them, and therefore it is not a good inspiration for us to offer to our company.

As trivial as that example may sound, we see CEOs make this mistake on behalf of their companies all the time. We work with a fairly small company which is local to one part of one state, and which is competitively disadvantaged and only marginally profitable. The company desperately needs to improve operations, upgrade the skill level of its employees, and re-craft its strategy to find a successful and profitable niche in its market. In the face of these pressures and a steady flow of bad news, the CEO tries to rally her troops by declaring that when the company gets it together it will ultimately become one of the largest companies in its industry, nationwide.

• •

> The key is for the CEO to strike just the right balance between "lofty" and "not too lofty," and it is in making that critical decision that you earn your title and pay grade.

• •

The attainment of this objective, while theoretically possible, is so far removed from the challenges that management and employees are facing today that it provides no meaningful guidance, alignment or inspiration. It would be far more useful for the CEO to craft an inspiration which identifies the most likely basis of competitive advantage for the company targeted at the right niche, and which points the way for management and employees out of the current morass. Once the company is well on its way to achieving that level of success, there will be plenty of time later for the CEO to broaden the vision and make it loftier should that be appropriate.

The key is for the CEO to strike just the right balance between "lofty" and "not too lofty," and it is in making that critical decision that you earn your title and pay grade. Your job as CEO is to inspire your team to stretch and reach high, but towards a vision that the team actually believes can be achieved. Your management and employees are out in the real world every day, and therefore they will be accurate evaluators of the realism of the vision. Therefore, if they are to believe that the vision is achievable, it must actually be so.

Set the goal too low, and you will lead a mediocre or satisfactory company, but not a superlative one which realizes its full potential. Set it too high, and for all intents and purposes your company has no vision, because your people will discount it and disconnect from it. The CEOs who have created the best inspiration for their companies have stretched their people toward a goal which is at the limit of what they can see as possible, but still realistically within that limit.

Finally, the vision must be stated in such a way that progress against it can actually be measured, so that you and your people will know where the company stands relative to the objective. If you were setting out on a long-distance bicycle trip, "let's go west" is not a measurable vision, but "let's make it to the foot of the Rocky Mountains and then return" is. Similarly, for a company, the statements "We will achieve excellence in all we do" or "we will maximize customer satisfaction" (how would you know that it has been "maximized"?) are not measurable. On the other hand, when the vision specifies that you will provide to your target market the lowest cost, best customer service or most rapid product innovation, then you have identified objectives against which your progress can in fact be measured.

Crafting your inspiration in measurable terms will help ensure that your inspiration is substantive and not of the vacuous variety described in Chapter 24. It will also help you hone in on your company's uniqueness, as discussed in Chapter 25. Lastly, because you will know that the company's progress against a measurable vision will be obvious to all, it will encourage you to strike just the right balance in answering the question of "how high," as you and your people stretch to achieve the full potential of your company.

Chapter 27

The Role of Rewards

One of the most significant business trends of the past several decades has been the increasing prominence of finance within the mix of issues considered by the CEO. It was fairly common twenty-five years ago to find CEOs who were operationally strong but financially naïve. However, the heightened sophistication and aggressiveness of investors has forced CEOs to focus on growth and profitability in order to keep owners happy — and to keep their jobs. This is clearly true for CEOs of large public companies, but CEOs of small companies have also increased their financial sophistication — either because they hope to attract potential sources of private capital, or just through a trickle-down effect as new financial perspectives have permeated the literature and the airwaves.

The two of us have been deeply immersed in the effort to spread financial sophistication through the ranks of CEOs and are big believers in a focus on profitability and growth, as we will discuss further in Part V. However, we do not believe that the vision statement, which should focus on inspiring and guiding, is necessarily the best place to speak of financial rewards.

Surely you and your management team need to remain keenly aware of the financial implications of all that you do. However, the vision statement is intended for a far broader audience, most of whom are not owners of the company and do not directly benefit when the company makes more money (although they may benefit indirectly in many ways). We ourselves have tried it both ways, and have learned that a more inspiring approach is to use your vision to describe how your company will be unique and will break new ground for the benefit of all — rather than explicitly trying to rally the troops around the notion of making more money for shareholders.

There is certainly a time and place (in fact many) for you to make the case to your employees that when the company is profitable and owners' needs are met, then the company will be better able to protect jobs, pay higher salaries and invest in growth which creates new and exciting career opportunities. However, financial returns accrue from strong strategies and execution in the context of a well-directed company vision. As a result, it is better to use the vision statement to set that direction and provide the context for strategy and operations, knowing that if each of these is well designed and executed then the rewards will in fact be there for all.

• •

> Think hard before actually articulating those rewards as a core of the vision, as company financial goals generally do not truly inspire a broad audience and do not specify a direction for your management and employees.

• •

<u>The Google Story</u> by David Vise profiles the company from its humble beginnings to its perch near the top of the business world, all in less than a decade. One of the striking themes of the book is that the company's leaders — Larry Page and Sergey Brin — kept the team and employees focused on creating the world's best search engine, and not on the pursuit of financial rewards. Time after time, when tempted by an opportunity to shift the focus to how best to cash out, Page and Brin demurred and single-mindedly stayed focused on their vision of creating a revolutionary product. The ultimate result was phenomenal financial reward for all. Yet even today Page and Brin continue to be speak primarily about the (now expanded) vision of the company in product and customer terms rather than financial ones — trusting that if they do so then over the long haul the stock price and all the corollary financial rewards will take care of themselves.

The best inspiration for your company is one that speaks of the unique way you will outshine competitors and better meet the needs of customers, and which encourages all on the team to reach high to realize the full potential of the company. Lead and communicate in a way that makes it clear that the more we achieve the vision, the more rewards there will be for all to share. However, think hard before actually articulating those rewards as a core of the vision, as company financial goals generally do not truly inspire a broad audience and do not specify a direction for your management and employees.

Chapter 28

Spreading the Gospel

Once you and your senior team have crafted an inspiration that uniquely defines how your company will make its mark, the next challenge is to instill that inspiration in everyone in your organization as well as outside of the company as appropriate. That is a communications undertaking of major proportions, yet in the absence of such an effort the effectiveness of the vision will be significantly diluted.

There are several keys to successful communication of your vision. First, the vision must be repeated frequently to every possible audience — today, tomorrow and forever. There is a reason why you see the same television commercial over and over again: Advertisers learned decades ago that it is the cumulative effect of that repetition which influences behavior, often in ways far more effective than the conscious thought that takes place the first time one hears an ad. Closer to home, you'll recall that in the chapter on Calm in Part III we described the CEO who claimed that the first 999 times he articulates his vision nothing sustainable happens, but on the thousandth time the organization "gets it" and long-term movement in the desired direction begins to take hold. One thousand repetitions may be an exaggeration, but his point is valid. Once you've crafted a substantive inspiration, it is your job to repeat it in every possible setting to every relevant audience, until it truly is internalized by everyone associated with the company.

Repetition, while essential, is not enough. We have all heard public speakers who sound like they are reading from a script or mouthing words which they don't truly believe. The messages of those speakers come across as hollow-sounding platitudes, and therefore they do not take hold inside of us and influence our opinions or behavior in sustainable ways. We have all also heard speakers who truly move us with a genuine passion that is communicated along with their words. If we believe that they are sincere, we reflect on their message more deeply, and are much more likely to take it to heart.

In other words, the *way* that you communicate the inspiration is as important as how often and to whom you communicate it. Like it or not, to your employees you are part business leader, part celebrity and part politician (among other things). And just as when they listen to those types of speakers, employees will apply a critical ear to anything you say and instinctively form an opinion as to whether you truly believe what you are saying. As you quote the inspiration again and again, they will listen for your passion, your sincerity and your absolute commitment to your message. If they sense that you are merely going through the motions of giving a speech, they will hear your words as platitudes and the inspiration will not take hold.

• •

> A well communicated vision not only motivates employees to work hard for the company, it inspires them to think hard for the company.

• •

There is one additional factor to consider. Your vision statement, although critical, will inevitably be expressed at a very high level of abstraction. Although we have implored you to make it specific to what makes your company unique, even then it is likely to be brief and fairly general — which creates a potential problem. You and your senior team likely will have had in-depth discussions to arrive at the words which comprise the vision statement — and that debate will help you understand the meaning, the power, and the implications *behind* the words. Others, however, will not have participated in that process and will not have had the chance as you did to explore several levels beyond the actual vision statement. As a result, what to you has depth beyond the actual words may sound shallow and less meaningful to a broader audience.

The solution to this conundrum lies in the third requirement for how you as CEO should communicate the vision. It is not enough for you to quote your inspiration for the company — you must also *explain* it.

When citing the vision to a given audience, you should describe how it is relevant for the particular challenges which they face, using examples and logic that best fit the situation. When speaking to a division which is reeling in the face of a competitive challenge, don't merely cite the vision and state how we will be unique — also translate the vision a couple of levels deeper and explain how it specifically points the way for the division to get back on its feet and prosper once again. When responding to a request for funding for a new product, plant, or business, start with the vision but then make the connection to show how the requested initiative does or does not fit within that inspiration.

Even if you are simply giving a speech to a broad audience, don't just quote the vision and assume that others will automatically drink the Kool-Aid and "get it." Instead, offer graphic examples which explain how the vision drives decisions and provides clarity for all that we do, as well as how that clarity has contributed to the success of the company. In short — *teach*, don't just speechify. When you offer your employees an explanation of the vision in combination with repetition and sincerity, you will have perfected the formula which over time will instill the inspiration into your entire organization and beyond.

Of course, dissemination of the vision is not a one-person job. As CEO you must lead the effort and cannot simply delegate it to others. Yet as you skillfully propagate the vision you will be setting an example for all the other leaders in the organization. Just like you, they need to learn to cite the vision repetitively, sincerely, and with in-depth explanation. In deputizing them you multiply your own effect, increasing the power of the vision and ensuring that it truly takes hold.

In fact, this multiplicative impact can extend all the way to the most junior members of your company. A well-crafted and well-communicated vision encourages employees at all levels to strive to advance the interests of the company. Since the beginning, Wal-Mart's vision has included broad product selection as one of its core tenets. A number of years ago one of us arrived at a beach vacation with his family, and went out the next morning to stock the rental house at the local Wal-Mart. As the store opened that morning he was the first customer to arrive, and as he did so the staff was still finishing up its morning meeting. He could hear a young employee describe to managers and peers how he had been in a competitor's store and had noticed that it stocked a broader range of fishing gear than Wal-Mart, including one new model which the employee thought would be popular that summer. The manager thanked the employee for the input, and promised that he would investigate broadening the line of fishing gear not only for this store, but for the entire company. Clearly, this was an employee who, despite being relatively new to a huge company and located deep within its hierarchy, not only had already internalized the corporate vision but was determined to do his part to help the company realize it.

As illustrated by this example, a well communicated vision not only motivates employees to work hard for the company, it inspires them to *think* hard for the company. It expands the number of innovative ideas well beyond the creative capacity of the CEO and his management team. Furthermore, a successfully communicated vision helps employees avoid wasting energy and resources on ideas that are too far afield and which distract from the company's vision. Finally, skillful dissemination of your inspiration for the company allows the broader constituencies — suppliers, joint venture partners, Board members, investors, and even customers — to understand how they can employ their own creativity in pursuit of the company's vision.

In Chapters 23 through 27 we focused on the keys to crafting a meaningful inspiration for your company. Yet the impact of that vision will be determined by how well it is communicated to all members of the corporate family. Through repetition, sincerity, and explanation you make it everyone's inspiration and not just your own — and in doing so dramatically multiply the power of the vision, and of yourself as CEO.

Chapter 29

Refining the Inspiration

The vision for your company should have a long shelf life. To instill your inspiration throughout your organization and beyond requires a major effort spread over a long period of time, and therefore it will be disruptive if the vision is altered too frequently or without sufficient reason to do so. We have been invited into companies which over the previous years had ricocheted from one vision to another, and inevitably that inconsistency translated into a management and employee team that lacked cohesiveness, direction and proper motivation. The foundering of the company was the usual corollary as well.

While fickleness of the vision statement is a problem, the opposite extreme — insisting that your inspiration can *never* be changed — can be equally deadly. As we've discussed, the vision should explain how you intend for your company to do a better job than your competitors of meeting the needs of your target market. Yet we all know that in the business world things change. With the passage of time, there may be major shifts in customer behavior, the nature of the competition, the technological underpinnings of your industry and other external factors. Alternatively, you may have miscalculated your own company's capability to outperform competitors in the intended ways, which means that you will need to re-assess your basis for competitive advantage. Indeed, it is likely that over time at least one and possibly both of these needs — to re-calibrate environmental factors or to re-evaluate your own relative capabilities — will become so critical that the vision will in fact have to be refined.

So what is a CEO to do? Should he keep the vision constant so as not to be fickle, or change it to reflect the new realities? To defer a direct answer for just a moment, the first imperative is to invest enough serious effort and forward-thinking analysis into the crafting of your inspiration so as to maximize the odds that it will have a long shelf life and be less likely to require refinement any time soon. We hope that with a full appreciation for the time required to "spread the gospel" of your vision as described in Chapter 28 — as well as the cost to your organization of changing it too frequently — you will see the merit in making the effort required to arrive at just the right vision. However, the *wrong* way to render a vision statement long-lasting is to make it overly broad and vacuous. The difficult but crucial task of the CEO is to craft an inspiration that is both substantive *and* likely to remain the direction of the company throughout a substantial period of growth.

> As companies succeed and move on to ever-broader visions, they often take on the increasing risk of loss of focus and a retreat to mediocrity.

As good a job as you do the first time, it will nonetheless be time to refine the vision if either of two conditions are met. First, when you've substantially achieved the vision, then it is time to move beyond it and set a new goal for your company. As founder of his company in 1923, Walt Disney first envisioned being a leading producer of cartoons. Once he realized that goal, he and his successors broadened the vision to include first animated feature films, then a theme park in California and then a vast tract of multiple theme parks in Florida. Today, the Walt Disney Company has expanded the vision again to reflect its role as a worldwide multimedia leader. If one reads the history of the company, its leaders did not change the fundamental vision capriciously or too often. Instead, perhaps half a dozen times in its eighty-four year history, as the company realized its prior vision, they set their sights higher and broadened the company's horizons. As they did so, they built around the company's core strength and brand image, constructing larger and larger concentric circles around that strength so that the company could stretch to conquer ever-larger opportunities.

Knowing that you can expand the vision from time to time as the company prospers has an important corollary: It helps you keep the *current* vision achievable in some reasonable period of time — and not craft one that is so far out there as to cease to be effective motivation for your organization. Although today Lance Armstrong is universally recognized as the greatest cyclist of all time, we doubt that when he got his first bike he started out with that vision. Instead, he probably first set his sights on learning to ride, and then on conquering some local challenge. As his proficiency grew, it is likely that one day he began dreaming of winning the Tour de France. Having done so, he may then have set a target of how many he wanted to win, and then eventually aimed for the seven in a row which crowned him as the greatest of all time. As he closed in on each of his visions, he moved on to inspirations which represented larger and larger circles built around the same core competence. Both successful business people and successful athletes understand this principle: You need a carrot in front of the horse, but you don't want it so far in front that the horse doesn't think he can get there in time for his next meal.

As companies succeed and move on to ever-broader visions, they often take on the increasing risk of loss of focus and a retreat to mediocrity. Each successive vision may be more lofty, but it also may be harder to achieve and further afield from what made the company successful in the first place. Wal-Mart has been phenomenally successful in achieving Sam Walton's original vision to offer broader selection and lower cost to rural America, but today the company has effectively saturated that market. In order to continue to challenge management and offer growth for shareholders, the company has expanded the vision in multiple directions, including urban America, international expansion, new product lines and new store formats. As of this writing, the company has hit significant stumbling blocks in all four of those areas and is finding consistent growth and success harder to come by.

Similarly, in just a few years Google achieved its vision of becoming the dominant search engine, but to keep the juices flowing today the company is investing in scores of new products ranging from near-in expansions in search and advertising all the way to the mapping of the genome. It may very well be just a matter of time before Google hits rocky patches just as Wal-Mart has, in its pursuit of ever-broader inspirations for the company.

To be clear, we are not suggesting that having achieved success companies should simply declare victory and go home. Growth is needed to both reward shareholders and to create attractive career paths for management and employees, and it is your job as CEO to conceive of broader visions once earlier ones have been achieved.

However, past achievement is no guarantee of future success, and it is also your job to figure out *how* to broaden the vision intelligently and carefully, and not to simply assume that the lines will always be pointing up because they have in the recent past. Expansions of the vision that appear logical because they are adjacent to the core business sometimes bring with them surprises about a new market segment or competitor, and therefore may be a lot harder to pull off than the CEO had anticipated. When Disney decided to replicate its successful theme park strategy abroad, it went first to Paris, where it

....
Fire yourself — then come back
and act like a new boss would.
....

struggled mightily, and later to Hong Kong, where the jury is still out. The company discovered that the precise formula that worked in California and Florida did not automatically work abroad.

When you as CEO expand your inspiration for the company, it is critical that you conduct as fresh and complete an analysis as when you conceived the original inspiration, and not subject the expansion to a lower level of scrutiny. It is the quality and rigor of your company's strategy — the topic of Part V — which will go a long way towards helping you develop broader visions for the company — visions which can become just as successful as the original.

Beyond achieving the vision, there is a second circumstance under which it should be refined — namely, when you have failed to achieve it, and you have convinced yourself that all reasonable avenues and efforts to do so have been exhausted. As described earlier, this may be either because the environment has changed significantly or because you have miscalculated your own company's capability relative to that of competitors. Either way, a stubborn refusal on your part to refine the vision when a change is truly needed can have disastrous consequences.

Sometimes, the CEO recognizes the need for a change considerably later than many of those around him. As CEO, you more than anyone have devoted yourself to your inspiration for the company, as well you should. If you've fulfilled this role properly, then you've espoused the vision over and over again to every audience you can find. It is often quite difficult to challenge that which you have been preaching so passionately, and it will require mental dexterity on your part for you to simultaneously both spread the gospel and, at an analytical level, periodically re-assess how it may need to be refined.

Yet you must do so, as the consequences of others recognizing the need for a change when you don't can be severe. When your staff knows that the vision as written is no longer right but you stubbornly cling to it, you will lose their respect and support. When your Board or investors are out in front of you in knowing that the vision needs to be changed, then you damage your credibility and your ability to work cohesively with them, possibly to the point of being replaced.

The key, as we discussed in Part III, is to separate in your mind the company from your own ego, and to recognize that the vision is something that defines the *company*, not you. Your job is to be a superlative CEO, which includes refining the inspiration for the company, as something separate from yourself, when that refinement is needed. The headline of an article by Carol Hymowitz in The Wall Street Journal provides a powerful reminder of the proper mindset: "Fire Yourself — Then Come Back and Act Like a New Boss Would." Her point is that when a fundamental change in direction is truly needed, don't wait for the Board to fire you and bring in a new CEO to make it happen. Instead, free yourself from your emotional attachment to the old vision, and act the part of that new CEO yourself.

In sum, you should not change your company's vision capriciously, but there are two junctures in your company's history when it is critical to change it — when the vision has been largely accomplished, or when it is not working. Knowing for sure when one of those moments has arrived — and knowing how to skillfully re-set the inspiration to ensure that the next phase of your company's progression will be successful — require that you fulfill your second non-negotiable role as CEO: charting a sound strategic course for the company. That is where we turn next, as the subject of Part V.

Part V: Charting the Course

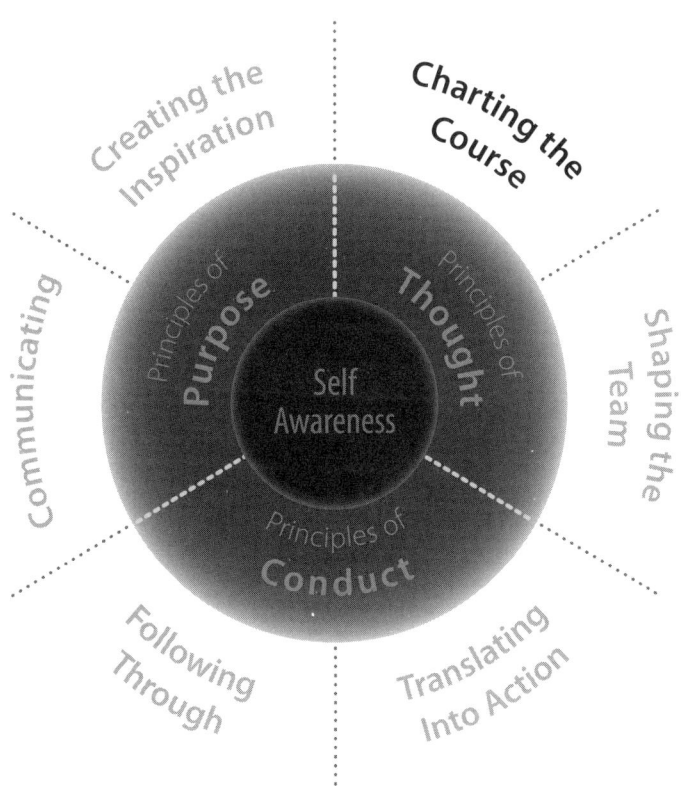

Chapter 30

Why You Need a Strategy

When you've inspired your organization with a vision of what is unique about your company, you will have fulfilled the first of your six roles as CEO. Yet there is still a long way to go if you are to translate that vision into reality. The remaining five roles comprise the balance of that journey, as you build on the vision and put in place increasingly specific levels of content and process to lead your organization to success. The next step beyond the vision is to chart a course or strategy which defines in more detail the basis for how your company will be successful.

In the end, companies succeed or fail as a result of two broad sets of factors. One of them is obvious to all CEOs: How well the company is managed. Most CEOs occupy the majority of their day with questions which fall into this category: Who needs to be hired or fired? How do we motivate people to work harder and get the job done? Are our various programs on time and on budget, and are they achieving the desired results? How efficient and effective are the various parts of the organization in delivering against our intended direction? How strong is the leadership of the management team? We will address management questions such as these — and many more — in Parts VI through IX.

Yet as important as good management is, it is only one of two factors which drive a company's success — and in terms of the logic flow, it is the second of the two. The first factor is the fundamental strategic positioning of the company: Given our company's strengths, weaknesses and potential capabilities, how competitively advantaged are we? What is our potential to create competitive advantage in the future? And how do the answers to those questions vary for different potential target markets? Are we directing our efforts and resources at the markets where we are most likely to be successful?

Suppose that in your non-working hours you are the coach of a youth soccer team comprised of players of generally average ability. Clearly, your team's won and loss record will be significantly influenced by how good a job you and your assistant coaches do of leading the players. Are you teaching them the necessary technical skills? Are you inspiring them to give their all and to play with heart? Under your leadership, do they play with cohesion as a team, or are they each out for individual glory? Are they enjoying the team sufficiently so that they show up at practices to hone their skills and at games so as not to leave you short-handed? If you've spent a Saturday at a youth soccer complex, it is easy to spot well-coached teams which win with average talent, as well as poorly-coached ones which lose with players of similar ability. The quality of leadership is a critical component of results.

Yet just as fundamental to your team's won-and-loss record will be whether you are playing in a league in which your team can be competitive. Place your team in a league with professionals, and no matter how great a coach you are your team will surely be winless — and probably on the way to the hospital as well. Enter it in the top-ranked youth "select" league, and if you've started with players of average ability you'll again no doubt suffer a series of blowouts. Yet in a lower-level select league you might, with great coaching, have a winning season — and with the same ingredient in the "house" league (intended for players of average ability) you could very well dominate.

In this very basic example, it is clear that choosing a "market" in which you are capable of being competitively advantaged is as important a determinant of results as the quality of leadership. As CEO of your company you should never fall prey to the assumption that the arena in which you compete is an unchangeable "given." Instead, you need to guide the company towards the target markets where it is most likely to be competitively advantaged and successful. Although the way to do so is likely to be more complicated and subtle than in the soccer example, you are also likely to have far more choices and degrees of freedom at your disposal in searching for the right target market.

There are countless examples of the importance of strategic positioning all around us in the business world. The old-line American auto giants, General Motors and Ford, are reeling and in risk of collapse — burdened with highly uncompetitive labor rates and legacy benefits costs, not to mention the momentum of decades of stagnation and strategic mistakes. There isn't a CEO anywhere, regardless of his skills, who wouldn't face extraordinarily high odds in trying to turn those ships around and win against competitors who enjoy far superior cost structures and strong momentum in the marketplace. Until a GM or Ford CEO is able to both craft a new strategy for competitive advantage and convince the necessary constituencies (most notably the labor unions) to allow it to be implemented, no amount of leadership skill will be sufficient for success.

• •

Spending time *planning* — writing out a whole lot of things you are going to do in an organized way — is not the same as actually having a sound, logically-tight, high quality *strategy*.

• •

In fact, entire industries can be strategically unattractive. Warren Buffett has noted that since the Wright Brothers the cumulative profits of the U.S. commercial airline industry are actually negative. After nearly a century the industry as a whole has yet to turn its first profit! It is unlikely that the reason for this is that scores of airline CEOs over the years have all happened to be weaker than their peers in other industries. Instead, there is something fundamental about the strategic structure of the airline industry which makes it very difficult for industry players to be profitable over the long term — and there exist just a very limited number of options for circumventing that tendency towards unprofitability. As a result, it is only a small minority of airlines with very particular industry positions which have been able to succeed and consistently earn strong returns.

More broadly, if any of us as CEO led a company with high costs in a commodity business, or one with nothing distinctive in an industry driven by differentiation, then we are simply not going to succeed, completely independent of how talented a CEO we may be. To paraphrase one of Buffett's adages: When you put a good CEO up against a bad business, your best bet is that the business' situation will prevail.

Conversely, a strong strategic position is a huge plus, although only up to a point. A CEO of a company in a fundamentally attractive industry or with strong competitive advantage is much more likely to lead his company to success. Yet the nature of capitalism is that a lot more companies fail or remain mediocre than truly excel — and while poor strategic position usually trumps good management, good strategic position will not necessarily enable a mediocre or poor CEO to glide his company in for a successful landing. There truly are two requirements for excellent performance of a company — strong strategic position *and* good management — and the absence of either is a prescription for serious trouble.

• •

> Equally important, a good strategy draws boundaries which define where and how your company will not compete, so that your limited resources can be concentrated where you are most likely to be successful.

• •

As indisputably critical as strategy is for success, it is remarkably common for it to be an area of weakness or neglect for CEOs, in any of a variety of ways. One category of CEOs is strongly biased towards detail, process and implementation, and tends to believe that good intentions and earnest effort are enough to succeed in any situation. Intentions and effort truly do count for a lot, but as the examples above illustrate they are not sufficient for success in the absence of a strong strategy. Of the six roles of the CEO, the second — Charting the Course — requires in some respect a different type of thinking than the other five, and as such it too often falls outside the ongoing practice of many CEOs. It's as if a lawyer were to handle a case without an understanding of the fundamental tenets of the relevant law, or a doctor were to treat patients without referring to the applicable medical science or pharmacology of her specialty.

Another category of CEOs is aware in a general sense that strategy is part of the job, yet has never truly studied and internalized the discipline. The companies which these CEOs lead tend to have structured, and often time-intensive and intricate, strategic planning processes which are more notable for the paper they generate than for how they create true competitive advantage for the company. Spending time *planning* — writing out a whole lot of things you are going to do in an organized way — is not the same as actually having a sound, logically-tight, high quality *strategy*. The former is a *process*, while the latter speaks to *content*, or the *result* of the process. It is just as easy (in fact a lot easier) to plan steps which when implemented will yield "me-too" performance than to construct a plan that truly will yield superlative results — just as a well-intentioned but poorly-schooled doctor might meticulously and faithfully administer a wholly ineffective treatment to her patient.

Finally, a third category of CEO not only appreciates the importance of strategy but also truly understands its tenets — which groups of actions will lead to competitive advantage and which won't. Yet, we have commonly witnessed even these CEOs get distracted and overwhelmed by the day-to-day pressures of the job, and in doing so lead in ways which are in direct violation of the rules of strategy. For these CEOs, the answer lies in part in remembering several of the principles described in Part III: the calm of the firemen who walk rather than run to the address the problem, as well as principles of thought based on knowledge and objectivity.

Combine all these categories of CEOs, and in our experience there may be no role which is more commonly neglected by company leaders. If you fall into one of the above categories, either in whole or part, it is our intent in the balance of Part V to set you on a journey to close that gap.

Scores of books have been devoted entirely to strategy, and it is not our intent here to write another one — this is instead a book about *all* that a CEO must do to be successful, with strategy being just one piece of the puzzle. However, the good news is that the truly non-negotiable things which every CEO needs to know about strategy can be boiled down into a short list of immutable laws, coupled with recommendations as to how to instill that sense of strategy into the rest of your organization. Beyond that fundamental understanding, any good strategy book will take you, sometimes helpfully, to deeper levels of detail and more intricate laws — but we encourage you to avoid becoming too enamored of the inevitable plethora of buzzwords, overly-complicated frameworks, and reputedly "must have," one-size-fits-all strategic processes which are all too often characteristic of the genre. In this book, we're going to stick to the basics since that's where most of the value lies — and because if you're not careful, the additional value of more involved frameworks can be obscured by the less helpful trappings in which they're wrapped.

At its most fundamental level, a good strategy is simply the path by which the company will realize the position of uniqueness defined by its vision. A strong strategy specifies in more detail than the vision:

- *Where* we will compete, and
- *How* we will compete and outperform the competition.

A good strategy also does so in a way that *stretches* your organization to achieve its full potential while remaining grounded in a *realistic* assessment of the market, the competition, and your own capabilities, so that it is likely to be achieved.

Equally important, a good strategy draws boundaries which define where and how your company will *not* compete, so that your limited resources can be concentrated where you are most likely to be successful. Couple such a strategy with strong management — as we'll discuss in Parts VI through IX — and you have the ingredients required to lead your company to excellence and to be the CEO you want to be. And with a strong strategy you'll also have something that the large majority of companies, large and small, in truth do not have.

In the latter half of Part V, we'll address the question of how to train your entire organization to think strategically. However, before turning there let's look first at the critical and immutable laws of strategy within which all companies — and all CEOs — must operate, whether they realize it or not.

Chapter 31

True Competitive Advantage

Every CEO and manager understands that in a capitalistic economy it is essential to outperform the competition. To a man and woman they preach in either formal plans, their day-to-day leadership or both that all in the organization must strive to beat the competition. In most cases this vocabulary of winning against the competition then extends throughout much of the company. Salespeople rally to win competitors' customers while protecting their own; the human resources department measures itself against competitive benchmarks for salaries, benefits and recruiting success; customer service strives to exceed industry benchmarks for responsiveness and customer satisfaction; and the manufacturing plant or operations center endeavors to stay state-of-the-art so as not to be leapfrogged by the competition. The notion of competitive advantage is ubiquitous in the business world and enjoys populist appeal, as well it should.

There is, however, a more focused and centralized step in the process to achieve competitive advantage — a role that can only be performed by the CEO and her management team. It is a role quite different from merely preaching and popularizing the notion that outperforming competitors is a good thing, and which provides a necessary foundation for that broader message. Yet it is a role which relatively few companies complete with the necessary quality and thoroughness.

The most fundamental component of the quest for competitive advantage is an informed, objective and *rigorous* thought process which ensures that the sum total of all that the company does will in fact create a position of *true* superiority over the competition, relative to the markets the company has targeted. Motivating your people by imploring them to beat the competition may generate a lot of positive energy, but if in the end those efforts add up to a position of parity with the competition or worse, then the company is unlikely to enjoy strong results that can be sustained over time. A *wish* to be the best in your industry coupled with an eloquent message will not produce *results*, no matter how often and skillfully it is repeated. Instead, your job as CEO is to lead the thinking and analysis required to chart a course that creates *real* and *sustainable* competitive advantage, and then to make that course the platform from which you and your management team direct the inspired efforts of the various groups within the company.

> A wish to be the best in your industry coupled with an eloquent message will not produce results, no matter how often and skillfully it is repeated.

There no doubt are pockets of competitive advantage scattered throughout your company, such as a functional group that is truly the best in your industry, or a metric for which you are the industry's top performer. But a more central question is whether the competitive standing of the different parts of the company together add up to the only type of competitive advantage that in the end truly matters: The ability to do a better job than the competition of meeting the most critical needs of your target market, in a way that is sustainable over time. You may have good people who work hard, but so do many of your competitors, and by itself that will not be enough for you to achieve and then sustain competitive advantage over the long haul. Instead, you must identify, nurture and protect one or more key structural, strategic advantages which then provide a barrier against potential inroads by your competition. That advantage must translate into a superior ability to satisfy customers, or your preaching about competitive advantage to the masses will be a pep talk more than a reality-based, winning game plan.

So what comprises real and sustainable competitive advantage? What does it mean to do a better job than the competition of meeting the needs of your target markets? Customers, of course, buy a product or service for a price. Therefore at the most fundamental level you can achieve competitive advantage only by being superior at one end of that purchasing equation or the other. You must either:

- Sell a product or service that is truly *differentiated* and superior in the eyes of the customer; or,

- Sell a product or service that is equivalent to that of the competition, but at a *lower price* — and the only way you can sustain that is to produce at *lower cost* than competitors.

The achievement of one or the other of these is the only reason why a group of customers will buy from you and then continue to do so over time.

Before reading on, ask yourself these questions: Is your offering *truly* superior to competitors' offerings in ways that are central and critical to the customer's purchasing decision — or is that just something you say to motivate the troops? Alternatively, are you *truly* producing the product at a lower cost than the competition? If you cannot clearly, confidently and honestly answer at least one of these questions "yes," then you do not yet have a winning strategy. To find a way to get there, let's delve one level deeper, starting first with the path towards creating a truly differentiated offering.

Each of the markets in which you compete can no doubt be segmented into groups of customers with different needs and purchasing criteria. As a result, there are multiple potential ways for you to successfully differentiate your company's offering, depending upon which segment of the market you choose to target. Yet most of those options will require you to do one of the following four things:

- Sell a higher *quality* product or service. If a customer is in the market for a car, television, restaurant, or business suit, he may buy from — and faithfully return to — the vendor who offers, respectively, the best ride, picture quality, food and service, or fit and look. Customers rapidly flocked to Google from its competitors because its search engine yielded the most useful results. A cell phone or pay television (cable or satellite) service may be chosen based on which vendor reliably offers the best reception. If your company can create the ability to deliver higher quality than the competition (however that is defined in your industry) and sustain that differential, then you've identified a potential source of competitive advantage.

* Sell a broader *variety* of products or features. The most famous competitive "win" in business history took place early in the twentieth century, when Alfred Sloan, at a predecessor of General Motors, captured the leading position in the U.S. auto industry from Henry Ford by offering a variety of colors and features to compete with Ford's "any car you want as long as its black." Ford bet on scale, standardization and low cost while Sloan bet on differentiation through variety, at a higher cost of production and therefore a higher price to the consumer. Sloan guessed right, Ford guessed wrong, and ever since GM has been the largest U.S.-based automotive company, with Ford trailing behind.

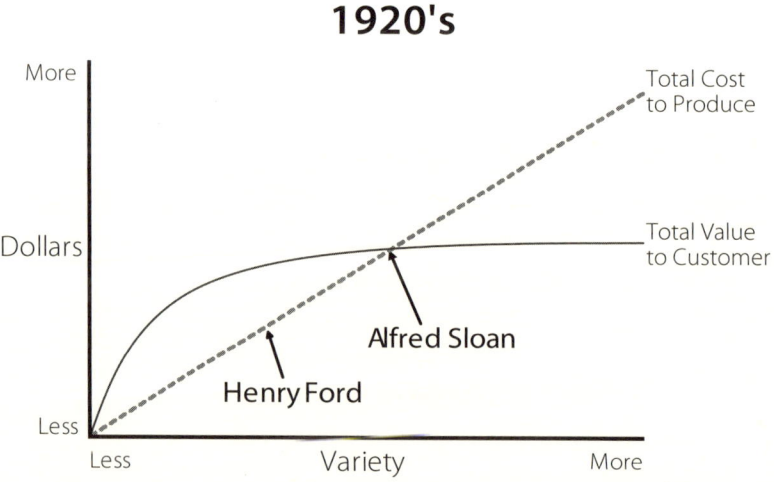

Today, Border's Books seeks advantage over your local book store by offering readers far greater selection; Baskin & Robbins bets that dozens of flavors will enhance the customer experience and bring him to the store; large law firms offer corporate clients an array of attorneys in every possible specialty from M&A to tax to labor law in the hope that a one-stop shop is what the client is looking for; and Disneyworld in Florida combines eight parks, countless restaurants, and varied nightlife options all under one "roof" to lure the family seeking the convenience of enjoying a whole week's vacation without ever leaving the premises.

- Offer superior *customer service* around the core offering. Whatever your company sells (product or service), there are inevitably a multitude of factors other than the offering itself which are part of the customer experience and which influence her choice of vendor. These may include elements as varied as: the accessibility and helpfulness of salespeople; payment terms; transaction speed; after-sale service; "return" policies; free "extras" ranging from a cup of coffee to gratis consulting advice around a large corporate product purchase; follow-up calls to ascertain whether the customer needs any further help; and so forth. In many cases, intense competition and product homogeneity have made these "peripheral" service elements the true differentiators which drive the customer's purchase decision.

   Talk to a loyal Nordstrom shopper, and more often than not they'll sing the praises of the service they receive not just when they're about to spend money, but year round as they hear from their designated sales representative that a key item has arrived which meets their tastes and needs. Why else would some consumers pay considerably more to use full service stock brokers when online brokers offer miniscule commissions, if not for the services that come with a personal relationship with the broker? As standards of living rise, more and more of customers' dollars are spent on convenience and service rather than the product offering itself, and with that trend has come an increased focus by many companies on building competitive advantage by offering the customer a superior overall experience.

+ Build a better brand *image* than the competition. Crest, Clorox, Federal Express, IBM, Disney, Coca Cola, the big accounting firms, Google, and Amazon.com all have powerful and ubiquitous brand images which give them enormous advantages over less well-known competitors, independent of any real product or service advantages they may have offered in the past or offer today. Customers are creatures of habit, and since these strong brands are top of mind and trusted, all other things being equal customers turn to them first.

Scanning the four categories above, you can probably identify a number of potential paths to differentiation for your company. However, choosing the right path is tricky, because regardless of the path chosen *creating and sustaining differentiation costs money*. It is expensive to build superior quality into your product, to provide a wide variety of offerings with the resultant added complexity to your operations, to supply higher levels of customer service or to invest in advertising to build brand image. For that reason, we have found the commonly stated strategy — to "maximize customer satisfaction" — to be a meaningless platitude. You can always satisfy your customer more by giving him more for his money — but that also costs you money. It's just not that simple.

The real goal — and the real challenge — is to figure out which types of differentiation truly create more value for the customer than the cost to produce them, and equally important, which don't. We call this — "What is the customer willing to pay for?" — and when this concept permeates your management processes, it is a powerful strategic mindset for driving investment and spending decisions. When you identify a way to differentiate that the customer truly values — which doesn't happen that often — this mindset should encourage you to invest aggressively and intelligently. Conversely, it should help you quell all sorts of requests for expenditures which might sound nice on paper but which do not create value for the customer which is greater than the added cost to your company.

At the same time that you are making these judgments your competitors are doing so as well. They are considering many of the same potential sources of differentiation, and looking at many of the same steps to reduce cost. The key to staking out a position of competitive advantage, whether you are a large company or small, is to make those decisions in a more disciplined way, and more intelligently and creatively, than the competition. In recent years, multiple companies have targeted the digital music player market, but it was only Apple and its iPod which crafted the brilliant combination of sleek design, just the right features (and not too many), and wide song selection which enabled them to take a huge lead in the market. Others tried to come up with the right combination, but as we write this book so far only Apple has. To build winning differentiation in your industry, you will need to draw upon the best minds you can find inside and outside of your company, but the importance of the decision necessitates that it rests with senior management and ultimately with you as CEO.

• •

"What is the customer willing to pay for?"
is a powerful strategic mindset for driving
investment and spending decisions.

• •

The Apple iPod story illustrates another key point about differentiation. It is most natural to think of pleasing customers in terms of what can be *added* to the product: more quality, better service, more features or variety, or more advertising to build brand image. Yet in today's electronics world (for example), many of us find that our gadgets — whether our VCR or personal computer — have far more features than we ever use, at the cost of reduced simplicity and user-friendliness. Part of the genius of the iPod is its utter simplicity, as Apple consciously decided not to add a variety of features which would have detracted from the product's elegance and ease of use.

Twenty-plus years ago the Japanese did something similar when they captured a huge chunk of the US auto industry from GM and Ford. Half a century after Alfred Sloan overtook Ford, companies like Honda bet that many consumers no longer sufficiently valued the almost infinite variety of colors and options offered by the U.S. companies, relative to what that variety added to the cost of the manufacturing process and distribution network — and therefore to the price to the customer. Instead, Honda offered its Accord in only four colors and two options packages, choosing not to give the customer (as American manufacturers did) dozens of independent options decisions. The company then used the substantial cost savings generated by that simplicity in three ways: to lower their prices, to invest in product quality and to enhance their own profitability. Honda then rode the combination of those three factors to huge success in the U.S. marketplace.

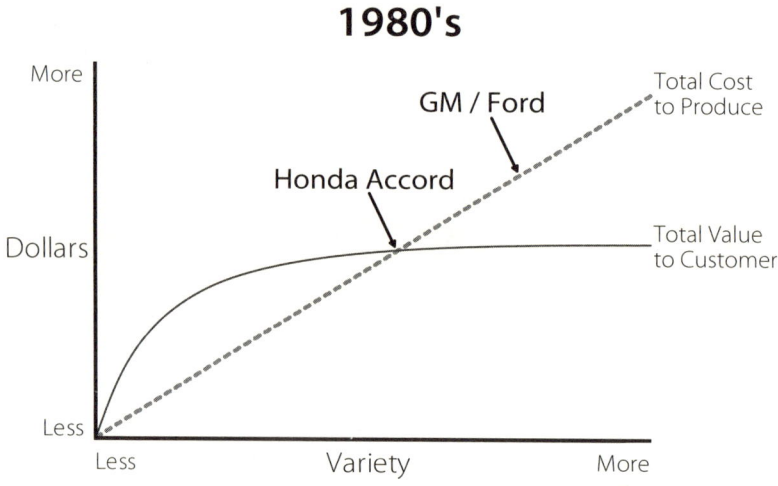

At about the same time, L'eggs captured a huge chunk of the U.S. pantyhose market by correctly guessing that women didn't need to pay department store costs for department store ambience when they made an everyday purchase of an unglamorous item, and instead offered it in lower-cost convenience stores and supermarkets. Because increasing differentiation adds cost — which the customer may or may not be willing to pay for — it is just as possible to gain competitive advantage by *decreasing* differentiation as it is by *increasing* it. The vast majority of people in your organization — whether in sales, marketing, R&D or product design — will think more naturally in terms of increasing differentiation, and therefore it is crucial that you and your management team take the complete view and look for opportunities in both directions.

If you are to achieve competitive advantage through differentiation, the bottom line is that you need to find a distinctive package of quality, variety, service and image which is better suited than competitor's offerings to the needs of your target market, *and* which the customer is willing to pay for. There are likely to be multiple paths to success (which is why more than one competitor can thrive in the same market), but you had better find one that is truly differentiated. Merely "going along" and booking a few more sales with a me-too strategy may get you through another day, but it will not build long-term success for your company.

The second potential path to competitive advantage is to offer an undifferentiated product or service, and to offer it at a lower price *by producing at a lower cost*. However, you are unlikely to maintain a position of lower cost merely by being vigilant and watching your pennies. Instead, *sustainable* cost advantage almost always derives from some type of structural strategic advantage, usually falling into one of the following categories:

- Greater market share and scale. The classic strategic prescription for low cost is to be larger than your competitors. In many cases, greater scale produces lower cost, both because costs can be spread over greater current volume and because of cumulative learning over time. The greater the fixed costs of a business the greater the potential benefits of scale. Hence industries such as pharmaceuticals (with large R&D cost), consumer packaged goods (where advertising to create brand image is very expensive), and oil (where a huge investment in production and distribution facilities is required) tend to evolve towards a model where most of the business is concentrated in the hands of very large players. Conversely, businesses with few fixed costs, in industries as diverse as long haul trucking and management consulting, tend to be highly fragmented.

- Access to lower input costs. In some competitive situations greater scale is trumped by asymmetric access to lower input costs, such as cheaper labor, raw materials, energy or capital. Call centers in India enjoyed lower cost even when they were smaller than rivals in America, because they were able to hire talent at far lower wages. In the metals business, access to raw minerals that by virtue of their location can be brought to the surface least expensively can be more important than overall size.

The recent globalization of scores of industries has provided many more companies with an opportunity to challenge traditional scale-based industry leaders. Competitors large or small who are clever about using global networks to find the least expensive labor and inputs for each step of their production and operating processes are finding new opportunities to achieve low cost and competitive advantage.

- Shared scale across businesses. Proctor and Gamble has its roots in cleaning-related businesses including soap and toothpaste, yet in recent decades it has successfully achieved cost and competitive leadership in industries such as diapers and beauty products where it started from way behind. What all of these businesses have in common is that they share the same target customers, distribution channels, and advertising vehicles — all of which are scale-sensitive, value-added steps where P&G's historical products gave them scale and cost advantages which they then transferred to their new businesses. Shared scale across businesses can trump scale in the business itself if the cost impact is real and if it is cleverly employed.

As you seek to craft a strategy of competitive advantage, the starting point is a realistic assessment of how your company stacks up today in terms of both cost and differentiation. That assessment should include not only a comparative rating of your offerings relative to competition, but also an understanding of the structural basis for your advantage or disadvantage to help you understand how your relative position might change in the future. Furthermore, you need to *quantify* the differences in cost and differentiation as best as they can be estimated, as in the absence of that quantification too many companies fall prey to claims of competitive advantage which are more wish than reality.

Once you have a realistic reading of where you stand today, you and your team need to blue-sky alternative future paths which will improve your differentiation or cost relative to competitors so as to create the best possible position of sustainable competitive advantage. Just as your company's current relative position must be quantified, you should do your best to quantify the likely impact on relative cost and differentiation of the various options which your company could pursue as its future strategy. This process can be substantial, as you consider a variety of different target markets and different paths to either low cost or differentiation. However, when you and your senior team, assisted by the right people from throughout the company, are constructively debating this multi-dimensional problem, then you are in the throes of a high-quality strategic process that will begin to lay the groundwork for sustainable competitive advantage and a leadership position in your targeted segment of the market.

There is one final crucial factor which must be considered, and that is the fact that competitors are moving targets. We have read many plans which document a company's current position of disadvantage, identify steps that will be taken to improve, and then calculate the resulting advantage relative to the competition — all based on the implicit assumption that in the time it takes the company to make its improvements, its competitors will be standing absolutely still. Obviously this fails a test of realism. In fact, it is quite possible that competitors will move even faster than you, causing you, during the time you implement your improvements, to fall even further behind your competition. Forward-looking strategy must consider likely future changes in the market, future progress by competitors *and* future steps by your company — and if the sum total of these, realistically assessed, does not yield a position of true competitive advantage for your company, then you do not yet have a strategy that will be successful over the long term.

The strategic process of determining the best course to competitive advantage is an ongoing and iterative one — yet at various points in time you have to put a stake in the ground and identify the course that will guide your management and your company's operating plans. The problem is difficult, but it is one that must be taken on by you and your team. One way or the other, you must create real differentiation or cost advantage based on the most important needs of your target market, and you must do so in a way that will be sustainable in the face of tough competition. If you fail to do so, the likely result will be a ticket towards a "me too" competitive position and mediocre financial results — for reasons we explore further in the next chapter.

Chapter 32

The Path to Profitability

Just as this is not a strategy book, it is also not one about finance. However, we do wish to address the one financial imperative which every CEO faces — to earn good returns for the company's owners, whether public shareholders, private investors, or the entrepreneur himself. Beyond the desire to reward risk-taking owners, without strong profitability your company will lack the resources to invest in the people, plant and programs which are needed to keep you strong and competitive over the long term. Profitability is both a result and cause of corporate excellence, and must be part of the equation if that excellence is to be sustained.

There are many complicated ways to think about profitability, but the simplest of all is also the most important: *Profit equals price minus cost.* The statement is an obvious one, but if combined with the lessons of competitive advantage, the implications are huge. Furthermore, in our experience those implications are ignored or papered over by far too many CEOs. Let's combine that simple profit equation with the principles of the previous chapter and see where that leads us.

All industries by definition have an overall average level of profitability. Some enjoy industry structures with characteristics which favor good profitability. Such characteristics might include non-price-sensitive customers, barriers to entry like patents or high customer switching costs which protect industry players from tough competition, and a relatively small number of competitors which keeps competition "gentlemanly." At the other end of the spectrum, there are industries characterized by factors such as too many competitors, powerful and price sensitive customers, and powerful suppliers, all of which squeeze industry profitability. Many other industries fall somewhere in between. On balance, the majority of companies large and small — and quite possibly yours — find themselves in competitive industries where the structural factors are challenging, and where the path to strong profitability is far from clear.

As a result, there is a huge difference between finding something that you can sell — *and actually achieving good profitability* as you do so. In fact, the empirical data is clear: There are far more companies, large and small, muddying up the waters while earning mediocre or weak profits, than there are companies which actually earn superior returns for their shareholders.

Yet you, as CEO of *your* company, surely intend to earn strong returns, as well you should. To do so, you need to chart a course for your company which ensures that it will achieve the desired level of profitability.

• •

To chart a truly successful course for your company over the long term, you must begin by embracing rigorous principles of competitive advantage and profitability, and by making them part of the fabric of your company.

• •

When we first are introduced to a company, we often go through the following exercise. First, we demonstrate to the CEO that his industry is quite competitive (as it usually is), and that the average company in the industry is not as profitable as the CEO wants his company to be (and neither is his company yet). Next, we point out that profit equals price minus cost. Third, we listen as he explains — either verbally or in a formal plan — the series of actions he is going to take to improve his company's operations and market position, in the hope of achieving the desired profitability. We then ask — "as a result of these actions, do you believe that your company will be able to differentiate to the point that you can sell at a higher price than the competition?" The answer usually comes back — "no, we will have to meet the price of competitors." Similarly, we ask if, by virtue of other of the company's intended actions, it will become the low cost producer in its segment of the market. Again the reply usually comes back, "no, we need to do these things just to keep up, because competitors are doing them too, and when we're done we won't be lower cost."

At this point we sum all of that up and reply — "Okay, so let's see what you're saying: The industry as a whole earns lower returns than you intend to, you will sell at the same price and produce at the same cost as the competition, yet magically — although profit equals price minus cost — you will earn stronger returns than they do." When stated that directly, it becomes clear that the math simply doesn't add up.

This story may *sound* simplistic, but in our experience it exemplifies a critical and costly gap in how many CEOs run their companies. Too often they get caught up in a series of strategic and operating actions, each of which independently may sound reasonable and make good sense. Yet they fail to rigorously test whether the sum total of those actions create enough of an advantage in differentiation or cost to yield the targeted level of profitability. You can run all the pro forma financials you'd like, and there is a good time and place to do so, but we all know that just because we forecast desired levels of future profitability does not mean that they will be achieved. For most companies, less time should be spent crunching the numbers and more devoted to thoughtfully exploring and defining the strategic path that will truly lead to strong profitability.

The irony is that, in our experience, most CEOs know how their company stacks up relative to the various pieces of the equation we describe above — they simply lack the discipline and resolve to squarely face the implications of that knowledge and tackle them head-on. Lacking a strong strategy the CEO instead finds solace, and much to keep her busy, in fine-tuning improvements to operations or the sales force and in re-running the financials — actions which may be useful, but which are simply not enough.

The fact that, in their gut, most CEOs understand the various components of their company's fundamental strategic position is also a cause for optimism: To get to the next level, the CEO need not acquire a whole new body of information — but instead to insist that she and her team simply face facts within a tight strategic mindset, and then work hard at crafting a truly profitable strategy. When the CEO fails to do so, she can fine-tune and re-crunch all she wants, but she is in effect "kicking the can down the road" rather than fulfilling the second of the CEO's non-negotiable roles — which is to craft a winning course for the company. Not surprisingly, the can-kicking CEO also often spends quarter after quarter and year after year frustrated with company profitability, all the while continually looking in the wrong places for the answer to that financial stagnation.

Perhaps at this point you're asking yourself — "but how can my company truly be the lowest cost producer, or how can it truly be differentiated from all those other competitors?" The answer lies in the fact that in your market there are many different groups of customers, each with different needs. Each of those market segments offer alternative ways to differentiate or achieve lowest cost, which is why there are usually multiple competitors who make good money in each industry, each identifying a different path to stand out and achieve competitive advantage. In our experience, perhaps ten to thirty percent of the competitors in a given industry — those who succeed in establishing competitive advantage through differentiation or low cost — earn strong returns, while the rest experience financial results which are mediocre or worse.

We could ask — "which of these two fates do you wish for your company?" — but we already know the answer to that question. We also know that if your company is to get there, then there is no getting around the requisite creativity, strategic understanding, hard work and discipline on the part of you and your team. To chart a truly successful course for your company over the long term, you must begin by embracing rigorous principles of competitive advantage and profitability, and by making them part of the fabric of your company.

Chapter 33

Strategy Up and Down the Organization

Up to this point we've described strategic principles — competitive advantage, differentiation, cost and profitability — as conceptual monoliths which apply to the entire company. In this chapter we look further at how different parts of your organization and members of your management team need to intersect with the various components of the strategic thought process.

There is in fact a hierarchy of strategic decisions which need to be made, consisting of three levels: *corporate* strategy, *business* strategy and *functional* strategy. For large companies, these different levels correspond to different parts of the organization: The corporate group and senior management team is responsible for corporate strategy, divisional or business leaders own business strategies, and the leaders of the various functional groups (such as sales, manufacturing, R&D or customer service) lead the various functional strategies. Smaller companies are likely to have more consolidated organizational structures, perhaps with each function reporting to the CEO but without any formal organization structure built around separate businesses. At the extreme, the entrepreneur may be his company's only employee, or he may have a small number of employees and no formal organizational structure at all.

However, regardless of organization structure, all companies and all CEOs need to analyze and craft strategies at all three of the conceptual levels — corporate, business and functional. Although the three levels may or may not correspond to organizational entities in your company, most fundamentally they are not about organization. Instead, they consist of questions which must be answered if you are to optimize your company's competitive position, marketplace success and financial performance. With that in mind, let's look further at what each of the three levels entails, beginning with corporate strategy.

At the corporate level, the goal (perhaps among others) is to deliver strong financial results to owners. In order to do so, corporate leaders have at their disposal three strategic levers which can be pulled. First, it is the job of the corporate strategists, including the CEO, to *select the businesses* in which the company will participate. For broadly diversified companies (of which there are fewer today than a few decades ago), the different "businesses" may be in completely separate industries — such as General Electric's financial services, entertainment and jet engines businesses. For companies which compete within a single industry sector (as most do), the different "businesses" might be different product lines, customer groups or geographies.

• •

> The strategic rigor with which resources are allocated is one of the most reliable indicators of the quality of a company's leadership.

• •

The dimensions along which you define your businesses can vary, but the determinant of how you do so should be this: For the purposes of strategic analysis, you should separate businesses which require different strategies to succeed — due to important differences in either the nature of the market, the basis of competitive advantage, or your company's position of strength relative to competitors. Microsoft no doubt views its Xbox gaming business as strategically separate from its software businesses, and its software geared to large businesses as separate from the offering to small businesses and consumers — because the needs of customers and the paths to differentiation are so different for those individual businesses. A local hotel might view its wedding/banquet business as separate from its individual customer business because the requirements for success are so different. And a U.S.-based multinational which sells the same product around the world might view its U.S., European and Asian businesses as strategically separate because it is the market share leader in the first geography, a weaker follower in the second, and just getting started in the third.

Whatever strategic businesses your company has today, there is no law that those are the businesses in which you must participate in the future. As CEO you have at your disposable many strategic options which can add to your company's mix of businesses, including product-line diversification, geographic expansion, sales or marketing initiatives to new groups of customers, R&D, joint ventures and acquisitions. Similarly, you can exit any business through discontinuance of a product line, geographic contraction, divestiture, and so forth. Your first responsibility as the lead corporate strategist is to assess both your current businesses and potential new ones, so as to select the mix of businesses in which you are most likely to be competitively advantaged, and which together will add up to the greatest success for your company.

That business selection process should take place implicitly and continually in all that you do, as well as formally at regular intervals, probably no less often than once a year. Too often companies and CEOs get locked into thinking that just because they have a certain mix of businesses today then that must also be their business mix in the future. By failing to rigorously explore both potential additions and subtractions with an open mind, those CEOs limit their degrees of freedom and render the challenge to achieve competitive advantage and financial success more difficult than it needs to be.

Beyond selecting businesses, it is the job of the corporate strategist to intelligently *allocate resources* among them. In every company there are limits to how much capital can be invested and how much can be budgeted for marketing, R&D, human talent and everything else. Every hour of every day, senior managers in your company make decisions which allocate these scarce resources among the company's various businesses — and the quality of those decisions can go a long way towards determining the success or failure of the company in achieving its financial objectives.

In fact, the strategic rigor with which resources are allocated is one of the most reliable indicators of the quality of a company's leadership. Non-strategic companies operate by a resource allocation process which dictates that "everyone gets a little." Requests come in from various parts of the company for money and resources, the sum total of which exceeds that which is available. Unsure of how to resolve this scarcity problem and reluctant to offend or disappoint, the CEO and his team cut all requests by roughly the same ratio, attempting to be "fair" to the various businesses and managers.

This sense of fairness is truly misguided. Different businesses within the company's portfolio have very different strategic prospects: Some offer great potential and others less so, while some good businesses require lots of additional investment and other good businesses don't. By spreading scarce resources around "equally," the CEO underfunds promising businesses, therefore handicapping their chance of future success. She also wastes money by over-spending on less attractive businesses or good ones which don't truly need that level of new discretionary investment. Spreading resources around in such a non-strategic manner is one of the surest paths to competitive and financial mediocrity for companies both large and small.

Well-run companies, on the other hand, are decisive and highly *differential* in how they divide scarce resources. In the large-company world, there is no better example of this principle than General Electric. For generations, GE has participated in a broad range of businesses, including many mature and "unsexy" industries which have bedeviled other companies' efforts to earn strong returns. Yet year in and year out GE has achieved strong financial results in those very same industries. What is their secret? A key part of the answer lies in the discipline with which they assess the prospects of their different businesses and then allocate resources among them.

At GE, truly strong and promising businesses are given all they need to grow. Solid businesses with more limited growth prospects are given enough resources to defend their position and to support more modest growth, but not so much as to waste money trying to find profitable growth where it doesn't exist. Finally, businesses where a true path to competitive advantage and strong profitability cannot be found are harvested for cash or sold — often to less strategically-managed companies which pay more for them than they may be worth. GE's objective strategic rigor ensures that the company devotes scarce resources where the payoff is greatest, giving the company a huge advantage over less disciplined competitors. That advantage then translates into GE's consistently strong profitability.

There is nothing about this principle of strategic resource allocation that is unique to large companies. The entrepreneur who faces day-to-day pressures and distractions must nonetheless remain objective and disciplined enough to invest resources in his company's most attractive opportunities, while limiting investment in (or even walking away from) the less promising ones. In doing so, he dramatically raises the odds that one day he will find himself running a much larger and more profitable company.

- -

> As corporate strategist, the CEO leads a rigorous process of selecting businesses, allocating resources among them and creating synergies.

- -

The third strategic lever available to the CEO as corporate strategist is to *create synergies* which make the whole of the company greater than the sum of its various parts. If a company is a collection of completely unrelated businesses, then one can question why it needs to exist. Instead, good companies inevitably possess shared overarching strengths which augment the competitive position of its individual businesses. In fact, those synergies may be the core of the vision for the company discussed in Part IV — the broad competitive advantage which serves as the foundation for the company's strategy.

As referenced in Chapter 31, the core strength of Proctor & Gamble resides in its understanding of its target customers, strength in key distribution channels and skill (and scale) in advertising and promotion — all of which are then used to empower each of its individual product lines well beyond the competitive position they would enjoy as stand-alone businesses. A local real estate company providing residential and commercial brokerage, as well as insurance, mortgage and other related offerings may very well be leveraging its local market knowledge and the contact network of its people as the overarching competitive advantage for each of its individual businesses. Even General Electric, with its diversified portfolio, would certainly acknowledge that a critical company strength is the depth of its management and the quality and rigor of its management processes, which it then applies across its wide range of businesses. For any company, the area of corporate synergy where the company truly excels can be its defining characteristic in its quest for competitive advantage and superior financial performance.

The importance of synergy means that for the purposes of corporate strategic analysis there is a fourth category of business beyond the three identified in the General Electric example — growth businesses justifying heavy investment, profitable but lower-growth businesses warranting less investment, and weak businesses to be harvested or sold. The fourth category consists of businesses which, in and of themselves, do not warrant investment, but which play an important role in supporting other, more promising businesses in the portfolio.

For a large vendor of computer equipment, a division offering training programs to customers may not be large or profitable enough to be of serious strategic interest as a stand-alone business, but may help serve and lock in customers to ensure that the hardware dollars keep on coming. The local real estate company we described might offer a school to train real estate agents, not because of the profit inherent in running the school, but instead to gain advantage over competitors in signing agents, which is a key to success in that business. Sometimes it is appropriate for the CEO and his team to direct a business leader to run his division in such a way as to contribute to the core businesses in the portfolio, rather than as an end in itself.

However, a word of caution is important here: One of the most common arguments made by managers of underperforming businesses is that the reason to continue to invest there is because of all that the business does to help the rest of the company. Yet it is far less common for the cited synergies to be truly important in creating competitive advantage. It is one of the roles of the corporate strategist to distinguish real synergies from superficial ones. If he is not rigorous in doing so, the result will be that *all* businesses will wind up getting funded, and the required differential investment and strategic allocation of resources will be lost.

As corporate strategist, the CEO leads a rigorous process of selecting businesses, allocating resources among them and creating synergies — the totality of which creates the strongest possible competitive platform and financial result for the company. It is within that context that the second level of analysis — business strategy — is formulated.

• •

Functional activities which are entirely operational in focus may get the company through another day, but they do not help enough in the difficult job of outperforming the competition.

• •

As the name implies, business strategy is the process of providing direction for each individual business within the company. The core of business strategy is what we discussed at length in Chapters 31 and 32 — the pursuit of true competitive advantage through the various potential paths to differentiation or low cost. The degree to which that advantage is created then correlates with the likely marketplace success and financial performance of the business.

Depending on the size and complexity of the business, it may also be useful to apply the corporate strategic thought process to the different sub-components of the business, such as different parts of the product line, different customer groups, or different geographies. The same three questions apply to this mini-portfolio: In which sub-businesses should we participate in the future, and therefore what needs to be added or subtracted? What is the best way to rigorously and differentially allocate resources among the sub-businesses? And what synergies are available to bind these sub-businesses together and enhance their ability to compete in their individual markets? As the strategic thought process is applied to lower and lower levels within the company it may be conducted more informally, but if you as CEO can train the organization to be disciplined in always asking and answering those questions, however informally, the impact on competitive and financial performance throughout the company will be quite powerful.

The third and final level of strategic analysis — the crafting of functional strategies — consists of the alignment of the various functions — sales, operations, IT and so forth — to the basis for competitive advantage identified in the corporate and business strategies. At many large companies, strategic planning has become an isolated activity: The CEO, senior management, the Board, or a group of MBA strategic planners design a strategy which, however brilliant, is not inculcated in the rest of the organization and therefore is limited in its effectiveness. At smaller companies, there may be no conscious strategic thought process at all.

In either case, the result will likely be functional activities which are entirely operational in focus. These activities may get the company through another day, but they do not help enough in the difficult job of outperforming the competition. The CEO may broadcast the vision and strategy throughout the entire company, but to the members of the sales force, manufacturing organization or R&D lab, those pronouncements are merely nice-sounding slogans — and they do not truly help them prioritize their activities in a way that maximizes the competitive strength of the entire organization.

On the other hand, companies which excel at developing strategies invest considerable energy to make sure that a solid understanding of the strategy, as well as the underlying thought process, is pushed down to include key people within the various functions. Once that understanding is achieved, the functional leaders and higher-level managers work together to craft strategies for each function which align its activities to the objectives of the business- and corporate-level strategies.

Specifically, functions need to be directed so as to produce the differentiation and cost positions which have been selected as the basis for competitive advantage and success in the marketplace: Is customer service, R&D or the IT group truly focusing its scarce resources on creating or supporting the differentiation that is the core of the business strategy? Are the various functions managing cost so as to create the targeted cost position (which sometimes means doing *less*, through the elimination of non-value-adding activities)? Functional leaders should then be held accountable for managing their functions in a manner consistent with these strategic principles and objectives.

If high quality strategic thought is pushed down from the CEO's office through the various levels of the company until it permeates the entire organization, it eventually becomes second nature in informing the myriad decisions which are made every day throughout the company. Furthermore, it becomes a powerful shared language whenever two or more people in the organization are engaged in constructive debate about a pending decision.

When the CEO fulfills this second of his six critical roles, then company leaders at all levels understand how to do their part to best support the company's direction and strategy. This guidance enables them to maximize their productivity and effectiveness, as well as that of their organizations, as they devote their energy and resources to the activities that are truly important for the company. At the same time, the strategic guidance enables individuals and groups throughout the company to minimize wasted motion and expenditures by providing them a conceptual platform to identify those activities which do not contribute to the intended direction of the company.

The net impact of all of this effectiveness and efficiency is to significantly raise the odds that the company as a whole will be successful at the difficult challenge of outperforming its inevitably tough competitors — and ultimately at achieving its objectives for growth and profitability. In addition, the corollary benefits of the investment in strategic thought include greater learning, motivation and retention rates for key employees, as they feel empowered by their strategic link to the larger purposes of the company.

Finally, by empowering them you are empowering yourself as CEO, as they collectively act as a huge force multiplier for your efforts to lead the company towards the vision which you have created. By aligning the various levels of your organization around your intended strategic direction, you've taken another major step towards solving the CEO's dilemma of powerlessness which we described way back in Chapter 1.

Chapter 34

Strategic Growth

Throughout the strategic thought process, you and your team will be making a myriad of decisions about growth: How fast should we grow? Where and how? What are the costs of growth? What are the risks? What will it take to achieve the growth we've targeted? "Growth" is a wonderful sounding word, but it is much more complicated in the application than the aspiration. A thoughtful, disciplined approach to growth is one of the key requirements of a good strategy.

Growth at some rate is a necessity for almost all businesses. First of all, few investors, whether public or private, are content to simply cash dividend checks which remain at a constant level. Instead they expect the CEO (or he expects himself as CEO/entrepreneur) to build on the company's strengths and find new areas of opportunity which enable both the top and bottom lines to grow over time.

However, an even more important reason to grow is to help your company create an environment which attracts and retains high-quality management and employees. All of your good people seek progression in their careers, as measured by their role in the company, their compensation and the challenges inherent in their work. When companies stop growing, all of those opportunities dry up: There are limited opportunities for promotion, fewer new and interesting challenges and no profit growth to fund increases in employee compensation. As a result, your best people — those most likely to have other options — are more likely to leave, making it even harder for your company to grow in the future. It is said that a shark has to either move forward or die, and that adage is just as true for corporations.

The search for growth is part of the entire strategy process. Each business seeks growth in its domain, while the corporate strategists prioritize existing and new businesses and allocate resources so as to capture as much profitable growth as possible. The company has many levers at its disposal to stimulate growth, including R&D, new product development, new target markets and customers, new distribution channels, joint ventures and acquisitions.

• •

One pivotal characteristic common to companies which grow consistently is that their people are trained to recognize industry disruptions as opportunities and not threats.

• •

Of these sources of growth, acquisitions comprise perhaps the most commonly misunderstood and mismanaged option. When growth is generated internally — as with the extension of the product line into a new distribution channel or the capturing of a new group of customers — the company is building on existing strengths and capturing value, in the form of revenue and profit, that often exceeds the incremental cost. On the other hand, growth through acquisition is achieved by paying for the acquired company, often based on projections of future growth. The competitive market for attractive acquisition targets means that the acquirer is likely to pay at least as much as — and often more than — the company is worth. Add in the inevitable unpleasant surprises which come with acquisitions, as well as the difficulty and cost of integrating the acquired company into your own, and in the vast majority of cases you will be starting from a position of value-to-cost deficit.

In fact, far too many acquisitions get made for the wrong reasons. Some are motivated primarily by the personal desire of senior managers to run a bigger company. While that may be good for managers in the short term, it will be costly to both owners and managers over the longer term if the acquisition does not make financial sense. Other acquisitions are pursued so as to give shareholders an illusion of growth, especially when management has been unable to stimulate growth internally. Management then can brag about results while glossing over the fact that the growth was purchased at a price equal to or in excess of its value — therefore creating no new value for shareholders. In fact, objective studies have demonstrated that the large majority of acquisitions benefit the acquired company but not the one doing the acquiring.

Of course, some acquisitions do make sense — specifically, when for some fundamental strategic reason the combined company is considerably more valuable than the sum of what each was worth individually. However, as with under-performing businesses trying to justify their role in the corporate portfolio, "synergy" as justification for an acquisition is much over-utilized in an attempt to paper over weak financial and strategic logic.

Because of the cost, risk and disruption inherent in acquisitions, it is particularly incumbent on the CEO to subject them to extremely rigorous tests to make sure that the claimed synergies are sufficiently powerful and achievable as to be worth the money and effort. Many a CEO of a company somewhat adrift has been seduced by the notion that the cure-all is an acquisition, only to wind up miring his company more deeply in the muck. In general, CEOs should be reluctant to buy other companies unless they are already confident that their own is being managed well — and even then only when the synergies are clear and compelling and the path to achieve them reasonably straightforward.

If internally-generated opportunities comprise the most reliably profitable way to grow, then what types of companies are best at capturing them? One pivotal characteristic common to companies which grow consistently is that their people are trained to recognize industry disruptions as opportunities and not threats. The natural tendency is to do the opposite: A change in technology, distribution channels or economics which does not fit the strengths of one's own company naturally seems to be something to be combated. Yet those changes are invariably caused by fundamental underlying forces that cannot be stopped, and fighting them is like standing on the beach and trying to stop the tide from coming in. Companies which grow consistently are constantly on the look-out for those forces of industry disruption, and when they see them they pounce and lead the way — even if the short-term implication is the uprooting of an existing business. They instinctively understand that it is better for *them* to be the "uprooter" than for someone else to do the job.

For many decades, railroads were dominant in the shipping of freight around America. At the time, they possessed three fundamental strategic assets which could serve as barriers against new competition. First, they owned a vast network of installed track, locomotives and rail cars. Second, they had a close relationship with every shipping customer in the country. And third, they had the nation's leading logistics capability and expertise, as they calculated on a daily basis how to move tens of thousands of shipments in as timely and economic a manner as possible.

Then along came an invention called the truck, which for many types of goods was a fundamentally more economical and flexible mode of transport. How did the railroads respond to this technological upheaval? They viewed it as a threat, and spent decades in the futile effort to stem the tide. The mistake they made was to view their business in terms of only *one* of their three strategic assets — the track and rolling stock — and with that as their business definition the truck truly was a threat, as it would render a big chunk of that investment in plant obsolete.

Yet if they had viewed their business as all three of their assets — physical plant, customer relationships and logistics capability — they would have recognized early on that two of the three applied equally well to the trucking business as to railroading. They then might have viewed the new technology as an opportunity, and had they done so it would have been theirs for the taking, as no new competitor could have caught up in the face of the railroad's huge installed base of customers. The railroads could have simply gone to their customers and said, "We're going to continue to pick up and deliver your goods on time and at lowest cost, only now using a new technology called a truck — but don't worry about that, that's our problem, not yours." Had that been their response, they would have remained the nation's dominant shippers, and the long string of railroad bankruptcies and restructurings which occupied the last half of the 20th century could have been avoided.

As old as this example is, it has powerful implications for many — in fact virtually all — of today's industries. Competitors who define their business so narrowly as to confine it to their physical technology are usually the last to adapt to changes — and then only when it is too late. Conversely, competitors who recognize the centrality of "softer" competitive strengths, such as customer relationships or core skills, are more likely to embrace disruptive industry changes and tie them into those existing strengths.

One of the places where this contrast is most publicly visible today is in the entertainment industry, where old-media companies struggle to develop strategies to deal with new media developments. If you are CEO of a network TV company, do you cling to the traditional broadcast model, show formats and advertising revenue streams — or instead, do you lead the way in offering programming via iPods, online

· ·

Excellent companies are vigilant about costs, yet at the same time, they consciously out-spend their competition on those areas of cost which are most important for future growth.

· ·

video services and other new media formats, even though the revenue model for those technologies is far less clear? If you are a movie production company, do you stick to rules which dictate that a movie isn't available on DVD or for sale online until a number of months after the theatrical release — or do you let the new media opportunities lead the strategy and give theatrical release — the older technology — a secondary role?

Interestingly, it is often the companies that are trailing in the old technologies who do the best job of embracing the new ones — because they have the least to lose. One sees this pattern in today's entertainment industry, yet some of the smarter "old media" leaders are beginning to realize that they too had better make the switch — if they want to remain leaders. The timing with which old and profitable paths to success are traded in for new but financially uncertain ones is an enormously challenging problem. Yet of one thing we are certain: In entertainment as in all industries, it will ultimately be customers, not vendors, who will decide what and how they will buy — and the winners will be those who seek out those trends and capitalize on them, rather than fight them to the death.

Beyond embracing the potential of industry change, the second thing that excellent CEOs do to ensure consistent growth is to make sure that the company is investing aggressively in those functions within the organization which are most important for growth. All companies are resource-constrained as they work to meet their targets for profitability and cash flow. As they pore over budgets in order to "make the numbers," the easiest thing to do is to shortchange the discretionary and more speculative expenditures, such as advertising, growth of the sales force, business development or R&D. Yet those discretionary items are also the ones which often are most important for growth. Companies who fall into this trap can start a vicious downward cycle: When times get tough they cut discretionary expenditures, which cuts off growth and weakens them competitively, thereby causing profits to stagnate further. When the market eventually cycles upward, these companies are usually the least well positioned to take advantage of the upturn, because they've stripped the company of its growth potential during the hard times.

Conversely, excellent companies understand what it takes to grow and therefore live by a different set of principles. They are vigilant about costs, as well they should be, and seek to eliminate waste and reduce cost wherever they can. Yet at the same time, they consciously *out-spend* their competition on those areas of cost which are most important for future growth. Depending on the sources of growth for their industry, they maintain a mindset that investment in a first-class and well-supported sales force, a top-notch advertising capability or a leading R&D function is the place where they would rather err on the side of over-spending than under-spending. And when times get tough they have the discipline to maintain that investment, knowing that they will need it more than ever to get through the downturn and to ride the crest of the recovery when it occurs.

While growth is an imperative, and the excellent CEO knows what it takes to achieve it, it is also crucial for her to keep it in perspective. Growth in and of itself gets you nothing — it is only *profitable* growth built on a position of sustainable competitive advantage which allows you to reward shareholders and employees. An exceedingly common mistake is for CEOs to get sloppy in assuming that a growth opportunity is worth pursuing simply because it produces new revenue — without subjecting it to the same tests of business attractiveness, competitive advantage, differentiation and low cost which need to be applied to existing businesses.

In fact, read the <u>Wall Street Journal</u> and about once a week you'll learn of another company which announces that it is cutting back on growth and focusing on its most profitable opportunities — and in most cases the article mentions that the company's stock price spiked upwards in response to the announcement. As detailed financial analysis reveals, it is not that the stock market doesn't value growth, because surely it does. Rather, the market values growth only when it believes it will be profitable, and in the cases cited above, it is rewarding the company for recognizing the difference between investment in profitable opportunities and growth for growth's sake. For privately-held or entrepreneurial ventures, there is no public stock market to help you by sending that signal, yet the principle is equally valid: You do your company's owners no good by investing in growth unless it is likely to yield strong profitability based on sustainable competitive advantage.

Furthermore, you should allow neither yourself nor your people to get away with the often-uttered excuse that "I can't analyze the profitability of this opportunity because the business doesn't exist yet." Strategic analysis, and in fact all business decisions, are about predicting the future based on the best available information, logic and analytical frameworks — and your role as a leader is to foresee your company's likely competitive position in the potential new business as a basis for predicting its profitability. A company that doesn't grow is in trouble, but so is one that views growth in an undisciplined way as opposed to basing it on high-quality strategic thought and disciplined leadership.

Ultimately, the most reliable way to test the merit of new growth opportunities is by analyzing their consistency with your vision and strategy, as described throughout Parts IV and V. Your role as CEO is to build a company that values growth and which does what is necessary to achieve it, but which also applies to growth opportunities the same tests of business selection and resource allocation which you apply to your existing businesses. Does the new opportunity fall within the sphere of the company's vision? Does it meet the criteria of competitive advantage, differentiation, cost and profitability?

Pursuing growth opportunities while testing them rigorously is a delicate balance to maintain — one that will require you to draw upon many of the principles of enlightenment, including knowledge, objectivity, focus on the company's objectives and not your own, and calm. The more you can keep the notion of growth solidly within the framework of enlightenment, vision and strategy which we've described, the more likely that you will capture it in a way that makes money for your owners, creates opportunity for your people, and propels your company strongly into the future.

Chapter 35

A Living Strategy

The best CEOs understand that strategy is a *mindset* even more than it is a *process*. Depending on the size of your company, strategic planning may be an extensive and fully-documented process, or it may be as basic as the key people getting in a room once or twice a year to debate the issues and chart the course. The difference between a strong strategy and a weaker one lies in the rigor of the strategic framework (are you asking the tough questions or avoiding them?) and in the creativity and quality of the answers — and not in the amount of paper generated.

In fact, we have often found that there is an *inverse* relationship between the length of written strategic plans and the quality of thinking contained therein. Conceiving of a path to true competitive advantage and supporting that direction with logic and evidence is a difficult challenge, but when you find a way to do so you should be able to describe it concisely — and if not, then the reasoning is probably suspect. Longer plans tend to drown the reader in extraneous information because their writers are not able conclusively make and prove the strategic case. As Mark Twain once wrote, "I'm sorry this letter is so long, but I didn't have time to make it shorter."

Of course, in companies of any significant size documenting plans in writing does serve a purpose. Yet good plans are kept focused through the use of a tight strategic framework — one which ties information to its strategic implications rather than just putting it down on paper to fill a binder. The strategic logic is the key, because the real payoff for the CEO is not when the plan is written down, but when decision-makers up and down the organization have been trained to *think* strategically every day. Instilling a high-quality strategic framework into the fabric of the company will not only produce better strategic plans, it will also help ensure that managers throughout the organization will know how to adjust on the fly to the inevitable surprises and bumps in the road.

Whatever the format, at too many companies the strategy remains the province of a small group of executives and planners, and the "document" spends most of its time sitting in desk drawers or on book shelves. If that is the case, then you have not fulfilled your objective of instilling the plan and a strategic framework throughout the organization. Your goal as CEO is for the strategy to be owned by all of the company's decision-makers, and to do so you will need to accomplish three things.

• •

If the reaction is a significant amount of resistance, then quite possibly there is something wrong with the strategy which you and your team have missed.

• •

First, regardless of who is involved when the plan is initially crafted, the strategy needs to be vetted by as wide an audience of the company's decision-makers as is practical, because they are the ones who will be responsible for its implementation. This iterative vetting by diverse groups of people will dramatically increase the quality of the plan — because inevitably there is information that is critical for the plan which is buried in different parts of the company far from the offices of the CEO, top executives or planners.

Sometimes, we find that the CEO or others are reluctant to include a manager or broader group in the process because it is believed that they don't "get" the strategy or are unhelpfully resisting it. In our experience, that person or group is usually neither completely wrong nor being completely obstructionist. Instead, they have unique data or a different perspective which causes them some legitimate concern about one part of the strategy. By including them in the process you ferret out that concern and identify any necessary adjustments. In addition, by giving them a seat at the table you have a shot at transforming their resistance into cooperation. It takes intellectual courage to subject your strategy to the vetting of a large number of people with diverse points of view, but the more people you include, the greater the opportunity to find potential flaws in the strategy and to increase the quality of the end product. Establishing true and sustainable competitive advantage is difficult, and the wise CEO would rather have his own people expose those flaws than for the marketplace or competitors to do so further down the road.

Second, for the strategy to permeate the organization it must be understandable. There is an old adage in business — "write it so that your grandmother could understand it." That may be an exaggeration (depending on who your grandmother is), but the point is an important one: If you can't express a strategy in clear, simple terms, then there is probably something lacking in your logic which the complexity of your communication is trying to obscure. The written version of the plan needs to be crystal clear with no potential for confusion as to its direction. When the strategy is communicated verbally, it may be described in general terms or in detail depending upon the audience. Yet in either case if the listener doesn't leave the room thinking "I understand this, it makes sense, and now I own the strategy too," then something is wrong and you have more work to do.

Third, the strategy must be supported by those with whom it is shared. If you've vetted the strategy and disseminated it in understandable terms, but the reaction is a significant amount of resistance, then something important is at work which you must address. Quite possibly, there is something wrong with the strategy which you and your team have missed — but which the people who are closer to the action and who have to implement it understand. Even if that is not the case and the strategy is in fact a good one, the fact remains that if it is not supported then it simply will not be implemented — or at best will be implemented in a highly inconsistent and inefficient manner. One way or the other, it is the job of you and your team to build the necessary support, and the presence of strong and clearly communicated strategic logic, coupled with empathy for your listeners, is the key to doing so.

Furthermore, even if the resistance is for the wrong reasons — such as political opposition to the de-emphasis of a business or to cost cuts — your job as CEO is to clearly communicate to as wide an audience as practical the strategic case for why it's the right course of action. The result may not be universal, full-throated support, but you will engender respect and appreciation, however grudging, for the thought process as well as the effort you made to share it with those who will be affected. The process of building support is an inherently healthy one, as while you do so you are spreading the language of strategic thought and discipline throughout the company.

Although the strategy must be clear and understandable, it should not be inflexible. All businesses face a continuous stream of changing circumstances and uncertainties, not just in the market and in the actions of competitors, but in its own capability to successfully implement the chosen course of action. As these changes take place, the strategy must be strong, yet flexible enough so that the company can react in ways that keep it on a course of competitive advantage.

To lay the groundwork for that flexibility, the assumptions, data and logic behind the chosen strategy should be laid out clearly for all to see. The strategy should also include recognition of the inherent uncertainties, as well as scenario planning for how the company should react based on how things actually play out. If the strategic logic is understood by all, then as the unexpected occurs decision-makers will know more readily how to adjust in response to an invalidated assumption or a critical new piece of data. The key to maintaining flexibility is a strategy based on a solid strategic framework, rather than one which reads like it came down from the mountaintop inscribed in stone.

In addition, when the plan is based on a solid strategic framework, then you and your team are more likely to remain objective about when the strategy is still correct and when it needs to be changed. When a strategy is created out of "whole cloth," CEOs are more prone to stick to it for too long as an article of faith, even when it may be obvious to others that the strategy is failing or that it needs a mid-course correction. Conversely, when the strategy is built upon clearly documented assumptions, data and logic, then smart CEOs stay wedded to the underlying framework and logic but not necessarily to every detail of the strategy — and therefore recognize early on when modification of the strategy is necessary. In the end a well-conceived and well-supported strategy should be refined considerably more often than the vision of the company. However, it should also be robust enough that it does not need to be abandoned altogether, except in very rare instances.

Throughout Part V we've described the characteristics of a strong strategy that creates real competitive advantage. The truth is, there are many more companies which *lack* a true strategy — one that is based on solid strategic thought and which is rigorous in its logic of competitive advantage — than there are companies which actually have one. The problem for the companies lacking a true strategy is that organizations, like nature, abhor a vacuum. When you don't have a solid strategy which is vetted, understood and supported throughout your organization, then what you *will* have is lots of independent "strategies" in different corners of the company — many of which will operate at cross-purposes. The latter is a formula for organizational discord and inefficiency as well as corporate stagnation, and certainly not one for competitive advantage and strong financial performance. That is why the second of your roles as CEO — to rigorously chart a winning course for your company — is a *non-negotiable* ingredient of success for you and your company.

For your strategy to ultimately translate into results, it must be reflected in the day-to-day actions of the company (the subject of Part VII), and there must be a good system of follow-through and accountability so that those action plans are actually implemented (the subject of Part VIII). However, before turning there let's look next in Part VI at what is required to shape the high-quality management team who will share your responsibility for all the steps in that progression.

Part VI:
Shaping the Team

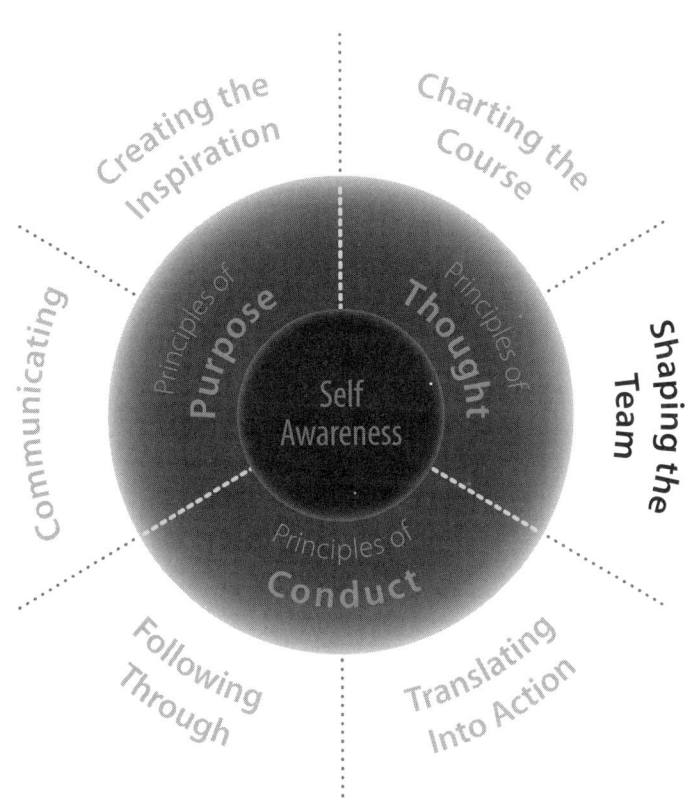

Chapter 36

Making the Investment

Parts IV and V explored the first two of your roles as CEO: To design a vision to inspire your company as well as a strategy to realize that vision. Both of these roles are "thinking" ones which address the question of *what* the company should be doing. Your remaining four roles concern *how* the organization will achieve those ends.

To design the vision and strategy, you need to immerse yourself and your company in the world of ideas. You need to be knowledgeable about your company, its environment and the rules of strategy, as well as underlying ideas in the realms of product possibilities, potential technological changes, market research and other disciplines. Based on all of that knowledge and analysis, you then must creatively craft the optimal path forward.

Immersing yourself and your company in a steady flow of creative concepts is very healthy. Yet the concepts themselves are inanimate and by themselves can accomplish nothing for your company. Instead, new ideas are only as good as the people you have to evaluate them and the ability of those people to work together as a team to get them implemented. In our experience, we've met a far greater number of CEOs who lament that they have plenty of promising ideas but not enough good people and teams to make them happen — than CEOs who claim to have a surplus of great people but not enough good ideas.

Yet as common as this view may be, it is at least as common — and strikingly so — for CEOs to under-invest in finding the right people and in shaping them into a highly effective team. Most CEOs understand that they need strong senior executives, but nonetheless go about the business of staffing and shaping that senior staff in too piecemeal and perfunctory a way. Such CEOs may wind up assembling a group which includes some talented individuals, but also one which lacks the "special sauce" that transforms a group of individuals into a superb, highly-functioning team.

CEOs who under-invest in shaping their teams do so for a number of reasons. The leader of a small company may believe that her own insight and charisma are enough to make her company a success, regardless of the team with which she surrounds herself. Caught up in the excitement of her business and focused on shorter-term issues, she fails to anticipate that if her company is to grow to any appreciable size, then she will need an effective team to support and drive the company's success.

> Cutting corners in shaping the team is one of the most penny-wise and dollar-foolish things that CEOs do.

Other CEOs fail to appreciate just how well high-functioning teams can truly function, and the powerful impact that they can have on the company's performance. As a result, they *believe* that their team is performing at a high level when in fact they are badly miscalculating: Their team may be an "average" one, but in accepting that level of performance they are squandering an opportunity for the team to do so much better on behalf of the company. Finally, many CEOs do sense that there is significant potential to improve the senior team, but they've tried with insufficient success and simply don't know what to do differently to get to the next level.

The net result, in our experience, is that most CEOs under-invest in the shaping of their teams. These CEOs may:

+ Lead limited rather than thorough searches for the best people to join their teams;

- In their anxiousness to complete the search, conduct only half-baked research on the previous track record of potential hires — research that could reveal how well the new hire will mesh with the existing team and company culture;

- Be deficient in providing regular, direct and helpful coaching to existing members of the team, preferring instead to sweep potentially contentious issues under the rug;

- Fail to design an effective process for the team to debate issues and reach decisions which are objective and best for the company — and therefore by default allow too many issues to be decided based on politics or expediency;

- Under-invest in learning what motivates their people both professionally and personally, therefore squandering an opportunity to reduce turnover and extend the tenure of the company's strongest leaders;

- Be too cavalier and unsystematic in their entire approach to shaping a highly-functioning team — assuming that "we're all adults" and that therefore issues among us will be worked out automatically — and ignore the need for consciously determined group behaviors and norms.

Cutting corners in addressing these critical building blocks for shaping the team is one of the most penny-wise and dollar-foolish things that CEOs do. There is huge leverage for any CEO in getting the right people onto his team and then having them work together as effectively as possible. A well-functioning team both dramatically reduces the number of problems the CEO must deal with on a day-to-day basis, and also creates all sorts of upside opportunities for the company that are not generated by less effective teams. Given the potential payoff of a well-shaped team, we have found relatively few CEOs who make the personal investment in time to match that payoff — yet *all* CEOs need to do so.

Think about your favorite professional sports team. Surely it has a vision, perhaps to win the championship this year, make the playoffs or embark upon a several-year rebuilding program. Now imagine the leaders of that team exhibiting only sporadic diligence in researching and deciding which players to add to the team. Furthermore, imagine them failing to do everything possible to help the players perform to the limit of their ability, as well as to get all the players to work seamlessly together in an inspired way, based on a carefully-designed set of rules and expectations. Surely you would view the team's leadership as foolish, and few professional teams would behave that way. For *any* organization or CEO to under-invest in selecting individuals and shaping the team is just as foolish, yet many in fact do just that. Because the time pressures of the job are omnipresent, and because the challenge of understanding and motivating talented but complicated people is difficult, too many CEOs shy away from this critical role.

If you are a CEO whose thoroughness in shaping the team ebbs and flows, the irony is that whenever it ebbs because you are pressed for time, you are in fact creating *more* work for yourself, not less. Fail to spend enough time carefully selecting the right person to add to the team, and you'll wind up having to repeat the process a second or third time when too often you discover that the initial hire was a mistake. Avoid regularly coaching your people, teaching them how to overcome areas of weakness, and you'll spend far more time fixing individual problems as they arise rather than leveraging yourself by instilling the requisite skills in the members of the team. Fail to explicitly define how the team will resolve disagreements and work together to make decisions, and you'll wind up wasting far too much time arbitrating misguided disputes which are based upon political agendas and conflicting sets of data.

Skillfully shaping a team requires intelligent reflection, sensitivity to human motivations, and a willingness to address conflict openly and honestly — and in the pressures of the job too many CEOs fail to fully engage those activities. *Yet if you aspire to excellence for your company and for your own performance, under-investing in shaping the team is a potentially fatal mistake.* That is why it is the third of your non-negotiable roles as CEO.

Shaping a team involves a range of specific activities, from selecting the right people to crafting how the team will work together to setting and enforcing expectations for levels of performance — and those issues will comprise Chapters 40 through 42. However, let's turn first in Chapters 37 through 39 to an even more fundamental set of questions: For you as CEO, what is your team? To what purpose should it be directed? And what is the key to getting the team to perform at the highest possible level?

Chapter 37

What is a Team?

As CEO, your innermost team consists of the group of senior executives with whom you work most closely. As the leader of the senior team, you are responsible for and can *directly* influence the effectiveness with which it functions.

However, you also have the ability to influence all of the other teams in your company. If yours is a company of any appreciable size, then each member of your senior team leads a team in his own part of the organization, and each of those people may in turn lead yet other teams. Your role as CEO is to not only set the right tone for *your* senior team, but also to set standards as to how *all the other teams* throughout the company will function. By shaping both the inner and outer teams based on principles of effectiveness and excellence, you create a consistent company culture and dramatically improve the odds that your vision and strategy will be successfully achieved.

Regardless of the location of a team within the organizational structure, a critical question is the purpose to which the team addresses its efforts. Said another way, to whom or what does the team owe its allegiance? To answer that question, let's first start by identifying where that allegiance should *not* be directed.

First of all, within a highly-functioning team the members of the group understand that their own personal agenda has to be subjugated to some larger purpose. In Chapters 9 and 12 we explored at length the legitimate needs, concerns and agenda of the CEO. However, we also concluded that the CEO is most likely to achieve that personal agenda when he directs his efforts at what is best for the company. The same principle applies to all employees: Each no doubt brings to the table her own agenda — but well-shaped teams insist that individual agendas remain in the background, to be realized only as a corollary of achieving what is best for the greater good.

• •

> Your role as CEO is to not only set the right tone for your senior team, but also to set standards as to how all the other teams throughout the company will function.

• •

To achieve that alignment for your senior team (and for other teams as well), you need first to understand what is driving the individual members of the team, and then to coach each of them as to how their needs can best be met within the context of the team's objectives. If a team member is looking for greater financial rewards, then you should specify the contribution to the team that you need from him, and make it clear that his performance against that standard will be a key basis of his next compensation review. For someone who is looking for a promotion, identify the transition from "functional" thinking to broader team or company perspective that such a career move would entail — and then coach him that the sooner he displays that perspective in his participation on the team the sooner he will be a candidate for promotion. People inevitably are motivated by their own self-interest, and it is your job as team leader to both identify those motivations and then match them to what the team wants to accomplish.

A second place where team members may misdirect their allegiance is to the CEO himself. Many CEOs demand unconditional personal loyalty, and mete out rewards — and punishments — to team members in direct proportion to the loyalty they believe they are receiving.

This is an easy and understandable trap for the CEO to fall into, which is why it is so common. The CEO needs the support of others, or he won't be able to get anything done. And once a CEO has made a decision, there is a time when the debate should stop and people must fall into line to implement it. For these reasons and others, a certain degree and type of loyalty to the CEO is entirely appropriate.

Too often, however, when the CEO feels challenged by his job or is faced with political intrigue, he goes beyond an expectation of reasonable loyalty and instead demands *absolute*, unquestioning loyalty, directed not at what needs to be done, but *at the CEO himself as an individual*. In essence, the CEO is asking someone to take sides, so that when debate about an issue arises, the CEO can count on that person to back him up, or at the minimum to keep her mouth shut regardless of her objective view of the merits of the argument.

At that point, the expectation of loyalty has reached unhealthy proportions in several critical ways. First of all, the CEO has replaced objective decision-making with politics, by responding to political pressure with even more politics of his own — which undermines the effectiveness of the team and is exactly the wrong answer. Second, by demanding and receiving blind loyalty from team members, he is in effect neutralizing their skills by asking them to be yes-men rather than to use their brains to do what is best for the team and the company. As a result, whatever short-term expediency the CEO may gain from this absolute loyalty is unimportant compared to the long-term decline in the quality of the team. In other words, by demanding and receiving loyalty to himself the CEO is ultimately reducing, and not augmenting, the support that he receives.

Finally, when the CEO demands blind loyalty he inevitably receives it from some members of the team, but not from others — those who are too smart to offer it or who believe that they have more to gain by forming an alliance in opposition to the CEO. At that point, the CEO has in effect split the team in two, creating a barely-beneath-the-surface civil war between the different factions. For all of these reasons, as tempting as it may be for the insecure CEO, the loyalty of the team should not be directed to the CEO as an individual.

There is yet a third place where team members often misdirect their loyalty. At too many companies the primary allegiance of managers is directed not towards the senior team of which they are a member, but instead towards the functional organizations or businesses which each of them leads. This focus is a natural outgrowth of who team members are and where they come from. Each is likely to have progressed for much of her career within the confines of a particular function or business, or for smaller companies, within a particular discipline such as sales or accounting. As a result, it is only natural that over the years each has developed an intellectual perspective and decision-making process that is heavily dominated by the needs of her own area.

Compounding these intellectual leanings may be a parochial sense of loyalty: As the leader of a function or business the senior team member may expect loyalty from those in her own organization, and in return may feel an obligation to protect the narrow interests of that organization — even when they conflict with the broader purpose of the senior team.

. . . .

> Within well-functioning teams individual members relate first and foremost to their shared purpose rather than to the needs of their own functional organizations.

. . . .

This silo-oriented thinking is extremely common, and in fact is more the rule than the exception. It is also highly destructive, leading to a wide variety of dysfunctional behaviors. When important issues are debated, team members who are narrow in their thinking distract the group by pushing their parochial agenda, making it more difficult for the team to objectively assess all the relevant facts and debate the issue on the merits. Even worse, silo-oriented team members may actively obstruct the team's output by sabotaging its efforts to implement a decision which they believe runs counter to the narrow interests of their own organizations.

Furthermore, when parochial behavior is allowed to persist within a team, what should be honest intellectual debate will in time mutate into personal friction or animosity. This in turn dramatically reduces open communication and causes team members to avoid the fact-based, substantive debate which is necessary to solve tough problems.

In contrast, within well-functioning teams individual members relate first and foremost to their shared purpose rather than to the needs of their own functional organizations. However, alignment of the team around what is best for the greater good simply will not happen unless you as CEO make it a critical part of your job to ensure that it does. The natural tendency towards parochialism is sufficiently strong, and the task of alignment sufficiently difficult, that it will not be achieved unless you dedicate yourself to a number of courses of action.

First, you must state *explicitly* — when a team is formed, when new members join, and then repeatedly over time — that senior team members owe their primary allegiance to the team and not to the organizations they lead. To drive the point home, it should be made clear that primary allegiance directed at the senior team *is the non-negotiable price of admission to — and retention on — the team*, and then you must lend credibility to that policy by backing it up with action.

Secondly, as team leader you must take the time to coach team members on a one-on-one basis to help them make the intellectual leap from silo-based to broader thinking. It is a challenging leap that runs counter to years of previous experience, and it is unlikely to happen automatically absent skillful coaching and clear direction from you.

Third, the principle of primary allegiance to the senior team needs to be reinforced continually in the way that you and other team members behave and lead. When silo-based behavior periodically re-surfaces, the team as a whole must openly recognize it for what it is, collectively legislate it back out of existence, and re-focus the group on team-based thinking.

Finally, as leaders of the company the senior team must work to ensure that its own non-parochial behavior becomes the model for the functioning of *all* the teams which exist throughout the organization.

Like so many other elements of your job as CEO, the harder part of building team cohesiveness is not in knowing what needs to be done, because the answers, once identified, are relatively straightforward. Instead, the challenge is to consistently maintain the discipline and principled leadership to set the right example and to demand it of other leaders of the company. The payoff of that discipline and consistency is likely to be huge, as well-functioning teams have the potential to dramatically multiply the effectiveness of the organization, as well as your own power as CEO.

In sum, the first requirement of shaping a team is to build a culture which makes it clear that team members owe their primary allegiance to a larger purpose, and not to their personal agenda, the CEO himself or to their own organization or discipline. Yet by itself the avoidance of those mistakes is not sufficient to create a superlative team which fully supports you in achieving the company's vision and objectives. For that to happen, the team must understand the true nature of the greater purpose towards which it owes its allegiance — the definition of which is both subtle and critically important. That greater purpose is also at the very core of what makes for a truly enlightened company, as we'll explore in the next two chapters.

Chapter 38

The Enlightened Team

It is not enough for you to insist that members of the team subordinate allegiance to their personal agenda, the CEO, and their own functional organizations and instead direct their allegiance to the team. A second and equally critical issue is the purpose to which the team then directs its efforts. While the answer to this question may *appear* obvious — to do what is best for the company — the path to successful implementation of that principle is not quite so simple.

One fundamental complication in stating that the team exists to do what is best for the company is the strong natural tendency of individuals to be motivated by self-interest. Although there is much that you can and should do to understand personal motivations and then align them with the objectives of the company, the self-interest of team members will be strong, persistent and ever-changing — and a difficult force for you manage. You will need to align as well as you can, but maintenance of perfect or even near-perfect alignment is an impossible state to achieve, no matter how skillful your leadership. In the end, team members must be truly inspired by the greater good for which they are being asked to subjugate their self-interest, or they will fall short of giving their all to the advancement of the broad interests of the company.

Yet CEOs who believe that eloquently conjuring up the greater corporate good will automatically be inspirational are not good observers of human nature. We've all heard CEOs who give such speeches, yet it is far more difficult to remember instances where that exhortation was successful in getting its audience to give their all to the company on a sustainable basis. To the extent that people do subjugate their needs to that of larger entities, it is more natural for them to do so on behalf of family, ethnic groups, religious institutions or charitable organizations. In contrast, devoting one's blood, sweat and tears to making more money for the company's owners is not an instinctively inspirational pursuit. People are too intelligent, self-interested and — when aggressively pushed for corporate loyalty that does not come naturally — cynical to be easily inspired by such an objective.

• •

> CEOs who believe that eloquently conjuring up the greater corporate good will automatically be inspirational are not good observers of human nature.

• •

Another problem arises when a team does coalesce, but does so in the absence of devotion to the greater corporate good. Quite often, such teams fall into an allegiance to comfortable team solidarity and process as an end in itself. Team dynamics on the surface will appear to be positive, but in reality the functioning of the team has become superficial, with the modus operandi becoming collegiality rather than candid discussion of the tough issues and the necessary (and healthy) tension involved in that debate. This superficiality is reinforced by people's natural aversion to confrontation and to the risk inherent in taking decisive new actions. The team then develops a bias towards the status quo, which runs counter to a notion of progress and the stretching of the company to achieve its vision.

In some cases, loyalty directed at the team as an end in itself may even progress to a point that it is only marginally superior to silo-oriented allegiance — as the operating principle of the team becomes mutual self-preservation rather than what is best for the company. These teams often assume an "us-vs.-them" mentality, with the "them" taking any of a variety of forms, including the Board (vs. management), the CEO (vs. senior executives), the business or function leader (vs. lower-level managers within the business or function), or even the outside world such as investors or customers (vs. people internal to the company). All of those conflicts are false ones created by misdirected loyalty, as the interests of both the "us" and "them" need to align if all parties involved are to achieve their objectives.

Loyalty is a tricky ethos to instill in an organization, and therefore to do so appropriately requires careful thought. Loyalty to the team is desirable and essential up to a point, but beyond that point it too easily mutates into *blind* loyalty which contradicts the larger purpose for which the team was originally formulated. For truly well-functioning teams, allegiance is not directed to oneself, to CEO, or to silo, *but neither is it directed to the team itself*. Instead, primary allegiance is owed to the *organization*, which means that *team members have a responsibility to speak the truth and to take each other on (within the bounds of acceptable behavior) when they feel that the team has diverged from what is best for the company*.

But how do you as CEO orient the team towards what is best for the company, if that is not an inherently inspirational cause? How do you overcome the natural allegiance to self-interest, the CEO, the team, or the status quo, and re-direct it towards the greater good? Where does the solution lie?

• •

> If you base your organization on the right principles, you won't have to beseech people to sign on, because they are looking for the right place to do so and are eager to find it.

• •

To discover the answer, think about the organizations, whether business or otherwise, to which you yourself have offered your allegiance, and to which you have willingly given your all over a sustained period of time. Our bet is that the common characteristic of those situations is that they include *principles of interaction among team members which you judge to be both right-minded and fair, and which make you feel valued as an individual*. In the end, all of us choose to spend our time and energy where we are made to feel good, and we are also smart enough to distinguish sincere, principled efforts to do so from fleeting or calculated ones. When we find an organization that is based on admirable and sincerely well-intentioned principles of human interaction, and which truly values our contribution, it is the *principled environment* which we instinctively want to be a part of, and to which we willingly offer our allegiance and enthusiastic support.

The truth is that people naturally *want* to believe in and commit themselves to something special. They want to admire the place of work where they spend such a large percentage of their waking hours and to be part of a greater purpose. If you base the human environment of your organization on the right principles, you won't have to contrive a story or beseech people to sign on, because they are looking for the right place to do so and are eager to find it. It is only because so many companies and CEOs either don't make the effort to create that environment or don't know how to do so that many people fail to give their all to the place where they work. And absent that environment, it is virtually impossible for the CEO to shape a truly effective team.

A highly-functioning and *enlightened* team consists of a group of individuals who work together on behalf of what is best for the company, based on a set of virtuous principles which make them feel valued for their contribution. So what are those principles? How do you as CEO achieve the enthusiastic devotion — the blood, sweat and tears — of all of the members of the team to the company's objectives? Read on.

Chapter 39

Openness, Candor and Respect

All of us are asked for our allegiance to a wide variety of organizations, whether explicitly or implicitly, in all walks of our life. We may temporarily give of ourselves to one or show up for a longer period of time at another, but it is rare for us to choose to give our all to an organization over a sustained period of time. When we ignore such an entreaty or give of ourselves only half-heartedly, it's often because the organization in question has failed to inspire us for any of a number of reasons:

- The organization's objectives are unclear and the path to achieve them even more so;

- Its leaders appear to put their own interests ahead of those of the organization;

- The leaders' overtures to us are perfunctory or clumsy, and their motivations transparently insincere;

- The decision-making process is inefficient and ineffective, too often leading to answers which do not appear to be optimal for the organization;

- The environment is characterized by politics and secrecy, and we feel that we are not being allowed "inside the tent" to understand the key aspects of the most important decisions facing the organization;

- We sense that we are valued for our work but not for our ideas, which the leaders rarely solicit and take seriously.

Some of the antidotes to these problems were addressed in Parts IV and V: For an organization to engender loyalty, it must have an inspiring, well-directed vision as well as a clear strategy to achieve it. However, many of the items on the list extend beyond those two factors. For an organization to engender allegiance to its cause, people must believe that they are contributing to the effort in meaningful ways and are also truly valued for doing so. Furthermore, people are smart enough to gauge the true motivations of the organization's leaders, and won't fall for insincere efforts to make them feel valued. The only way to build and sustain a fully motivated team over a long period of time is to instill an environment which is right-minded in thought and process, led by leaders who sincerely believe in and foster that environment. If you try to build a team with anything less, the allegiance and efforts of its members will be correspondingly diluted, with equivalent results for your company.

• •

Companies build in organizational layers of secrecy which in truth are not needed, but which instead are intended to protect power bases and advance political and personal agendas.

• •

The precise definition of that environment can take a number of forms, but to be optimal for both engendering loyalty and for doing what is best for the company, it must include three characteristics.

First, it should be as open as reasonably possible. One of the most striking things about the human interactions in most companies is how rarely people — particularly managers — simply say what they mean and mean what they say. Instead, too much that is important to the company's future is avoided, hinted at, or even disguised and misrepresented. Information is hoarded, and too many interactions revolve around achieving some short-term political (and often trivial) aim, rather than getting all the facts on the table so that the best decision can be made. Companies build in organizational layers of secrecy which in truth are not needed, but which instead are intended to protect power bases and advance political and personal agendas.

Many companies tolerate such an environment, yet that tolerance undermines their objective of building a motivated team. Think about what a secretive or overly political environment says to someone deciding whether to give her all to the organization: "We don't trust you"; or "We don't think you can contribute to the decision to be made, so we're not going to give you the information you would need to do so"; or, "Our decision-making process is so political that any effort you might make to contribute would be so diluted by the politics as to be a waste of your time." All of these messages are highly de-motivational and lead to the outcome you would expect — employees who may do what is necessary to collect a paycheck but who are unlikely to give their all for the company.

Conversely, companies which insist on and embrace an environment of openness provide employees a tremendous breath of fresh air. Within such an environment employees are likely to feel any and all of the following: "I'm valued — they truly care about what I think. I'm part of the inner circle. And by being exposed to higher-level decisions and all the relevant information, I'm continuing to learn and am willing to be open-minded about finding new answers that are optimal for the company. On top of all that, so much of the dysfunctional political behavior has disappeared, along with the resultant waste of time and energy." In short, a culture of openness serves as a "welcome mat," communicating to people — "come on in and join us, we sincerely want you here and we need you to sign up as an important part of a well-functioning team."

While openness is critical, it will in any group of individuals initially uncover at least as much conflict as consensus. Yet humans by nature are not comfortable with conflict, so when it surfaces it can quickly lead to any of a variety of unhelpful behaviors and non-objective thought processes. The most senior person in the room might simply make the decision, without a full airing of all of the relevant information and views. A difficult item may be quickly bypassed, with the team instead turning to less urgent areas where there is more agreement. Or the intellectual disagreement may be transformed into personal animosities or friction.

For these poor decision-making modes to be avoided, the second requirement of an enlightened team is that its members communicate candidly with each other, particularly when a valid intellectual disagreement has surfaced. Members need to be continually encouraged to speak frankly about what they believe, even when it flies in the face of the views of other, and perhaps more senior, people in the room. Issues need to be decided objectively based on the true merits, which requires honest debate. And you as the leader must insist on a culture that rewards the candid airing of views, whether or not those views ultimately carry the day. Without that culture of candor, too often the organization will arrive at the wrong answers to tough problems, which is a luxury you can't afford if you are to build a truly successful company.

Being consistently candid among one's co-workers is difficult, because of the natural aversion to conflict. However, like any learned behavior, once initiated and reinforced it can build momentum over time until it can sustain itself naturally. If you conduct yourself in an objective and forthright manner, and if you make it clear that you value that in others who are in the room, they will pick up those signals and try it themselves. When you reward candor with recognition and kudos (rather than with ostracism or political retribution), the desired behavior will increase in frequency until it becomes the behavioral norm of the group. Once it does, it will become more natural for all members of the group to recognize behavior that is overly secretive, political or even dishonest, and to root it out. Building a culture of openness and candor is difficult, but once achieved it can sustain itself and serve as a cornerstone of truly great and enlightened companies.

A number of years ago we were invited as a guest to a dinner of senior executives of General Electric, a company renowned for its superb management processes and long-term financial results. Seated at a table with leaders of various of the company's businesses, we were introduced to each of those leaders by the most senior person at the table, who as part of his introduction included a hard-hitting synopsis of what was going right at each business as well as what was going wrong. The candor and seriousness of the information shared was truly striking and, compared to the mode of communication in scores of similar situations, quite rare indeed.

Yet at the same time it was clear that the executives at the table spoke this way in each other's presence all the time, and therefore had grown completely comfortable with open and candid communication, even with a newcomer at the table. The conversation that subsequently ensued was highly productive and valuable, with the introductions serving as a starting point for all involved to delve deeply into potential improvements to each of the businesses represented at the table. If the senior leader had been overly concerned about hurting the feelings of the various participants, the conversation would neither have started so frankly nor proceeded nearly as far and productively. Clearly, openness and candor are key ingredients of the "special sauce" that enables GE to build management teams which are universally recognized for their excellence.

> Unconditional personal respect is the oxygen which openness and candor need if they are to flourish on a sustainable basis.

Yet there is a third principle of human interaction which was exhibited at GE that night, and which is common to all strong teams. As we've discussed, openness and candor are difficult modes of interaction to promote, and can be inhibited by people's aversion to conflict. How can you as leader temper people's potential discomfort, so that they embrace honest intellectual debate as a standard mode of operation? The answer lies in *personal respect* — an ethos which demands that while *ideas* should be debated unequivocally, the people offering them are to be treated with appreciation and respect, regardless of rank or whose view ultimately carries the day. The way you encourage consistently candid debate about the tough issues is to re-assure with the behavioral norms of the team that the argument is not personal — the winner or loser is the idea, not the person.

Building such a culture is difficult, because people tend to keep score of whose ideas are adopted by the group, and also are naturally inclined to take it personally when theirs is not. To encourage such openness and risk-taking without people taking it personally requires constant reinforcement that you appreciate the ideas being offered and the candor being displayed. Furthermore, that appreciation had better be heartfelt and not perfunctory, because people, particularly someone whose idea has just been passed over, have the antennae to tell the difference between the two.

More fundamentally, an environment that is based on personal respect must be devoid of any of a number of common but counterproductive behaviors. These include intellectual or emotional bullying based on whose title is more lofty, playing out one's own personal frustrations by being aggressive towards others, and Machiavellian game-playing in order to achieve one's own personal objectives. All of those behaviors both demean people and get in the way of optimal decision-making — and consistent legislation against them is necessary to continually encourage people to be open and candid and to give their all to the group effort.

There is a mental leap of enlightenment here which, if achieved, renders personal respect for all a very natural and instinctive behavior. It is the recognition that not only do ideas win and lose rather than people, but that people who may be less naturally bright or talented, or whose ideas carry the day less frequently, are just as fundamentally "good" as more gifted individuals — as long as the former are well-intentioned and exhibit behavior which is consistent with the norms of an enlightened culture. Tangible *rewards* can and should be distributed differentially based on who makes the greatest contribution, but *respect* must be distributed universally.

When you instinctively believe that the minimum-wage restaurant worker doing a great job of bussing your table is every bit as good a person as you are — as is even the busboy doing a mediocre job of it but giving his all — then you are on your way to understanding a culture of merit-based pursuit of excellence supported by unconditional personal respect. Take that mindset into your company, and teach others to adopt it as well, and you are truly on the path to something special. Unconditional personal respect is the oxygen which openness and candor need if they are to flourish on a sustainable basis.

Your people are constantly buffeted by change in both their professional and personal lives. Markets undergo technological upheaval, competitors surprise, internal plans go awry, personnel turn over, and challenges present themselves at home which can seep into the workplace. If your team is to stay on course in the face of constant change, what its members need are rock-solid principles upon which they can rely. Properly constructed, principles are constants, much as the North Star is for navigators, and together serve as a fixed point of reference from which to view the change and uncertainty that surrounds us. You will know that you have built a truly enlightened team when in the face of confusion or doubt its members fall back on the three principles we've described in this chapter and agree: "Let's get the issue out in the open where everyone can see it. Let's debate it with objectivity and candor. And let's do so while treating each other with unconditional respect rather than personal attacks."

Openness, candor and respect are the key ingredients which lead to objective decision-making and which build the right type of loyalty in your organization — loyalty directed towards seeking the truth and the optimal answer, rather than to self, CEO, silo or comfortable team process. When these principles become the default behaviors of your team, then you will have created a truly admirable human environment which will attract the allegiance of team members and make them feel valued for their contribution. Furthermore, these principles will become the foundation of all of your more specific team-building processes, such as recruitment, coaching and review, which are the subject of the next several chapters.

Chapter 40

Selecting the Players

Ask any sports coach to build a winning team, and his chances improve in direct proportion to the quality of his players. Provide him with a roster of top recruits or first-round draft picks, and he's much more likely to capture a championship than if all he has to work with are other teams' rejects. This principle applies equally well for the CEO of a corporation: The stronger the individuals on your team, the more likely you will achieve superb results. For that reason, it's almost impossible to spend too much effort getting the right players into your company and onto your team.

That said, it is mistake to believe that all you have to do is select top-ranked players and then the rest will simply fall into place. Even a team of superstars will fall short unless it is coached and managed well. As with any sports team, it is essential that you are skillful in both teaching the individuals and blending them into a well-integrated unit — and that you never stop doing so. In fact, as CEO you will inevitably oversee a team of highly imperfect individuals, yet it is nonetheless your job to mold them into a strong team. You help yourself enormously when you recognize that an intense focus on selecting the best possible players enables you to build from a position of much greater strength.

Selecting the players is an inexact science, as it is very difficult to get a thorough and accurate read on a candidate, and then to anticipate how he will fit into the organization over the long haul. In the end it will be a judgment call, and only a percentage — hopefully a high one — of your picks will turn out well. However, the wrong way to respond to this inherent uncertainty is to make only a rough pass at the process, because you know that you can't be sure any candidate is right, or because you think you are too busy. To the contrary, given both the importance and the difficulty of the process, the only appropriate way for the CEO to respond is to be extremely thorough and disciplined, so as to maximize his "hit rate" of selecting excellent people for the team.

The first step in the selection process is to become clear in your mind as to what types of people you want on the team. Leaders develop different lists of key criteria, but the good lists usually include some variant of the following four factors: Intellect, knowledge and skills, energy and attitude. Identify a candidate who passes these four tests, and the odds increase significantly that you've found someone who will be a strong contributor to the team.

The first of the four criteria is intellect, but that doesn't mean that you need to find geniuses or that you should be administering IQ tests to candidates. In our experience, there is nothing even close to a direct correlation between some pure and uniform measure of intelligence and success in business, or for that matter in many other careers. (Jimmy Carter is universally regarded as highly intelligent, yet most historians rate his presidency as one that achieved relatively few of its aims. Ronald Reagan was never suspected of being a genius, yet in terms of achieving his vision had one of the most successful presidencies of recent times.) Instead of some quantifiable measure of intelligence, what you are looking for in candidates is an ability to think logically and analytically. Business is a social science with an infinite number of variables, uncertainties and unquantifiable factors. Strong executives have the ability to deal with abstract complexity, and then to boil a problem down to a focused list of issues, sort them out and make a decision. Absent clear-headed logical thinking, it is very difficult to consistently make good decisions or to explain those decisions to the people who have to implement them.

For starters, intellect can be gauged from elements of the candidate's resume and by speaking with references. However, we have found that a particularly good way to test for analytical thinking is through the interview process. Start by posing questions such as "How does this job fit within your long-term career path? Go back a few steps on your resume, explain to me how you made each decision along the way and why this is the next step in the progression." Or, "What other jobs are you considering and what are the pros and cons of this one relative to those other options?" It really doesn't matter which questions you ask (although you might as well kill two birds with one stone and ask questions to which you'd like to know the answer anyway).

What you are really doing is listening for the candidate's thought process — not so much the specific content of the answers, but rather *how* they are delivered. Did the candidate provide a focused, clear, well-reasoned response? Or did he ramble in a disorganized and unconvincing fashion? Get the wrong type of answer enough times, and you probably have a candidate who is not a particularly logical thinker. Receive consistently well-organized and concise answers, and that is a good sign — as an intelligent communicator is usually an indicator of an intelligent thinker, and for most business positions the latter without the former is not of much use anyway.

• •

> There are two types of people in this world —
> those who believe that there are only 24
> hours in a day, and those who don't.

• •

There are plenty of smart people out there who don't have the experience necessary for the position you are filling — so knowledge and skills form the second of the candidate criteria. However, it is important that you go beyond general knowledge of a discipline or industry, and think hard about the specific skills required for the job in question. Whether you are hiring a leader for sales, operations or human resources, consider where that function is in its evolution and therefore what skills will be critical for its next leader. Do you need someone who will find new technologies to re-invent the organization and take it to the next level? Is it time for someone to look towards the marketplace and competition and craft a new strategy? Do you need someone who is a team-builder, and who can unite warring factions and build skill bases across the organization? *Before* considering individual candidates and establishing biases based on the available pool, the more work you can do to hone in specifically on what you are looking for, the better job you will do of evaluating the various candidates.

A third criterion is the energy level of the applicant. We've all met three types of people in our companies — those who do the minimum possible to keep their jobs; those who apply themselves in a perfectly acceptable and satisfactory way; and those who go above and beyond, exuding dedication to the organization in a fashion which contagiously energizes those around them. Obviously you don't want any of the first category, and the more of the last group you can find the better. References are one place to search for answers to this question, as are interviews — because a candidate's energy level is not something that is easily faked or hidden. Did you come out of the interview charged up yourself and eager to spend more time around the candidate? Did the time fly by or did it drag?

When it comes to energy level, there are two types of people in this world — those who believe that there are only 24 hours in a day, and those who don't. The former see their efforts as a zero-sum game: "If I do more of this, I have less time to do that." The latter, on the other hand, are highly motivated by tough challenges and innovative solutions — and the more of them they attack the more energy they find to take on others. As a result, they truly believe in some motivational sense that good, hard work creates more capacity, not less. Such people are wonderful influences on co-workers and the dynamism of the team, which is why "energy" is a criterion worth focusing on.

High energy can be a very good thing, but only if it mobilized in the proper direction. Therefore, the fourth criterion is attitude, encompassing a range of basic questions about the candidate's character and motivation. Is she ethical? Can she be trusted? Is she a team player, or only in it for herself? Is she a positive-thinking person, or full of doom-and-gloom? And — to be consistent with the critical tenets of Chapter 39 — can she be counted on to be open and candid rather than a yes-woman, and will she treat others with respect rather than abusively?

Beyond these four characteristics, there are two sets of questions which should be explored to ensure that not only is the candidate right for the job, but that the job is right for the candidate. First, be sure to fully understand the career arc of the applicant (whether an internal candidate or someone from outside the company), and how the currently available position fits within that arc. Where does the person want to be in ten years and how does he intend to get there? Is this position truly the right move for him given his long-term objectives?

If he can't answer those questions convincingly or hasn't thought them out sufficiently, you may experience problems down the road after he is hired. Either he is taking this position out of necessity and expediency, and will leave it for the next better one that comes along, or he will discover after accepting the job that this is not the right career-building opportunity, and his tenure will be limited. The two of you should work together during the interview process, just as you would in an internal review, to determine that this is truly the right next step for the candidate's career, and if you can't do so satisfactorily then you have learned something which may be a deal-breaker.

• •

Of all the senior hires you've made, how many were still on the team and performing at a high level three years later? If you are like most managers, the number will be less than half.

• •

Secondly, you must ensure that the candidate, however talented and motivated, fits well within your existing process and team. On the one hand, one would hope that anyone with the proper intellect, knowledge, energy and attitude would be a good team player, and to the extent that she has a little different style, that the team would welcome her and adapt. However, there are limits to how far the team will be willing or able to change to accommodate a new member, and you should test through openness and candor whether the team process you have designed and the existing team members are reasonably compatible with the potential new addition.

In the end there are no perfect candidates, and there is a diversity of types of people who can and will succeed in your organization — particularly if you are a skilled builder of teams and treat the role with the emphasis that it deserves. The criteria outlined above — or analogous criteria which you might develop — are important to ensure that you evaluate candidates in a rigorous way rather than simply relying on your gut. Most CEOs do have strong instincts, but if you subject those instincts to a disciplined and logical thought process you will further enhance the odds that you will secure the best possible players, and in the process avoid some costly mistakes.

Similarly, it is worth the investment to maintain a disciplined hiring process. It is common for CEOs to cut too many corners here, either because they are "cowboys" who rely only on instinct or because they set the wrong priorities and think they are too busy to do what is necessary to get the best possible people on the team. To reflect on whether you expend enough energy hiring the best possible people, try this analysis: Of all the senior hires you've made, how many were still on the team and performing at a high level three years later? If you are like most managers, the number will be less than half, and part of that shortfall stems from inadequate upfront investment in finding the right people. Given the many costs of making a hiring mistake — including lowered individual and team productivity, and the distraction and cost of having to repeat the process to find a replacement — it is difficult to imagine how greater upfront investment wouldn't pay for itself many times over.

That investment should manifest itself in a number of ways. Make sure that all team members who will work closely with the new addition participate in the interview process. Carefully coordinate the various interviews, agreeing in advance who will cover what issues and which questions each of you will ask. Before even beginning the interviews, you should have a clear picture in your mind of how in the end you will all come together to get a full picture of the candidate and to make a decision.

In selecting interviewers, include at least one person who has a knack for "smelling a rat" — someone who can get beneath a smooth interview veneer and ferret out the truth about the candidate and his track record. Contact multiple references, and when you do so probe deeply, getting well beyond the polite endorsements that are typically offered. Work to get references to open up and be candid about a candidate's shortcomings, such as by asking: "We are a coaching company, so were we to hire the candidate what counseling will he most need to ensure that he succeeds?"

Whether you use an outside recruiter or your internal HR department, remember that the quality of the job they do will be directly proportional to the specificity of the guidance you give them: What exactly are you looking for? What concerns do you have? Let them inside the tent so that they can fully understand the team's thinking, and then insist that they do the legwork to eliminate unqualified or mediocre candidates — enabling you and your team to focus on truly getting to know and evaluating only the most attractive candidates.

When it is time to make the decision, convene your team, listen carefully for their input, and lead an open and candid analysis and evaluation. In your anxiousness to fill the position, don't try to ram the candidate through or attribute the objections of team members to the wrong motivations, such as not wanting to bring someone in who may outshine them. In the end, you may be the decision-maker, but if you can't convince the team in advance that the decision is correct then something is amiss — and you may not have found as strong a candidate as you had believed.

Finally, when you have made your choice you will need to sell the candidate on the position, but it is critical that you don't oversell or "fool" them by exaggerating the company's prospects or the job's attractiveness. Nor should you paper over the negatives. All of the downsides will be apparent soon enough once the candidate has arrived, and assuming he is a strong individual, he will have as many options after he is hired as before. If once hired, he is then surprised by the negatives, he very well may leave, particularly if he feels that you were intentionally less than the candid in the hiring process. If that happens, you will be forced to start the process all over again.

To the contrary, we have found that the most effective thing to do at this point in the process is to candidly lay out your greatest concerns as to why the candidate might *not* like the job, and then see if she can get past them and accept anyway because she is convinced that the positives outweigh the negatives. If she is smart then she has already sensed those negatives, at least to some degree, and you will impress her with your openness — making it more likely, not less, that she will sign on. Rather than attempt to hide the skeletons in the closet you should acknowledge them candidly, at the same time that you inspire the candidate by describing the attractive attributes of the company, the team and the position.

In sum, in the hiring process as with all elements of shaping the team, you serve yourself best by keeping top of mind the three core principles explored in Chapter 39: openness, candor and respect. Actively solicit both the candidate and his references to be open and candid in laying out the full picture of his skills and motivations. Encourage the existing members of the team to objectively weigh in during the evaluation process, and listen carefully to their input. Communicate candidly with the candidate as you would if he were a trusted and long-tenured member of the team. By relying with discipline on those three core principles, you are most likely to select the players who will provide you the best possible starting point for the shaping of your team.

Chapter 41

Making Decisions

No responsibility of the CEO is more important than to drive good decisions throughout the company — yet neither is there a responsibility that is so rarely fulfilled with excellence on a consistent basis. The cost of this deficiency is huge. Inevitably, a CEO who tolerates weak or even "average" decision-making processes will lead a company with a predominance of correspondingly weak or average-quality decisions. Furthermore, the ultimate result of the accumulation of those decisions will be a mediocre company struggling to truly distinguish itself in the marketplace and to achieve superlative financial results. It is far from a coincidence that the majority of companies suffer from mediocre bottom-line results, and that at the core, most tolerate undisciplined decision-making.

The responsibility for that lack of discipline lies squarely with the CEO. The quality of the decision-making processes throughout the company inevitably reflects the leadership of the senior team and its own decision-making process, which in turn reflects upon the CEO. While a "cowboy" CEO may instinctively make some good decisions on his own, he and the company will not do so consistently enough until he has instilled a disciplined decision-making process which pervades his senior team and the entire organization.

Teams with poorly structured decision-making processes are recognizable by any of a variety of flaws. Take inventory of your own company, and ask yourself if all too commonly your teams:

- Employ their time together inefficiently, rambling from issue to issue and then running out of time before some of the most important factors are fully understood, debated and resolved;

- Avoid conflict, choosing to move on when things get sticky in the room rather than to get to the bottom of honest intellectual disagreements;

- Fall back on political or parochial reasoning, rather than what is best for the company;

- Go through the motions of making a decision together without truly doing so, because the CEO has already made up his mind and isn't interested in the input of others;

- Resort to personal game-playing and even attack — often passive-aggressive rather than overt — and in the process undermine their ability to be objective and get to the right answer.

- Leave the room at the end of a meeting with no clear path forward — with either no answer or one that is insufficiently understood — and as a result, with team members subsequently operating at cross-purposes rather than as a unit.

The way to avoid these common flaws is obvious, particularly for the reader of Chapter 39. Like so much of your role as CEO, what is needed to get to the next level is not further complexity, but rather a disciplined focus on a short list of key principles. To dramatically upgrade your company's decision-making processes, start by keeping top of mind the three core principles of shaping your team: *openness, candor and respect*. As we've explored in depth throughout this section, when you welcome — in fact insist upon — the honest input of all members of the team, and keep the debate focused on issues and not people, then you've laid the foundation for strong decision-making.

Others of the principles of enlightenment described in Part III are also particularly relevant here. Teams which consistently make excellent decisions embrace *the quest for knowledge*, digging deep to get as much of the relevant information on the table as possible — eliciting it from both the various members of the team and a wider circle of resources as needed. Strong team leaders set the tone by staying *calm* and resolutely focused, keeping the debate on target and not letting it degenerate into personal attack or wander aimlessly in an unproductive direction.

In addition, what is needed for consistently strong decisions is a decision-making process that is *well-structured from start to finish*. This is something that we have found to be rare in companies (or organizations of any kind), and also universally admired and appreciated when present. To improve the structure of the decision-making process for your team, you need to think through each of its various elements.

> No responsibility of the CEO is more important than to drive good decisions throughout the company — yet neither is there a responsibility that is so rarely fulfilled with excellence on a consistent basis.

To begin with, when scheduling a meeting of your team, the first step is to make clear why you will be getting together. Is it simply to share information or sound people out with regard to an issue? Or are you gathering to make a decision? Very often, people arrive at a meeting without a clear expectation of the desired outcome, and therefore come unprepared and in the wrong frame of mind to commit to a decision. If it is worth peoples' time to meet, then it is also worth the investment of a few minutes beforehand to specify the desired outcome and allow people to do their homework and some offline preparatory thinking. That way, rather than having people arrive with a blank slate, the meeting will be considerably more productive and will move the team several steps further towards action.

Next, think carefully about how much time you have for a meeting and how you want to use it. What data do you need to get on the table for review and debate? Should certain information be distributed before the meeting? Which people do you most need to hear from, and with regard to which issues? Too often, airtime is allocated by default based on personality and loquaciousness, and not proportionally to the value which each team member is likely to bring to the issue in question. Before the meeting begins you should have a couple of checkpoints in mind: Where should we be twenty-five percent of the way through the meeting, half-way, and at the three-quarters mark? At what point should a preliminary decision be offered, with time allowed to question, test and understand it?

In leading the meeting, don't be afraid to be assertive in keeping it on track and the time well employed — doing so with personal respect so as not to embarrass those whom you may be cutting off. Be discerning in your management of the meeting, maintaining the discipline to let useful input continue while cutting off less valuable discussion, and to know the difference between the two. The guiding principle of the team should be that we are here to employ our valuable collective time in as productive and meaningful way as possible — and not to docilely sit back and allow each person to go through

• •

> When you are reluctant to justify your decision to others it may be an indication that the logic is flawed, or that it is being made for political and not objective reasons.

• •

every one of his PowerPoint slides, way past the point of diminishing returns. Too often, meeting leaders abdicate their responsibility to devote the group's time to its highest and best use, instead allowing themselves to become slaves to the inertia of an unproductive discussion or meeting flow. Suddenly you discover that there are only ten minutes left, with important data unexplored and key people insufficiently heard — and yet a decision now must be made.

You should also be purposeful and take the lead in drawing people out — particularly those whose input is important or those who will be responsible for implementation — and whom you know to be quiet or unassertive by nature. Continually read the faces in the room, and when you sense that someone has a concern or a countervailing view, ask them to share it. When people offer their views, remember as team leader an adage expressed in Part III: Listen, listen hard, and then listen again, as often the most important message is a level or two beneath the surface, and too often leaders react or cut people off before it is out in the open. And whatever you do, don't try to avoid or paper over honest and substantive disagreements, as they often point to where the truly critical issues lie, and where further analysis is needed so as to ensure an optimal decision. Instead, keep probing those disagreements until either a consensus is reached or you as leader are in a position to make a well-informed and high-quality judgment call.

When a meeting is complete, state clearly and concisely what has been accomplished and agreed. Has a decision been made and, if so, what are its implications for each member of the team as well as the organizations they lead? What uncertainties remain, what progress checks are needed, and what potential mid-course corrections remain options for the future? Alternatively, has a decision been postponed, and if so what further work is needed and when will the decision be re-visited?

Whatever you do, don't end the meeting with only a vague sense of where the team is to go from here. If you do, people may resent what they view as a poor use of their time, and far worse, they may each leave with a different understanding of what was agreed.

It is remarkable how often team leaders skip the simple and critical step of ending a meeting by summarizing what has been agreed — with predictable results. The team leader may believe that a decision has been made and that the path forward is clear, but since it was not explicitly stated the team members may not share that understanding, and may respond in one of two unhelpful ways. They may fail to implement what the leader intends, or, based on different interpretations of what was agreed, they may each go off in different directions and implement at cross-purposes. In either case, a good discussion which could have resulted in decisive action instead was wasted, because you failed to check that all understood the path forward.

Finally, as referenced in Part III it is a highly useful discipline to clearly explain the rationale for a decision, not only to team members, but to as wide an audience as appropriate. When you are reluctant to justify your decision to others it may be an indication that it is not an optimal one: Either the logic is incomplete or flawed, or it is being made for political and not objective reasons. Holding yourself and the logic of your decisions accountable to others is an effective way to raise your game and improve your skill at shaping the team.

The degree to which you achieve well-structured meetings and strong decision-making processes is a reliable and very public indicator of your strength as a leader and CEO. Subject team members to mediocre decision-making processes, and they are likely to regard you as a mediocre CEO. Make decisions with openness, candor and respect; with knowledge, objectivity and calm; and with a well-structured process from start to finish — and the benefits will be many. Your decisions will be on target a much higher percentage of the time. You will build an environment and a company to which people want to give their all and their allegiance. And you will engender the respect and admiration of others of you as CEO.

Chapter 42

Managing for Excellence

Statisticians speak of regression to the mean, and in business there is an analogous principle, which is regression to the mediocre. The selection of top players and the instillation of high-quality decision-making processes are critical steps, but those two alone are not enough to maintain excellence. If having achieved the first two you then sit back and watch, assuming that the rest will take care of itself, then over the long-haul bureaucratic inertia will set in and the performance of most of your people will regress from excellent to average. To shape high-quality teams, the final part of the equation is to inspire the ongoing excellence of all in the organization, and to proactively and skillfully manage so as to achieve it.

Throughout this book, we've spoken of the enlightened CEO as someone who is sensitive to others as human beings. We've implored you to listen for and address the concerns of your people, to lead with humility, to forgo personally abusive behavior and to distribute rewards equitably. However, there is nothing in any of these principles of enlightenment which argues for extending your interpersonal sensitivity to include the tolerance of mediocrity. Quite the contrary, the predominant theme throughout the book has been the pursuit of excellence for you and your company — and an expectation of excellence from your people is both a requirement for, and an element of that pursuit.

The enlightened CEO demands excellence of all in the organization, but does so in an open and objective way which respects and inspires others as people. By basing his leadership on inspiration and respect rather than fear or bravado, the enlightened CEO builds a culture of excellence which can pervade his entire company and which can be sustained indefinitely.

The first requirement for building a culture of excellence is to broadcast your expectations clearly, widely and repetitively. As CEO, you should be absolutely unapologetic that nothing less than excellence is expected from every employee of your company. You then need to spell out what personal excellence means, rather than merely mouthing it as a vague and unspecified platitude, as is the case at so many companies.

There are several dimensions to personal excellence. Most fundamentally, it is about the achievement of results. Every business, function, team and person in the company should be measured by what they produce, and not by good intentions or impressive form. Standards for both the quantity and quality of results should be high, and it should be made clear that the standard is not a wish or a target, but the minimum level which needs to be achieved by all.

In addition, you should be clear that you expect people to carry themselves and interact with each other in a manner consistent with the principles of enlightenment — as your goal is not simply to become an enlightened CEO, but also to lead an enlightened *company*. In other words, in addition to the achievement of results, personal excellence means being a good team player by conducting oneself openly, candidly and respectfully, and by contributing to the strong, objective decision-making process of one's team.

Finally, personal excellence means that people are expected to give their all to the company — but not as measured by the number of hours they work, as you should respect people's need for a life outside the office. Instead, their effort should be measured by the *nature* of their dedication to the company — a dedication that translates into a relentless, passionate and never-ending drive to increase their contribution to the success of the company.

The truth is that you don't need to employ people with supernatural powers in order to achieve excellence and set yourself apart from other companies. Most companies *do* regress to the mean, with an indistinctive vision, indecisive strategies, and unenlightened team dynamics and decision-making processes. Yet the mediocrity of most companies creates the opportunity for yours to stand out, as all that is needed is to remain focused in a disciplined way on the enlightened core — a vision that describes how your company can be truly distinctive, a strategy that directs resources highly selectively only to the right places, and teams which rely upon enlightened people dynamics and which objectively cut to the important essence of key decisions. In other words, inspired by your enlightened leadership, a group of people who at another company might yield mediocre results can produce excellence at yours.

> Employees are lacking not for an additional incentive but for knowledge about *how* to succeed.

Furthermore, it is important that the expectation for excellence be translated into very specific terms for each individual employee. When the employee is hired, and then periodically forever, she should be told orally and in writing exactly what is expected of her — what the company needs her to achieve, to what standard, and in what timeframe. It is rare for companies to apply this practice universally to all employees regardless of rank, yet when it is practiced it inevitably is greatly appreciated. Everyone wants to know in as specific terms as possible what is expected of them, because it makes it easier for them to figure out how to do their job well. And when you hold them to a high standard, they appreciate that they are in effect being "promoted," giving them the opportunity to take their career to the next level.

Expecting the most from the employee is the right thing to do, but sometimes her performance is not commensurate with the expectation. In our work with CEOs, we often are asked the following question: "Jane is not producing at the level she needs to. I've tried a variety of both carrots and sticks, but none of them has worked. What should I do now to get the performance from her that the company needs?"

When we explore the question with these CEOs, it is clear that they are looking for some new carrot or stick — one they may have overlooked. They expect that some new incentive will magically unlock superlative performance — but they are looking in the wrong place for the answer. Jane knows that she is disappointing her boss, and *badly wants to succeed for her own sense of self-worth.* Jane is lacking not for an additional incentive but for knowledge about *how* to succeed: She wants to perform, but doesn't know how to get there, no matter how hard she tries. The missing piece of the puzzle is not an incentive, but *teaching* — and there is no part of the CEO's job that is more important or empowering for you and your organization.

As CEO you have a unique vantage point and experience, and it is your job to impart that perspective in specific ways which help the members of your team perform at a higher level. The answer for the CEO who asked the question above is that he needs to roll up his sleeves and get down in the trenches with Jane, so that he can identify with specificity the barriers to her success and then teach her how to surmount them. There is no avoiding this responsibility and no shortcut around it: If you sit in your ivory tower and demand excellence without teaching people how to achieve it with specificity, you will face chronic under-performance from many parts of your team, the sum total of which will prevent the company from achieving its objectives.

This teaching philosophy should also permeate your formal review process. For reviews to have maximum impact, they should focus not on grading the employee, but on coaching him. A good review should be structured as follows: "Congratulations on all that you've achieved and all the skills which you've already mastered. Please keep doing more of the same. Now let's identify the skills you need to develop in order to get to the next level, to the mutual benefit of you and the company." Then you need once again to roll up your sleeves and invest the time and energy to coach the employee in very specific terms, so that he can learn in tangible ways how he can further upgrade his performance. As CEO it is your job to both provide this coaching for those who work directly for you, and also to insist that it is part of the management and review process at all levels and in all corners of the company.

However, don't underestimate just how many people you yourself can teach directly. In his book <u>Execution</u>, Larry Bossidy describes how as CEO of Honeywell he traveled far and wide to spend days at a time with the leadership teams of the company's many businesses, offering coaching in specific terms as to how to improve results and upgrade individual performance.

Strong leaders coach all the time, all day long and every day of the year. When a leader makes teaching an everyday part of his job, then the employee's formal annual review becomes a routine confirmation of what has already been communicated many times before, and there should be no surprises. Furthermore, if you've interacted well with the employee throughout the year and listened carefully, nothing he has to say at a formal review should be a surprise to you — because you've encouraged him throughout the year to share his concerns and to ask you for help whenever he's needed it to perform with excellence.

In order to lend credibility to your expectation for excellence, it is essential that you lead your company as a true meritocracy and distribute rewards accordingly. First of all, the overall level of rewards at your company should be better than the average for comparable companies and jobs, or employees will wonder what's in it for them in contributing to a truly distinctive and excellent company. However, you will only be able to *afford* better-than-average rewards across-the-board if you outperform your competitors. Strong performance and superior rewards are mutually reinforcing and dependent variables.

Secondly, nothing de-motivates strong employees more than rewards which are distributed evenly regardless of performance, or differentially but not sufficiently so. In any part of any company there is inevitably a wide range of performance among different employees, yet too often there are smaller percentage differences among compensation levels. The problem with this approach is that it produces exactly the opposite of the result you need: Strong performers feel cheated and begin to look elsewhere for opportunities, while weak performers are unduly rewarded and stay forever. Ask yourself which group it is more important to keep happy. Obviously, the answer is the stronger performers, and the way to do so is to maintain differences in compensation which are as great in percentage terms as the underlying differences in performance.

Third, the basis for differentiation — the results and behavior which are rewarded — must be carefully defined and then consistently reinforced. Companies are usually comfortable tying compensation to results for jobs such as sales, since sales dollars generated can be measured in relatively indisputable ways. Yet it is no less important to enforce differential rewards based on performance for jobs where output is more qualitative and subjective. It is the job of all managers to deal with that subjectivity and to make an accurate and logically supported judgment call, rather than avoiding it and paying everyone more or less the same because precise performance can't be measured. It is far better to be approximately right than exactly wrong, and until every employee has a personal standard of excellence defined for him and can count on rewards to approximately track with his performance, then you have not put in place the conditions which will produce excellence across the company.

In sum, to sustain excellence the company's rewards must in general exceed industry averages, and then must be differentially distributed based on careful definition and measurement of performance. If you do anything less, your exhortations for excellence ultimately will fall on deaf ears.

Of course, disciplined adherence to a standard of excellence means that there will at times be employees who simply cannot meet the standard and therefore no longer belong at the company. This is true for every company large and small — and for every individual team within the company. Too often, managers are overly reluctant to terminate employees, yet unless you are comfortable doing so the company cannot achieve excellence. Keeping consistently underperforming employees on the payroll simply becomes too dysfunctional to the efforts of the team as a whole and too de-motivational to the stronger performers. It also undermines your entire message of excellence, as well as your credibility as CEO.

However, the determined pursuit of excellence does not mean that you should terminate people lightly or before all other options are pursued. When deciding whether to fire someone, ask yourself a series of questions, and begin by putting the onus on yourself (or on whoever oversees the employee). Have you communicated in specific terms, clearly and repetitively, what it is that you need the employee to achieve? Have you given him every chance to identify the roadblocks for you and share his concerns? Have you coached him, coached some more, and then coached again? If in fact you've done your part and the employee's performance is still not up to par, then it is time to act. But before you do, make sure that you can clearly articulate for your own purposes as well as the employee's specifically what the problem is — whether in skills or attitude — and that you can convince yourself that it can't be solved.

The rationale for these steps goes beyond concern for the employee: It is in fact is in the best interest of the company. The cost and difficulty of finding good people, training them and then integrating them into the company is substantial. In many cases you'd be better off putting the same energy into coaching those already on board so as to raise their performance — because despite what it looks like, the grass out there is not always greener. Yet there are times when it is clear that the employee simply does not have what it takes, and in those cases you should act decisively and send them on their way.

• •

> When you are consistent in setting expectations, coaching relentlessly, rewarding differentially and replacing people as necessary, then you have the ingredients necessary to manage for excellence.

• •

When you've managed this process correctly, the final decision to terminate should not be a surprise to the employee, because you've coached and communicated so openly and consistently every step of the way. In fact, it should be a relief, because the employee will know that they have been given every consideration and that they are just not right for the job. At some level, they will be glad that you have made the final decision and are cutting them loose to find a job with a better fit — and with appropriate assistance or severance to help them make the transition.

The departure of such an employee should also be a teaching opportunity for those who remain. When someone has departed, employees will know or suspect that it was not voluntary, and they will speculate as to the reason. Without resorting to personal attack or disrespect, you should be sure that the team understands the reason for your decision so that you reinforce for them the standards of excellence valued by you and the company. In fact, people will continually look to all of your personnel decisions for signals about what behaviors are and are not rewarded — and the more you can help them understand by communicating the rationale for those decisions, openly and explicitly, the more dramatically you multiply the good that will come from each individual decision.

Managing to consistently high standards of excellence is the third leg — along with selecting the players and instilling objective decision-making processes — which together enable you to shape a superb team. When you are consistent in setting expectations, coaching relentlessly, rewarding differentially and replacing people as necessary, then you have the ingredients necessary to manage for excellence. And when you reinforce these practices in all that you say and do, and instill them in all the teams throughout the organization, then you will be leading a company whose people are optimally empowered to achieve its objectives. In the process you will have created something which is pretty rare, and something which will not only attract and retain people in general, but in particular *excellent* people — in other words, precisely the ones you most want in your company.

Chapter 43

Creating the Spark

An engineer can combine atoms into molecules, aggregate molecules to produce synthetic materials, and then shape those synthetic materials into something approximating limbs and a torso. He can even add some level of artificial intelligence and what he would then have is a robot. Yet until he learns how to add an indefinable spark — something whose nature we can debate but which we all agree would be lacking — he hasn't created a human being.

And so it is with teams and with companies. As CEO you can define the organizational structure, hire the people, specify strategies and put processes in place. Yet you no doubt still sense the need for something indefinable — some spark — that can transform the team you've created into something truly special, one that will make your company superior to its competitors. You search for ways to stir passion in your employees, and for them to be willing to give their all to help the company achieve an unusual level of success. You are looking for the spark which will be the difference between an average team and a superlative one that is self-motivated, psyched up and operating on all cylinders.

CEOs resort to a variety of means to motivate their people. They schedule company picnics, give Christmas bonuses, make impassioned speeches and institute broad stock options plans. All of these are good things when employed in the right way, at the right time and in the right place. Yet in your heart you know that neither a picnic nor stock options can create lasting motivation, absent something much broader, more fundamental and systemic.

Fortunately, if you've been reading along then you don't have to search far for the answer, nor do you have to do anything different from what we have described to this point. CEOs who lead truly motivated, special companies — those that possess that magic spark — are so blessed because they are consistent in their pursuit of three ideals.

• •

The pursuit of these three ideals is the magic trifecta
which creates truly special teams and companies.

• •

First, they are disciplined in insisting upon organizational excellence. Such CEOs embrace their six roles, so that their company's vision is crisp, the strategy decisive, the team shaped with purpose, and — as we'll discuss in Parts VII, VIII and IX— all of the above is translated into action, followed through and properly communicated. Consistent focus on true organizational excellence is so rare that when employees — who naturally want to be part of something special — are exposed to it they invariably are highly motivated.

Second, as we've described throughout Part VI, companies with teams that possess that spark treat their people with openness, candor and respect — as well as all of the other principles of enlightenment. They minimize the noise of politics, parochialism and personal attack, and replace it with objectivity, a sense of equity and personal empowerment. By doing so, they extend the welcome mat, inviting employees to join the team and do their part to help build a great company.

Third and last, these CEOs insist not just on organizational excellence but on personal excellence from every employee. They select for it, coach for it, review for it and reward for it. In the process, they provide the opportunity for each employee to realize his full potential, making it possible for him to progress further at this company than elsewhere — which is another powerful motivator.

The pursuit of these three ideals — an unrelenting focus on organizational excellence; human interactions based on the principles of enlightenment; and the active promotion of the individual excellence of each employee — is the magic trifecta which creates truly special teams and companies. Insist on these three, every day and in all that you do, and you'll build team strength at every level — organizational, personal, and in the interactions which form the pathway from one to the other. Furthermore, the three are mutually reinforcing, with the strengthening of any one making it easier to achieve the other two. Taken together, the three comprise the magic motivational spark that you are looking for, and create an environment which will attract and retain the very best people.

So continue to schedule your company outings and give your speeches, bonuses and stock options, as they are part of the everyday fabric of most good companies. But most important of all, keep directly in your line of sight at all times your vision of organizational and personal excellence, and of enlightenment — and you will have shaped a truly motivated and superlative team.

Part VII: Translating Into Action

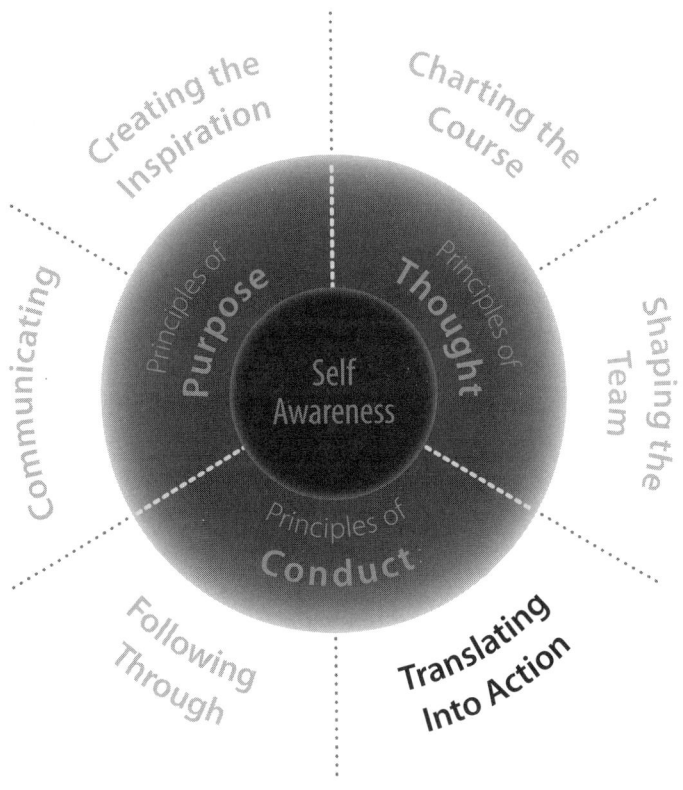

Chapter 44

Your Fourth Role

The Washington Redskins were getting ready for the big game against their arch rival, the Dallas Cowboys. Coach Gibbs convened his assistant coaches, studied the game film and identified where the Redskins could play off their strengths and exploit Cowboy weaknesses. Collectively, the coaches concluded that their game plan was strong and that the Redskins' chances were very good.

Next they called a series of team meetings to share the game plan with the players. By game day all of them understood the strategy, and before they took the field Coach Gibbs exhorted them to go out and execute the plan! Charged up, the players raced onto the field, convinced that this was the week when that they would reverse recent failures and return the team to its winning tradition. (Representatives of the media, forever believing in the team, wistfully agreed.)

When the game ended and the Redskins had suffered their fourth defeat in a row — by 31 points — Coach Gibbs berated the coaches and players for not executing the game plan. Nothing had transpired as it had been drawn up on the chalkboard, and he was beside himself that such a well-designed strategy should all be for naught. He announced a 7:00 am meeting the following day to get to the bottom of what had gone wrong.

At the meeting, Gibbs encouraged people to share their thoughts, and then sat back and listened carefully. Among other things, he learned the following:

- Once the overall game plan had been agreed, he had assumed that the offensive and defensive coordinators and the various position coaches would use it as a starting point and then translate it into more specific plans for each part of the team. He further assumed that these plans would be as rigorous and well-communicated as the overall strategy. In fact, two-thirds of the coaches had designed and communicated their plans effectively, but several had dropped the ball.

- A number of the coaches overly relied on the fact that the players were pros who had been playing football since they were kids. They assumed that by now the right guard surely knew what was expected of him during a sweep to the left, and that the cornerback knew what to do in two-deep coverage on third and eleven — even though there were unusual aspects of the Cowboy's formations which presented some unique challenges on those plays. In fact, on any given play nine or ten of the eleven players on the field had successfully scoped out the situation and executed properly. Unfortunately, it only took one player who was out of position to provide the Cowboys an opening to complete a key pass or make a drive-killing tackle.

- Unbeknownst to Gibbs, the running back's chronically bad back had been acting up, and the defensive secondary had been feuding based on a combination of on- and off-field issues. Although a couple of the assistant coaches were generally aware of the problems, the players successfully downplayed the issues and hid them from Gibbs. As a result, the game plan over-relied on players who were not ready to be at the top of their games.

- When the running back, hampered by his bad back, was consistently stymied throughout the first half, there was no plan B, and with no alternative ready the team stuck stubbornly and unsuccessfully to the original plan.

- In an effort to bolster the Redskins' performance on kick-offs and kick returns, the special teams coach inserted several defensive team starters onto those units, at the same time that the defensive coordinator had independently decided to give them a larger role in the defense, including more plays on the field. By mid-way through the second quarter they were dragging, at which time the Cowboy offense began marching down the field more or less at will.

From Coach Gibbs to the coordinators to the assistant coaches to the players, the Redskins had signed some of the most renowned and highest-paid talent in the game. They had an owner who was sincerely willing — if not desperate — to do and spend whatever it would take to get the team to the Super Bowl. Gibbs had designed a strategy for the game that was sound and which could and should have led to a more positive result. But in this hypothetical example, a key link in the chain was missing: The translation of that strategy into solid and detailed plans for action.

The failure to translate the broad strategy into specific and detailed actions is common to far too many CEOs, and is at the core of their frustration with both their company's and their own performance.

Part of the reason why it is relatively rare for CEOs to fulfill their fourth role properly is that in order to do so a very delicate balance must be struck. Somehow, the CEO must delegate to and trust his team at the same time he ensures that they have in fact crafted plans of action which are sufficiently strong and detailed. Unfortunately, most CEOs don't understand how to reconcile these competing objectives, and instead fall too far to either one side or the other of the optimal balance.

On one side are the "meddlers." These CEOs commonly — but not exclusively — reside in small and medium-sized companies. Although the meddlers may have hired good people and put in place potentially effective team processes, they find themselves unable to stand back, trust their team and let them do their jobs. Instead, they take on tasks that should reside with the team, and jump in and out of various parts of the organization, undermining the authority of functional leaders. They cannot resist personally tinkering on team members' turf, in the process de-motivating their people and doing more harm than good.

Well-intentioned CEOs fall into this destructive behavior pattern for any of a number of reasons:

- They are "operators" by background and by nature. It is in working the details of a problem that they find their comfort zone, so they naturally gravitate in that direction. When not sure what to do next, they dive down into the weeds and step on the toes of a team member by doing his job, rather than focusing with discipline on *their* six roles as CEO.

- They are convinced that they can implement solutions better and faster than the members of their team, so rather than take the time to teach a team member, they simply go do it themselves.

- In truth they do not have faith in the team which they have assembled, because they are too conscious of its imperfections. Unwilling to trust that the team will get the job done they jump in and try to fix every little thing themselves. While this may temporarily improve one aspect of the action plan, these CEOs are preventing themselves from ever building a team and team process which will enable the company to sustain growth over the long haul. If the company is of any appreciable size, then no CEO can manage it all himself, and the only alternative is to skillfully nurture and manage the team, rather than circumvent and undermine it.

- They are uncomfortable in the role of teacher, or feel that they do not have the requisite skills, so instead they simply try to go and solve the problem themselves. To invert an old joke, "those who can't teach, do."

No CEO intentionally sets out to be a "meddler," yet many wind up there. Often the CEO's natural inclinations, as described above, start him out in that direction. Over time, when he discovers that "despite" his meddling things are not going as planned, he re-doubles his efforts to fix the problem himself, thereby increasing his meddling quotient. Sometimes this downward cycle leads to a situation that is unsalvageable, as the relationship between the CEO and his team becomes poisoned, leaving team members irretrievably confused or de-motivated by his behavior. At that point, it is time for the CEO to leave and for a new one to take over — one who is more capable in this fourth role.

At the other end of the spectrum are CEOs who fancy themselves as exclusively "big thinkers," and who take the concept of delegation to an unhelpful extreme. Of the many perks of rising to the top of the company, a favorite of many CEOs is that finally they "don't have to do the work themselves," but instead can get others to do it for them. These CEOs may fully occupy their day preaching the company's vision to whoever will listen, contemplating broad strategy, or schmoozing with Board members, public figures or representatives of the media. They hire good people to join their team — as of course they should — but mistakenly assume that "good people" are enough to ensure that the strategy will successfully be translated into action.

As with the first group of CEOs, these CEOs fail to fulfill their fourth role, not because they intentionally decide to do so, but because of their natural likes and dislikes, compounded by a lack of discipline. They may fall into this pattern of behavior for any of a number of reasons:

- Most commonly, they find the details of operating plans and implementation to be boring, and too much drudgery. It's no fun for them to pour into the details, and as a result they are quick to accept the assurances of the team that the strategy will be successfully translated into action without the CEO's involvement.

- They remind themselves that the members of the team are skilled, well compensated and highly motivated, so why do they need to involve themselves in the design of action plans?

- Translating the strategy into action is time-consuming, and they are busy people.

- They tell themselves that in any case external and internal events will soon render action plans outdated, so why spend too much time specifying them in detail?

- They don't understand what strong operating plans really look like, nor do they appreciate how essential they are for the achievement of the company's — and the CEO's — objectives.

Yet without question there is *great* value in your fourth role — and in fact as with the other five roles, it is impossible for you to be a strong CEO over a sustained period of time unless you fulfill it in high-quality way. Go back and re-read the first six sentences of Chapter 1. So much of what lies at the root of CEO frustration is about execution: "I know what needs to be done, but it's just not getting done!" Unless the CEO takes an active role in ensuring that the strategy is translated into action, there are simply too many opportunities for things to go wrong. On the other hand, when you as CEO fulfill this role, the circle from vision to strategy to team to action remains unbroken, and — along with your remaining two roles as CEO (the subject of Parts VIII and IX) — lead all the way to the results and performance which you are looking for.

So what is the right way for the CEO to be involved in the translation of the strategy into action? If the answer is neither to do it yourself nor to abdicate your responsibility, then where does the proper balance lie?

It *is* your non-negotiable responsibility to ensure that the strategy is translated into action with sufficient rigor. To do so, you must fulfill four key elements of this role.

First, you must articulate and then insist upon the *accountability* of the various members of the team to produce thorough, well-conceived and documented plans of action which tie to and support the strategy. At far too many companies, the strategy is agreed to, but when everyone leaves the room the team leader — like Coach Gibbs in our football example — blindly assumes that every team member will do his part and take it from there. In most cases, a number of the team members will be both diligent and skilled enough to independently craft a strong operating plan. And there will be others who fail to do so but luck out in the execution — this time — because market conditions were fortuitous, or because even though they were winging it they guessed right.

However, at least some and perhaps even most of the team members will not produce operating plans of sufficient strength unless you explicitly hold them accountable for doing so. And as in our football example, it takes only one member of the team to bring the others down with him, as the plans inevitably are highly interdependent. When you blindly trust your team to design their plans, absent clearly defined accountability, you'll inevitably find yourself asking, as did Coach Gibbs — "Why can't they simply execute my beautiful game plan?"

Second, it is not nearly enough for the CEO to ask for operating plans and simply "check the box," calling it a day when they are submitted. The second element of your role is to use your experience and your vantage point as CEO to rigorously *test the logic* of each team member's plan until it is as strong as it possibly can be.

• •

If the answer is neither to do it yourself nor to abdicate your responsibility, then where does the proper balance lie?

• •

When superb CEOs review action plans, they question, probe, drill down and explore, until both they and the team member responsible are satisfied that the plan is as powerful and logically tight as it can be — and that it deals with important risks and contingencies. What parts of the plan sound nice as wishes, but are not backed up by the resources or skills that can truly get the job done? Where is the plan not sufficient to produce the targeted strategic advantage? And what potential developments does the plan ignore which could throw it off course? Inevitably this testing process — as with the review of a manuscript or engineering design by someone with an experienced eye — will lead to significant upgrades to the plan, and only after the testing is complete will you have maximized both the potential impact of the plan and the likelihood that it will be achieved.

Some CEOs may be afraid that such a process will offend team members, as it could suggest that you don't trust them to do their jobs well, and that you are in fact meddling. The answer lies in *how* you fulfill this element of your role. When you make it clear that you respect the skill of the team member and have no intention of reaching down into their organization to subvert their authority, then you've laid the foundation for them to be open rather than defensive. When you conduct the "test" in an objective way, searching only for the best possible answers and introducing helpful ideas that the team member might have overlooked, then he will recognize that all you are trying to do is ensure both his success and that of the company as a whole. In doing so, you will engender their respect and appreciation, and not their resentment. Remember, just as every Redskin aches to go home Sunday night a winner, the desire to come out on top is just as strong for the members of your team. When you test the logic of their plans respectfully and objectively, consistent with the principles of enlightenment, then team members will appreciate the help and recognize the value of the process.

• •

> As you subject the operating plan to a tight logical grilling, you should avoid the temptation to "fix" whatever is wrong with the plan yourself.

• •

Beyond holding team members accountable to produce good operating plans and then logically testing them, the third element of your role is to *teach*. We spoke of this responsibility at length in Part VI (Shaping the Team), and the optimizing of operating plans is one important venue where that teaching should take place. Your VPs of Human Resources, Sales and Operations, or the leaders of your businesses, are in a sense your assistant coaches, and it is their responsibility to go out and get the job done.

However, you are the head coach, and the most fundamental thing a coach does is teach those who report to him. We have often heard from team members who longingly remember earlier times when the CEO was truly their mentor, nurturing their skills and giving advice along the way. Today, they feel as if they've "graduated" to a place where it is assumed they know it all, and the CEO is reluctant to mentor them as he once did. Yet everyone at every level needs and values effective coaching, and your responsibility to teach your direct reports never ends, no manner how senior a title they assume.

In reality, the "testing" and "teaching" processes occur simultaneously. As you subject the operating plan to a tight logical grilling, you should avoid the temptation to "fix" whatever is wrong with the plan yourself — for as we've all learned about both our professional subordinates and our children, unless *they* internalize what is wrong with the plan and what *they* must do to fix it, any value gained by you fixing it will be short-lived. If you are to build a team and company, then as the adage goes your role is to teach others how to fish and not simply hand them a fish.

Finally, there is a fourth element of your role which is at least as critical as any of the others: You must ensure that the action plans of the different team members are integrated and well-*coordinated*. This task should be a regular responsibility of the entire team, but as team leader it is ultimately your responsibility to make sure that it happens. Inevitably, there are many ways in which the operating plans of the various team members must be coordinated — as well as many opportunities for them to undermine each other absent that coordination. Does the product demand which we expect to generate through the marketing and sales plans match our manufacturing plan and service delivery capability? Will the Human Resources plan deliver the people and training upon which the other operating plans are dependent? Do the resources required by each of the company's businesses add up to a total that the company can afford and is prepared to supply? Of all the reasons why plans fail to get achieved, some of the most difficult to foresee stem from unexamined or unanticipated ways in which they are interdependent, and only if you are disciplined and purposeful in leading coordination of the plans will those pitfalls be avoided.

In sum, you ensure that the strategy will be translated into action — fulfilling your fourth non-negotiable role as CEO — not by "doing it yourself" and not by handing it over to the team and simply trusting that it will be done effectively. Instead, through accountability, testing, teaching and coordination, you put your experience and vantage point to work to ensure the design of strong operating plans. Your job is not to "do" or simply "trust," but to coach and oversee, and by doing so you lead the process to its successful completion.

It may seem to some that there are not enough hours in the day and days in the year for the CEO to play such an active and disciplined role in the design of action plans — yet it has been demonstrated repeatedly by strong CEOs that it can and must be done. You can take the time to do it up front — or you can spend many times the upfront investment correcting problems that surface later. And if you choose the latter course, you can also continue to ask yourself why your team cannot seem to execute your strategy.

• •

Through accountability, testing, teaching and coordination, you put your experience and vantage point to work to ensure the design of strong operating plans.

• •

The most admired and consistently successful Fortune 500 CEOs are able to describe a detailed range of operating issues and challenges, and a plan to attack them, for every function and business within their organization. This understanding has been gleaned from rigorous and consistent involvement as a tester of those plans. Similarly, we've known CEOs of small- and mid-sized companies who are superb at teaching the members of their team to produce strong, logically tight action plans, while at the same time respecting their turf and avoiding the temptation to meddle. These CEOs are not necessarily smarter than less effective CEOs, but they do have a superior understanding of their fourth role — and with resolve and practice virtually any CEO can do the same.

So let's assume that you have that resolve and are determined for your team to effectively translate your strategy into action. The next question is just what does a good operating plan look like — and let's turn next to that question.

Chapter 45

From Strategy to Operations

A good operating plan can take a variety of forms, and it is not our intent to advocate one in particular. The right format for your company will depend upon a variety of factors, including the issues specific to your industry, strategy and company culture, as well as the personal preferences of you and your senior team. In particular, the nature of the operating plan will vary dramatically as a function of the size of the company. A large company should expect each individual business to develop an operating plan — and each of those plans in turn is likely to be far more detailed and thorough than one prepared by a small company, as the effort expended must be realistic given the available company resources.

Nonetheless, there are universal principles for what constitutes an effective operating plan, regardless of the nature or size of the company or the length of the written plan. You may opt for a relatively detailed or succinct operating plan, but in either case the plan needs to be consistent with these principles.

The first principle is the most central: *When implemented, the operating plan must ensure achievement of the strategy.* No statement could be more self-evident, yet in our experience it is the exception rather than the rule for companies to adhere to it. Too often, the writing of the operating plan becomes a time-consuming paper-production exercise, and those writing the plan are sloppy in tying the specifics of the plan to the ultimate objectives of the strategy. These plans may be quite impressive when measured by length or degree of detail, but amidst all that detail they lack conclusive demonstration that the various actions prescribed in the operating plan, when taken together, will produce the outcome stipulated by the strategy. In fact, too often we find that the length of the operating plan is *inversely* proportional to its linkage to the key elements of the strategy.

Recall the core strategic principle explored in Chapters 31 and 32: A good strategy must establish a real and significant advantage over your competitors in either differentiation or cost, aimed specifically at your target market. Correspondingly, the tactics enumerated in the operating plan must, when aggregated, produce the intended competitive advantage. When we review an operating plan the most important questions we ask of its authors are these: "We see all the good things you intend to do, and at first blush it is difficult to argue with any of them. But which tasks, when taken together, are the ones which will produce the core competitive advantage stipulated by the strategy? And where is the evidence that they will in fact add up to the advantaged position which you have targeted?" When you insist that in creating the operating plan team members consistently focus on these questions — and when you as the ultimate arbiter of the plan stick with these questions until you are fully satisfied with the answers — then your team is much more likely to produce an operating plan which truly supports the strategy.

The inter-relationship between your strategy and operating plan works in the other direction as well. *It's all fine and good to posit a strategy and a desired competitive advantage, but sometimes it is not until your team dives into the detail of the operating plan that the realism of the strategy can truly be tested.*

When, despite their best efforts, your team cannot design a set of actions which will produce the envisioned competitive advantage, then the strategy needs to be re-visited. But if you've done a good job of designing the strategy, you are unlikely to have to go to the extreme of throwing it away and starting over. Instead, the strategy may need to be refined in subtle but important ways so that an operating plan can be designed to ensure that it is achieved. The linkage between the strategic and operating plans is a two-way street, and testing it in both directions is a crucial step.

The operating plan needs to be entirely consistent with the strategy, but its content should extend to much lower levels of tactical detail. If the strategy calls for a major increase in sales effort aimed at a particular market, then the operating plan should specify how many salespeople need to be added, where you will find them, how you will train them, what support they will need and where they will be deployed. If the strategy prescribes a ten percent reduction in cost, then the operating plan should identify how much — and how — various parts of the organization will reduce cost so that the total reduction is in fact ten percent. If the strategy includes an increase in capacity to deliver your product or service, then the operating plan should specify how the new capacity will be configured and what the implications are for re-allocation of existing capacity.

> The real cost of overly cluttered operating plans is that, as a corollary, the analysis of the truly critical issues is usually insufficiently detailed.

Again, just how much of this is put on paper will depend upon your individual situation and the resources available, but however concise or detailed your written operating plan, the logic of it and its tie to the strategy had better be tight and thorough. If not, you are likely to miss critical operating issues which may doom the strategy to failure, regardless of the level of documentation. However, if in the past you have not put much of the operating plan on paper, we encourage you to find a way to do so, as the process of writing it down will focus your team on the logic of the plan and thereby improve your chances of success.

Although operating plans should include considerable tactical detail, they nonetheless should be hard-hitting and to the point, and should not be allowed to become a voluminous busy-work chore to be dreaded. If you allow the latter to transpire, not only are you wasting the time of some of your best people, but the process of generating plans will become rote and unthinking, and therefore lose its real value. The plan should get down to tactical specifics, but not so the team can "check the box" when they have successfully generated a large stack of paper. Instead, you want them to engage with and debate the critical details until they are sure that they are on target and can effectively implement the strategy. Operating plans which are as hard-hitting and concise as possible are much more likely to be fully read, understood and appropriately debated.

One important way to ensure the relevance and readability of the operating plan is to devote most of it to the critical initiatives where the risk of failure is higher than for business-as-usual activities. Much of what the team is responsible for each year is relatively routine, or subject to only minor modification relative to the prior year. These action items should be acknowledged in the plan, but discussion of them can be kept brief so as not to distract from the more challenging issues that require more thoughtful discussion and execution.

We've reviewed numerous operating plans where we've found ourselves suspecting and hoping that discussion of the truly new and challenging initiatives is included somewhere in the plan — but it has taken us multiple readings in order to cut through all the clutter and find them. The real cost of that clutter is that, as a corollary, the analysis of the truly critical issues is usually insufficiently detailed. For the operating plan to be properly focused, the emphasis on various issues should be proportional to their importance — and in particular to the degree of difficulty of their implementation.

Not only should the critical issues make up the bulk of the operating plan, they should also be the focus of your review and scrutiny as the leader of the team. The plan and your review should focus on initiatives for which:

- The resources invested are changing to a significant degree. This category includes initiatives which are brand new, being scaled up or down by a considerable amount, or being discontinued so that resources can be focused elsewhere. These types of actions imply a conscious re-allocation of effort, and such decisions should be highlighted and reviewed for consistency with the strategy. Furthermore, whenever there is new or increased investment in an initiative, there are also any number of ways in which the implementation can disappoint relative to the intention. As a result, these items are worthy of particular scrutiny to ensure that they proceed as expected.

- There are significant functional interdependencies. Sometimes, an initiative by one function will succeed only with the support and related initiatives of a second one. Alternatively, the actions of one function may have hidden consequences for other parts of the organization which need to be brought to their attention. Finally, a crucial initiative of one function may require staff support — such as from human resources or the legal department — which will limit the availability of those resources to the rest of the organization for a period of time. Quite often, these functional interdependencies trip up or slow down companies which are not disciplined in creating their operating plan. To ensure that the year proceeds as smoothly as possible, the operating plan is the right place to highlight these inter-relationships so that they are understood and anticipated by all.

In sum, a strong operating plan should be focused first and foremost on the critical initiatives, cordoning them off and highlighting them relative to business-as-usual items. For large and medium-sized companies this distinction between new and ongoing issues should also be reflected in the structure of other components of the planning process. For these companies, the operating plan typically will be the second link in a four-step process which includes:

- The strategic plan, which sets the fundamental direction of the company as well as its basis for competitive advantage;

- The operating plan, which includes a thorough detailing of what the organization needs to accomplish during the upcoming year in order to achieve the strategy; and which focuses on and explores in depth the key high-risk initiatives but not the routine items;

- The functional plans (for sales, manufacturing or operations, customer service, IT, human resources, R&D and so forth), which include the next level of detail for all items — both new and routine — and which is the focus of each functional group rather than the senior team;

- Individual plans, which specify the personal objectives for every member of each team throughout the organization.

Seen in this context, the operating plan is not the final step, but an intermediate one between the big-picture strategy and the details of functional and individual plans. That perspective highlights the role of the operating plan, which is not to be exhaustively detailed but rather to focus the team on a short list of hard-hitting initiatives which will make the greatest difference between success and failure in the year to come.

• •

A critical fork in the road is to decide whether the root of the problem is in the strategy or in the execution.

• •

Smaller companies may not have the resources for a written four-level planning process, but the thought process should nonetheless be the same, only typically with less documentation. As the CEO of a small company, if your thought process clearly identifies and separates the game-changing and more difficult operating initiatives from business-as-usual, you increase the odds that you will give the former the attention they require in order to be successfully implemented.

By its nature the operating plan should be concrete, and not abstract or wishful. One way to ground the plan in reality is to make it as tangible and quantifiable as possible. A strong operating plan should include:

- Specific actions stated in unambiguous terms, rather than broad directional statements;
- Clearly stated, quantified results to be achieved;
- Timelines, milestones and progress checks;
- Identification of specific key risks, and clearly articulated contingency plans to deal with them should a Plan B become necessary.

In addition to providing the team with unambiguous guidance, there is another benefit to clear measurability: When performance is not "up to plan" during the year, the quantifiable specificity can help pinpoint the cause of the shortfall. The only thing you know for sure about your operating plan is that events will not unfold exactly as it is written — because for every company there inevitably will be disappointments and surprises. (Of course navigating those unforeseen events is one of the reasons most of us enjoy being executives — if we wanted precision and certainty we would have become mathematicians or accountants.) And although the operating plan should anticipate all that it can, it remains the job of the CEO and her team to adjust to the problems as they occur, and in doing so keep the company on course.

In making the necessary adjustments, *a critical fork in the road is to decide whether the root of the problem is in the strategy or in the execution.* Depending upon the answer, the intervention of you and your team needs to take an entirely different form, and choosing the wrong solution is likely to be ineffective as well as de-motivating to your people. You want to avoid the futile exhortation of your team to step up their performance when the true problem lies in a strategy that is no longer right due to unanticipated changes in the environment. Similarly, you don't want to alter a good strategy when the real answer lies in more determined or skillful execution. The identification in the operating plan of clear actions and milestones provides you with a roadmap against which you can compare actual performance, giving you important clues as to the true nature of the problem.

We began this chapter by pointing out that there is no single correct format for an operating plan, nor is there only one correct process to produce one. Even if there were a "right" process, it would need to be different for companies of varying sizes. However, as a starting point for companies which do not currently produce an operating plan, or as a point of reference against which you can compare your existing process, we describe in the next chapter the broad outline of what makes for a successful planning process.

Chapter 46

Focus and Clarity

The starting point for development of your operating plan is your strategy. There is an almost infinite variety of potentially worthwhile endeavors towards which your people will devote their time and resources if left to their own devices. *The real value of the operating plan is to focus your team selectively on those activities which are the most valuable — and which together add up to a position of true competitive advantage for the company.* As we discussed in the previous chapter, it is unfortunately the exception and not the rule for CEOs to insist on operating plans which are tightly focused around the strategy. As a result, too often the operating plan is an amalgamation of pieces, each of which makes sense when reviewed in isolation, but which when added together are not likely to produce the targeted strategic and financial results. To make the operating plan truly worthwhile, you must maintain the discipline and focus to drive everything in the plan off of your strategy.

To make the translation from the strategy to the operating plan, begin by extracting from the strategy the key change elements, including both new initiatives and areas where performance needs to be significantly improved if the strategy is to be achieved. There should be a limited number of these key items, typically no more than four to eight. If the list is too long, there may be a question about the realism of the strategy and the ability of your team to implement it. Each of these change elements should be described explicitly and clearly, and you should test for concurrence among your team as to their precise meaning.

Next, each of these initiatives should be assigned an "owner" from among the senior team. In many cases the identification of the owner will be obvious and clear-cut, with little opportunity for choice or debate. However, in other instances selection of the owner will be a critical decision with important implications for the odds of success. Some initiatives will be cross-functional in nature, and the owner should be the person who not only can implement the required change within her own organization, but who also has the skills to secure the necessary cooperation from other parts of the company. In other cases you may decide that the best way to achieve a new direction or marked improvement is to assign ownership to a less obvious person who is more likely to take a fresh approach. Finally, you may sometimes find it useful to tie ownership of an initiative to a professional development objective which has been identified for a particular team member, or to use ownership to preview or test a change in responsibilities among the senior team.

It is the responsibility of the owner of each initiative to break it down into the component tasks necessary for its successful implementation. For each of those tasks, the owner should specify who has a role to play, the support they will need, and any other organizational interdependencies. Each task then needs to be translated into specific deliverables and timetables, along with identifiable risks and contingency plans.

The resultant detailed description of each initiative and its component tasks should be discussed, debated, refined and ultimately agreed to by the entire team, at which point firm commitments should be secured from all who will be involved in the initiative's implementation. Until each initiative is agreed to in completely unambiguous terms you have not completed this step, as you've allowed too much potential for things to go wrong as the year progresses. One of the key things which separates companies which successfully execute their plans from those where things go astray is their insistence on absolute clarity and tested concurrence with regard to each initiative and task within the operating plan.

Once the critical change initiatives and supporting tasks have been specified, the operating plan should place them in the context of a full list of responsibilities for each functional organization for the upcoming year, including business-as-usual items. As mentioned in the previous chapter, these routine items need not be explored in the operating plan in the depth with which they will be addressed in functional plans. However, they do need to be recognized and summarized in the operating plan so that the senior team has a complete view of what lies ahead as well as the implications for what resources will be required.

> In some cases the best way to achieve a marked improvement is to assign ownership to a less obvious person who is more likely to take a fresh approach.

It is usually instructive to separate the discussion of routine items into "line" and "staff" categories. Start with the line functions — consisting of those focused on developing, producing and selling your product or service — and express them in terms of deliverables, measures of performance and resources required. For example, the operating plan is likely to include specific sales targets, customer service level commitments, and performance targets for manufacturing or operations — as well as the tasks to be completed and the resources required to ensure the achievement of those deliverables.

The "staff" functions — such as human resources, legal or finance — should develop their plans in terms of what is needed to support the line organizations as they execute their plans. The staff plans should also include any tasks specific to the staff function itself, such as financial reporting. As with the line plans, the staff plans should be specific and action-oriented, including deliverables, timetables and resources devoted to each task.

For every function (whether line or staff), a critical yet often neglected step is to look for activities which can be *discontinued or scaled back* from prior years because of the company's progress or changes to the strategy. This part of the process runs counter to the basic nature of almost all organizations (whether business, governmental or non-profit), because it is easiest for people to simply do in the future what they have done in the past. However, all companies face tough competitive challenges which must be conquered with finite resources, and without a willingness to discontinue less valuable activities it becomes difficult to muster the resources required to successfully attack new opportunities and problems.

To help overcome inertia and resistance, it's often helpful to make the search for less valuable activities a conscious step in the development of the operating plan, to be conducted at least in part by the team as a group. The scrutiny of peers is often the best way for a functional leader to recognize when one of his organization's activities is ready to be scaled back. In any case, one of the most reliable indicators of whether a company achieves consistently strong or mediocre results is whether its CEO and leadership team insist upon a culture which continually pares items from previous operating plans at the same time that they add new ones.

Finally, all of the change elements and business-as-usual items need to be combined to produce an integrated operating plan which is then assessed for viability. You and your team need to rigorously test the plan along a variety of dimensions, asking questions such as:

- Do we have the resources to successfully achieve the plan, including types of people, skill levels and necessary support systems? If not, can those resources be added in a timely fashion?

- Can we afford the plan in light of our financial objectives? Is it too aggressive, with an unacceptable hit to profitability or cash flow? Or is it not aggressive enough, missing available opportunities which we could afford to pursue?

- Is the plan clear and focused? Can it be understood in consistent and unambiguous terms by all who will be responsible for its implementation? Are not only the tasks clear, but also the underlying logic? Testing by asking these questions is a critical step in producing a plan which is likely to be successfully implemented, and it is typically well worth the effort to test and refine the plan multiple times until it is crystal clear and agreed to by all.

- Does the operating plan get us to where we need to be? If we successfully execute the plan, will the strategy and targeted levels of financial performance truly be achieved?

- Is the plan realistic? Are we confident that we will pull it off, or is it merely a "wish" which includes critical elements which are likely to fail?

> Every hour which you skillfully invest in producing a superb operating plan is likely to save you and your team tens or even hundreds of hours later trying to correct problems which could have been avoided.

As CEO it is your role to be tough and disciplined in asking these questions, and to keep at it until the team has produced an operating plan which is on target and tightly focused. Inevitably, the payoff from your rigorous testing of the plan will be huge. Far from being an imposition on your time and that of your team, the testing is where the greatest value lies and is the most important determinant of whether you will produce a successful plan or a mediocre one. When you as CEO are disciplined and skilled in asking the right questions about the operating plan, then all elements of the plan will be improved: Key initiatives will be refined in order to raise their odds of success, each function will allocate its resources to the most valuable activities, and expectations for performance can realistically be raised for all parts of the organization. Finally, a tightly reasoned operating plan will uncover ways to refine and upgrade the strategy which gave birth to it in the first place, as you iterate back and forth between the two.

Throughout the process of developing your operating plan, the goal should be focus, absolute clarity and integration of the efforts of the various parts of the organization — and *not* complexity. To the contrary, unless the plan is reasonably straightforward and simple, both taken as a whole and for each function, then you've significantly handicapped its chances for successful execution. Your role as team leader is to tighten the logic so that it is focused and closely aligned with the strategy. When you have done so, then the path forward will be consistently and unambiguously understood by all.

Every hour which you skillfully invest in producing a superb operating plan is likely to save you and your team tens or even hundreds of hours later trying to correct problems which could have been avoided. Even more to the point, this upfront investment is typically the difference between companies which consistently achieve their strategic and financial objectives, and those whose CEOs and leadership teams are constantly scrambling either to plug holes in the execution of their operating plan or to needlessly re-cast their strategy. For all of these reasons, translation of your strategy into a strong and comprehensive operating plan is the fourth of your non-negotiable roles as CEO.

Chapter 47

Giving Them What it Takes

As we've observed throughout the previous three chapters, too many companies allow the development of the operating plan to become a relatively rote, unthinking process, resulting in failed implementation of the strategy as well as mediocre financial results. The same can be said for another activity which occurs downstream of the operating plan — the budgeting process. We find that most people, including CEOs, think of budgeting as an administrative process. *However, budgeting should instead be viewed from a much more enlightened perspective — as the means for allocating scarce resources to the strategic objectives of the company.* As such, it is a crucial step in the successful implementation of your plans and the achievement of the goals which you have set for yourself and your company.

As companies grow in size and budgeting becomes increasingly formalized, CEOs and other leaders often cease to engage with it intelligently, instead viewing it as a number-crunching exercise or political negotiation. However, if you are going to be true to your strategy and operating plan — if you are going to put your money where your mouth is — then the thought process around the allocation of resources needs to be as discriminating and intelligent as that for the operating plan and strategy. There is no point in rigorously testing and focusing the operating plan if you don't match that with an equal insistence on thoughtful and discriminating resource allocation, because without that you are dooming the operating plan, as well as the business, to failure.

While detailed discussion of budgeting is outside the scope of this book, in order to complete our discussion of what makes for a strong operating plan we want to briefly highlight some of the most common budgeting mistakes. They are all closely related, and may in fact all exist concurrently in the same company — and perhaps yours. We know from experience that if you reflect honestly, then more likely than not you will recognize some of these mistakes as being present in your company. By identifying these common errors in simple terms we hope to help you eliminate them — and in doing so continue the transformation of your company into an enlightened one which achieves enhanced levels of growth and profitability.

• •

If you are going to put your money where your mouth is, then the allocation of resources needs to be as discriminating and intelligent as the operating plan and strategy.

• •

The first point is that to ensure that budgeting is an intelligent process and not a rote one, it is critical that the plan lead the budget and not the other way around. Too often we have observed leadership teams which are able to conceptualize an inspirational vision, a winning strategy and a focused plan of action — only to abandon them because they assumed too quickly that the money wouldn't be available to fund critical components of the plan. Often what is lacking in these leadership teams is the requisite level of imagination and guts.

Why should it be surprising that a truly winning plan requires a marked departure in how resources are allocated throughout the organization? Aren't we looking for a marked upgrade in our marketplace and competitive success? Doesn't it stand to reason that to produce real change in our results we will also need real changes in how we allocate our resources? If you truly intend to break the mold of your historical results, then you have to back up the strategy and operating plan by giving managers the money it takes to win in the places that they truly need it. Then it is up to them to be both bold enough and organized enough to spend it well and to deliver tight, effective implementation.

Of course, as you craft the strategy and operating plan you have to keep in the back of your mind a general sense of what is affordable. But in doing so too many leadership teams keep themselves on too short a leash. There is a natural human tendency to stick to the familiar, yet what you are ultimately seeking are unfamiliar results. To achieve them, you and your team need to stretch to produce the most powerful strategy and operating plan possible. And for the team to deliver against that stretch plan, it has to liberate itself from budget-leads-planning thinking and turn it the other way around. While keeping a holistic sense of affordability in mind, the team needs to be reminded to creatively explore a strategy and operating plan with as long a mental leash as possible, and only later in the process to go about the business of creating a budget that fits the plan.

When you as CEO ensure that sequence of events, you'll find your team proposing bolder and more progressive changes, and also more decisively augmenting budgets in key places while saving money in others. This approach becomes more natural when you think of the process as one of resource allocation, and not just traditional budgeting.

> Doesn't it stand to reason that to produce real change in our results we will also need real changes in how we allocate our resources?

A related mistake is to budget based on the previous year. No budgeting approach could be more obviously rote and unthinking, yet because it is the easiest thing to do it is also the most common. Through your leadership as CEO, you need to establish a pervasive principle that resources are scarce and precious, to be allocated to only truly worthy causes. Every year (and in fact on an ongoing basis throughout the year), every business and function has to re-justify and re-earn the right to receive these scarce resources, and not just assume that this year's budget will be a few percentage points different from that of last year. Budgeting based on the previous year is a bureaucratic way of thinking and not a capitalist one, and if your company is to continue to thrive as it grows it had better maintain the latter mindset and not fall prey to the former.

Where the previous year's numbers *are* helpful is as a communications vehicle and as a check on the consistency of a proposed budget with the strategy and operating plan. Resource allocation, and hence the budget, should be based on fresh thinking every year, but that thinking is often best communicated by relating it to what has transpired in the past. A team member might explain, "I've proposed a 10% increase in call center expenses, to match our targeted 30% growth in our customer base coupled with a dramatic improvement in efficiency based on our recently implemented upgrade in technology." Or she might describe, "I've budgeted 40% less for product development because my business is approaching maturity and I know we are looking elsewhere for future growth."

• •

> "Let us understand this," we say to our CEO friends, "You're telling us that things are not going nearly as well as you'd like. So now you're going to cut everyone's budget a little in the hope that it will somehow lead to a dramatic turnaround. How does *that* work?"

• •

Proposed budget changes relative to the prior year, both positive and negative, should be expressible in terms of the key elements of the strategy and operating plan. You will know that you have a truly intelligent budgeting process when your team relates their budget proposals to key strategic initiatives and expresses them relative to the prior year — and in doing so proposes considerably more year-to-year variability in their budgets than they have in the past.

A third and related manifestation of ineffective budgeting is to treat all parts of the organization too similarly. Too often, companies budget by applying uniform percentage increases, or increases tightly grouped in a narrow band. Similarly, in tough times they may ask all departments to cut their budgets by a similar percentage. When we come across the latter example in particular, all sorts of alarm bells go off in our heads.

"Let us understand this," we say to our CEO friends, "You're telling us that things are not going nearly as well as you'd like. So now you're going to cut everyone's budget a little in the hope that it will somehow lead to a dramatic turnaround. How does *that* work?" In truth, the only way to achieve a major change in results is to actually *do* something that is markedly different and better, and then to back that up with an equally decisive re-distribution of budgeted resources. Budgets which go up and down annually by similar percentages across the company provide one of the surest clues that you're in the presence of a run-of-the-mill company and not a superior one. Yet decisiveness and differentiation, critical determinants of a sound budget, are relatively rare.

As CEO, the most all-encompassing budgeting decision you are faced with — and the one which you decide most directly — is the total level of resources to invest in the upcoming year. In doing so, you will be addressing one of the most fundamental and pervasive trade-offs in business — whether to pursue more growth or more profits, and in what proportion. Should we invest more aggressively now, taking a hit in short-term profitability, in the pursuit of growth and longer-term payoff? Or should we invest less in order to give our owners more return now rather than promises of an uncertain future? Not only is this one of the most critical decisions you face as CEO, it is also one of the most public: In addition to convincing yourself and your team of the right answer, you undoubtedly will also have to justify and sell it to your Board and shareholders — or perhaps to your family members (and your own wallet) if you are an owner/entrepreneur.

This critical decision is invariably a tough one to make. However, if you've fulfilled with discipline and focus the CEO roles which we've described throughout the book, then your profit-vs.-growth decision will be greatly leveraged and much more likely to be made in a high-quality way. Is your vision for the company substantive and well-directed? Will your strategy truly achieve the vision, and is your company capable of pulling it off? Do you have the right team and enlightened team processes in place to effectively manage the company? Is the operating plan logically tight and is it focused on the strategy? And — as we'll describe in Parts VIII and IX — do you have the right processes in place to follow through and communicate so that all of the above actually transpires as planned?

When you've skillfully fulfilled all of these roles, then the profit-vs.-growth decision, while still tough, is leveraged in several ways. First, you will be able to conceptualize and weigh the trade-off more clearly and precisely, because you've focused your thinking on the truly critical variables while clearing away much of the distracting clutter. Second, a strong vision, strategy, team and operating plan greatly raises the odds that the decision and targets you set for profit and growth will actually be achieved. And finally, by maintaining focus and decisiveness in carrying out all of your roles you provide yourself with a longer leash to attack the profit-vs.-growth trade-off — because you will have cut out inertial but unproductive and unprofitable activities and freed up additional resources to focus on the truly game-changing and growth-producing initiatives.

At the end of the day, what every owner or shareholder really wants is profitability *and* growth. And in today's highly competitive economy the only way you'll simultaneously achieve strong levels of both is by budgeting in an intelligent, decisive way — and by closely tying your resource allocation process to the enlightened fulfillment of all of your roles as CEO.

Chapter 48

You're Almost Home

We began this book by acknowledging the limits of power for the CEO. He has the title, recognition and prestige, yet in most cases remains frustrated with his ability to move the organization with all due speed in the direction he has chosen. In our experience this frustration is virtually universal, and among the greatest challenges facing the CEO.

We promised that the answer was not complex, and that it resided in disciplined and enlightened fulfillment of a short list of key roles. Now that we've completed exploration of the first four of those roles, most of that list is in clear focus. When you are doing a good job of those four — creating the inspiration, charting the course, shaping the team and translating into action — then you are almost home.

Of course, the job of the CEO (thankfully) is never done or even nearly so, as there are always unresolved issues, unfortunate surprises and new opportunities. So in that sense you are never "home." Even when you skillfully tend to the roles we have defined, you will continually have to return to them — updating, refining, and improving — for as long as you have the job.

Yet when you have turned the corner towards enlightened leadership and mastery of the roles you *will* be home in the most fundamental way: You will have conquered the CEO's dilemma of powerlessness. For when the vision clearly defines what is unique about your company; when the strategy charts a clear path towards competitive advantage; when you have shaped a team of strong players which operates with openness, candor and respect; and when you have translated the strategy into a crisp and focused plan of action — then you will have created enormous leverage for yourself and multiplied your power many times over. Now, as you envision the path forward, you have a focused and highly effective pyramid of people and processes in place to turn it into reality.

But before welcoming you *all* the way home, we first need to explore your two remaining roles: *Following Through* to ensure that your plan of action is in fact implemented; and *Communicating* effectively throughout your corporate world so as to continually support and reinforce all of your other roles. Let's turn next to the first of these, Following Through, in Part VIII.

Part VIII:
Following Through

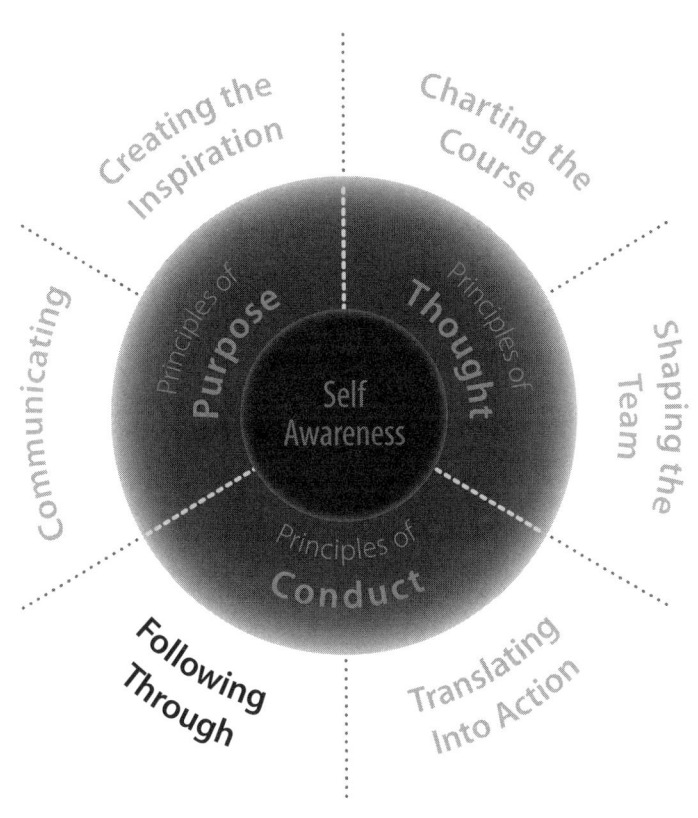

Chapter 49

Getting Results

One of the most common complaints we hear from CEOs (and have experienced ourselves) is the inability to get the team to follow through and deliver against the plan. Even when the path forward is agreed to by all, it inevitably seems that results are inconsistent and behind schedule. We doubt there is a single CEO anywhere who doesn't recognize this scenario and wish that there were more that she could do about it.

Of course, without follow-through all of the hard work that preceded it is significantly diluted. In the end, what matters for the CEO and the company are results — and not simply a great vision, strategy, team or operating plan, all of which are merely means to an end. For that simple but compelling reason, unless you as CEO are as committed to the skilled fulfillment of your fifth role — Following Through — as to the first four, you will never be as satisfied with your own performance as you would like to be.

The explanations for why many CEOs do not give this fifth role the attention that it deserves are familiar ones. They'd prefer to assume that their people are competent and will keep their commitments, and that for the CEO to focus on follow-through would constitute inappropriate micro-management. They find it drudgery. They are pressed for time, and the detail of follow-through strikes them as beneath their position and title. And it's more fun to focus on the "next problem" rather than to follow up and ensure that the previous one — which they've already "solved" — is successfully taken care of. The sum total of these avoidance mechanisms produces the universal frustration which we've described above: When you are derelict in ensuring follow-through, the actions which you and the team have prescribed simply do not occur with the regularity required to ensure that your efforts at your first four roles do in fact pay off in full.

• •

> When you as CEO become skilled at maintaining a good early warning system, you supply everyone — the Board, investors, the senior team and the organization at large — with confidence that the company is in good hands.

• •

There are many reasons why disciplined follow-through is necessary. First of all, you'll recall that a well-designed operating plan is focused primarily on those items which are most critical to the company *and* which carry the highest risk of failure. These are not business-as-usual items, but rather they are initiatives which by their very nature are challenging to implement. When you as CEO assume that with the mere identification of these actions your work is done and it's time for the team to take over, you are leaving far too much to chance. Instead, these critical but risky initiatives need to be monitored and managed in an organized way, so that the plan is not upended when an action item is either only partially implemented, or is completed too late to coordinate with other elements of the plan.

Second, a good operating plan also focuses on those initiatives which require a significant degree of cross-functional cooperation. That cross-functionality creates a different category of risk: Will the lead team member (the owner of the initiative) get the support he needs from other functions in order to deliver? Will the efforts of different parts of the organization be closely coordinated from a timing perspective, so that they work in tandem? Will politics and turf issues enter the equation and throw the effort off course? Is communication among different functions working as it needs to? By definition, the organization is not set up to deal with cross-functional issues as cleanly as single-function ones. As a result, particular attention is required to ensure the successful delivery of initiatives with cross-functional implications — which is likely to be a characteristic of many of the key elements of the operating plan. Just as you would expect each member of your team to ensure coordination among the different disciplines within his own organization, you as CEO must do the same for the senior team.

Third, it is the nature of business that the implementation of all initiatives, regardless of their focus, will require mid-course corrections. These adjustments will be necessitated both by unforeseen events in the external environment as well as internal implementation that does not proceed as planned. No doubt many relatively minor mid-course corrections can be handled exclusively by the owner of the action item. However, to the extent that the initiative in its original conception required the collective wisdom and concurrence of the entire team, it stands to reason that significant mid-course corrections may similarly need group buy-in and cooperation. As team leader, it is your job to manage an ongoing process which involves the entire team in important adjustments to the plan so that both the individual item and the overall plan can stay on track.

The fourth argument for your focus on follow-through stems from your role as motivator of the team. We all know that no matter how good the team, there will be variability in their level of energy and reliability, both across different team members and for individual people at different points in time. They also will be subject to distractions which will periodically impede their delivery of important initiatives. Near the top of the list of your responsibilities as CEO is to continually throw motivational logs onto the fire, so that all members of the team consistently move forward with urgency and focus.

Furthermore, you are far more likely to secure universal motivation and execution when the way in which you manage includes the use of nearer-term deliverables, and not just broad commitments to be completed over the course of a year. To fulfill your fifth role, you need to put in place a system which requires each owner of an initiative to define and deliver against its component parts, and to provide regular and frequent progress reports to both you and the entire team.

Fifth, as we described at length in Part VI (Shaping the Team), as CEO you are responsible to continually develop the skills and improve the performance of all who report to you. However, coaching is far more helpful when it is cast in specific terms relating to real-world problems, and not just in the abstract. As you work with team members to ensure follow-through, you are learning about who needs coaching and when, and around what types of issues. When a situation arises which requires coaching, you then kill two birds with one stone: You provide the help needed to keep the initiative on track, while also using that "teaching moment" to build the capability of the team member to attack not only this endeavor, but future ones as well.

Finally, *there is an overarching argument for a disciplined approach to follow-through, and that is to build an early warning system for your company which will dramatically raise the odds for effective execution.* All implementation problems — whether stemming from external surprises, cross-functional miscommunication, motivational lapses or the need for coaching — will come to light eventually, with or without an organized system of follow-through. However, absent that system, the problems will be recognized too late to be dealt with as efficiently and effectively as they should be. Delayed awareness of these issues will force you to waste valuable manpower repeating and reworking activities that should have been executed correctly the first time, or to create patchwork solutions which may create further, unanticipated problems elsewhere. In the process, you are also likely to throw delivery of the entire plan behind schedule.

With an effective early warning system, you and the team can address problems early on and make any necessary adjustments. The sooner the owner of an initiative shares the need for a mid-course correction with you and the team, the sooner all team members can update their own plans and expectations to fit the revised course of action. The same principle applies to relevant external constituencies, such as business partners and suppliers. And when you as CEO become skilled at maintaining a good early warning system, you supply everyone — the Board, investors, the senior team and the organization at large — with confidence that you are in control and that the company is in good hands. All of those constituencies have an intense desire for you to be a strong leader, and they are also very accurate observers and judges of your performance.

One of the things which will be most obvious to all is whether you are a CEO who can ferret out and deal with problems early on, or whether you're always back-filling and scrambling to keep up — and their confidence in you, the company and their own ability to do their jobs well will rise and fall accordingly.

In sum, there are numerous and powerful arguments for why CEOs need to apply the same focus and skill to ensuring follow-through as to the first four of their roles. These arguments are intuitive ones, and no doubt you've sensed them in the past — yet most CEOs struggle with giving their fifth role the consistent attention it deserves. Typically what is missing is a straightforward and disciplined approach to managing follow-through, based on a short list of key principles — which is the subject of the next two chapters.

Chapter 50

Monitoring Progress

An effective approach to follow-through, to an even greater extent than any of the other CEO roles, requires nothing more than basic common sense. In fact, every CEO works on follow-through every day, whether he is calling a meeting to work on a problem or picking up the phone to check up on his people and see how things are going. Quite naturally, the CEO focuses his inquiries on those initiatives about which he is most nervous. Perhaps the owner of the initiative is someone who has disappointed him in the past, or he suspects a particular item is the hardest to pull off, or earlier progress reports on an initiative have not been encouraging. He hopes that if he checks up on those situations with enough urgency in his voice, the heat will be turned up and the motivation will be provided to get a potentially problematic initiative over the hump and moving towards completion.

However, the behavior we've just described is not sufficient to constitute effective follow-through and the enlightened fulfillment of your fifth role. It may be effective in isolated ways, but it is too ad hoc: While some initiatives are being monitored others which are equally critical — and which may prove to be greater impediments to achievement of the plan — are being ignored. Often, even those initiatives which the CEO is inquiring about are being checked on with only erratic frequency and without thorough analysis and help. Effective follow-through *is* simply common sense, but it is *not* ad hoc. If you need further convincing of this point, ask yourself this question: "How often have I found out we were going to miss a key deliverable just before it was due — or in any case considerably later than would have been most helpful?"

The difference between CEOs who are strong at this fifth role and those who are not is that the former approach follow-through in a *regular, structured and thorough* way. In doing so, they minimize the odds that something will go wrong, and also provide themselves the greatest opportunity to take timely corrective action when it does. As a result, these CEOs see their vision, strategy, team and operating plan translated into the desired results, while the "ad hoc" managers are more likely to allow this fifth role to be the one that becomes their undoing by breaking the chain.

Fulfilling the role of follow-through in a structured, thorough way involves five steps:

- Setting milestones for key operating plan deliverables;
- Measuring results against those milestones;
- Analyzing any results that fall short of the milestones;
- Prescribing corrective actions;
- Updating the operating plan.

As promised, these steps are nothing more than common sense. However, the key is to stick to them in a regular, objective and relentlessly calm way — rather than scramble to plug holes when something doesn't proceed as planned or to simply berate an underling for missing a target as an expression of your frustration or panic. Too many CEOs rely on the latter approach to follow-through, but we've also been pleased to know CEOs (at companies both large and small) who conduct these five steps reliably and skillfully. For the latter, the usual reward is consistently strong bottom-line results for their companies.

The first step of follow-through — the setting of milestones — can take place either as part of the operating plan itself or shortly thereafter. The idea is to take each of the key initiatives in the operating plan and break it down into smaller deliverables with regular due dates, so that progress can be checked frequently. Each deliverable needs to be specific in terms of what will be done and when it will be completed.

Most importantly, it must be expressed in such a way that results are clearly defined and *measurable*, as without measurability there is no structured way to check on progress.

If as a key initiative you intend to increase the size of the sales force by 20%, then milestones might include specifying the search process, identifying a sufficient pool of candidates, interviewing them, making offers, hiring them and completing their introduction into the company — all expressed in terms of numbers of candidates at each step of the process and delivery dates. If the initiative is to bring a recently developed product to market, then milestones might include putting the final touches on development, conducting various types of market research, selecting the initial target market and marketing approach, readying the marketing materials and program, training of the sales force, and readying customer service and production for the new introduction.

> Effective follow-through is *not* ad hoc.

A useful way to think about milestones is in terms of "angst" (or the risk of failure). We know one CEO who, early in his tenure, had an involuntary reaction as he got ready to head to work each morning: He would instinctively take mental inventory of what was going on around different parts of his company that day, and hone in on the three or four things that he was most worried would not be delivered as promised. When he arrived at the office, he called the relevant people and checked up on those items. While his instincts regarding what to worry about were fairly good, the approach wasn't: It was ad hoc, identifying some items for follow-through but completely missing more critical ones which were hidden from view. Furthermore, the last-minute urgency of his follow-through disrupted the management processes of the people reporting to him, and left the impression that he was a bright but too impulsive leader, ricocheting from one issue to another without discipline and a steady hand at the wheel.

Eventually, he learned to channel his instincts and angst in a more consistently effective way. He came to appreciate the value of a disciplined and regular approach to follow-through, including the five steps described above. Furthermore, in defining milestones for each key initiative, he learned that the most useful milestones are those which correspond to where the risk of failure — or "angst" — is the highest. While focusing milestones on routine or easy-to-implement tasks may make the owner of an initiative feel or look good as they are checked off, that is not where the true pay-off lies.

The greatest value of milestones is to serve as the foundation of your early warning system — allowing you to uncover potential problems before they get out of hand and in doing so to keep the plan on track and on schedule. In other words, milestones should hone in on where problems are most likely to occur, and in selecting milestones you and the team would be well-served to start with the question, "What are the aspects of this initiative that concern us the most?"

• •

Companies which execute with consistency anticipate what might go wrong, and then build enough slack so that in any reasonable eventuality, the chain will remain unbroken.

• •

However they are defined, the sum total of the milestones for each initiative, once achieved, should ensure the successful completion of the initiative. If it is possible for the milestones to be met but implementation of the initiative to fail, then something critical is missing and your milestone list is not yet complete. As with all aspects of your planning process, the value lies not just in writing things down but in the intelligent discussion about what is written — and an important check on the process is to ask the initiative owner and the team whether they could imagine the initiative failing even if the milestones are achieved. In doing so, you may point the group towards an important issue which has not been considered but which needs to be added to the plan.

There is an additional point to be made about milestones — relating to the "margin of error." It is a more subtle point, but one which often makes the difference between successful and unsuccessful accomplishment of the plan. Too often, an initiative is broken into component milestones which collectively leave almost no margin for error. These initiatives are based on a "best case" scenario — a very thin and fragile string of action items, each narrowly dependent on the precise achievement of the previous one. In reviewing these initiatives, it often feels like it would take only one karate chop — or even gust of wind — from an unexpected source for the string to be broken, the initiative to fail, and the overall plan to be undermined. The owners of these initiatives have defined an action plan and milestones that *will* achieve the initiative if everything goes exactly as planned, but *only if* everything goes exactly as planned — and that is a bet that no good manager should be comfortable with.

Clearly, a plan with an insufficient margin for error is not a prescription for consistent, predictable success. Companies which execute with consistency anticipate what might go wrong, and then build enough slack into their milestones that in any reasonable eventuality, the chain achieving the initiative will remain unbroken. If you need three new productive salespeople to successfully grow in a target market but your past experience tells you that your hit rate for new salespeople to become productive is only 50%, then you had better hire six and not three or you are leaving too much risk in the plan. If an outside IT vendor has promised that a new system will be up and running in six months, but their track record is that they sometimes miss deadlines by as much as 33%, then the plan had better assume eight months or the system may not be operational when others are ready to depend upon it.

What we are advocating here is not a lack of aggressiveness or urgency, as we firmly believe in both, but rather aggressiveness based not on mindless exhortation and hope, but on real-world practicality. CEOs who consistently achieve the most impressive levels of execution inspire their team to stretch the farthest — but at the same time they expect them to remain level-headed in anticipating potential problems and to build in sufficient margin of error to prevent those problems from undermining the entire plan. This is particularly important for the key initiatives of your operating plan, because they are typically cross-functional in nature. When one member of the team misses a deliverable, the tightly developed plans of others may very well be disrupted.

With the milestones defined, the second step of follow-through is to measure results against those milestones. This should take place on a regular schedule — perhaps monthly — and with the whole team present. At these meetings, the owner of each initiative should report on his progress against each milestone, allowing the team to ask questions, identify additional issues and provide assistance as needed. If the setting of milestones (Step 1) was conducted thoroughly and thoughtfully, then this second step should follow in a logical, self-evident way.

> When you instill such a system, a culture of politics, obfuscation and "wiggle room" transforms into one based on determined follow-through and actual facts on the ground.

These regular report-backs should be documented in writing as well as delivered orally. The written version should be concise — because as with all parts of the planning process, length often obscures the most critical elements of the progress report — but it is important to put it on paper. First of all, doing so leaves less room for misinterpretation of exactly where things stand. Secondly, insisting that the report be documented in writing makes it less likely that an important item will be forgotten, either by the owner of the initiative in his oral report, or by the other team members as they check the report for thoroughness.

As the initiative owner reports on his progress, he should be encouraged to do so in *measurable* terms. It is not enough to say "things are going well," or "we're working hard on it," as such vague thinking is unverifiable. Too often, that approach leaves room for problems to grow undetected, until much later when the initiative owner is finally ready to say, "sorry, but things didn't go quite so well after all." Every milestone for each initiative should have been defined in measurable terms in Step 1, and in his report to the team in Step 2, the initiative's owner should present specific data comparing actual results to plan.

While many action items can be quantified in detail, the quantification of others can be more challenging. Many of the things which we all do as executives are qualitative in nature, with only subjective measurement possible. However, that subjectivity is not an excuse to avoid measurement. It is the responsibility of the owner of the initiative to define what is to be accomplished in as measurable terms as possible, even if subjective. Then at each report-back session, he needs to report on his progress in those same subjective terms as honestly and accurately as he can, backing up that assessment with whatever data is available. It is then the responsibility of you and your team to ask probing questions until you are confident that you agree with the team leader's subjective assessment.

More broadly speaking, both you and the team need to assess the quality of the initiative owner's progress report: Have the right milestones been identified or is something missing? Does the progress report have the ring of truth, or is the owner struggling but trying to appear self-assured? Does he have the skills and knowledge to bring the initiative to fruition, or are we headed for trouble? If these follow-up meetings become boring, polite and rote, then they are a complete waste of everyone's time. The only reason to invest all this time and energy is to get the critical and potentially troublesome issues on the table, and then to attack them honestly and objectively, while maintaining a tone of personal respect.

In doing so, you should insist on a culture that deals in reality and facts, and not in verbal gamesmanship or politics. A good, tight follow-through process should have the effect of minimizing "wiggle room." Rather than entrusting our hard-won vision, strategy and operating plan to a hope and a prayer — or merely to people's good intentions and vague assurances — an effective process of follow-through employs logic to break the plan down into bite-sized, verifiable pieces. On a regular schedule, as much objective data as possible is put on the table for all to see, and progress is checked to make sure that nothing is being left behind.

When you instill such a system and stick to it with resolve, it should not be too long before a culture of politics, obfuscation and "wiggle room" transforms into one based on determined follow-through and actual facts on the ground. In the process, you will build everyone's confidence — in the team, in you as CEO, and in their own ability to deliver against their initiatives.

Finally, as the initiative owner provides his progress report, it is important that you remember that this is *not* the time to be conducting a performance review. This is simply the time to report the facts and deal with the issues.

When you assume a tone that implies that you are grading personal performance, then team members will become defensive and will be inclined to hide the bad news — and that defeats the whole purpose of an early warning system. Step 2 of the follow-through process needs to be conducted with openness, candor and respect — as discussed at length in Part VI — and based on the enlightenment principle of calm. Your tone should be, "We need to hear both the good news and bad, and then to work together to solve problems and keep the initiatives on track. We are here to help and leverage each other, and not to pass judgment." Of course, there is a time and place for performance reviews, but they should be conducted holistically at a distance from the problems of the moment, and not in the context of a detailed session of progress reporting and follow-through.

Once the milestones have been set and progress against them has been measured, it is time to proceed to the last three steps of the follow-through process. We turn to these in the following chapter.

Chapter 51

Staying on Course

When progress against an initiative falls behind plan, many CEOs proceed immediately to trying to fix the problem. After all, they have ascended to their current position in part because of their bias towards action, and it is their nature to move with urgency to eliminate any barriers that stand in their way. When a barrier doesn't immediately succumb they re-double their efforts, raising the intensity and impatience with which they personally intervene — under the assumption that mere will is enough to solve the problem.

However, these CEOs are neglecting to first figure out the true reason why the given initiative is off-track — which is Step 3 of the Follow-Through process. As the owners of the various initiatives present their performance relative to milestones, the team needs to intelligently analyze the areas where results are disappointing, so as to determine the underlying reason for failure or delay.

In order to instill discipline into this analysis, you and the team should proceed through a mental checklist which is organized around two groups of factors. The first set of factors include structural and externally-generated issues, and you should ask questions such as: Is the plan fundamentally flawed in some important way, such as an objective that is unrealistically optimistic or parts of the plan that contradict each other? Is a key assumption off-base and in need of adjustment? (For example, you may have expected customers to be attracted by a new product offering, but in reality they are underwhelmed.) Has an unexpected action by a supplier, distributor or business partner thrown the initiative off track? Has the initiative been buffeted by an unexpected competitive attack?

Alternatively, the plan may be fine but the problem may be one of performance. If so, there are different types of performance problems, and you need to probe more deeply to determine the precise cause. Has the owner of the initiative been either disorganized or distracted by other requirements of her job — and has she therefore neglected to give the initiative the priority that it deserves? Has she failed to garner the necessary resources to get the job done? If so, is that because her function is over-extended and more resources are required? Or, does she have sufficient resources but needs more discipline in focusing them on the right priorities? Have resources and focus been sufficient, while the real problem lies in a skill deficiency of the initiative owner?

Remember, the initiatives included in the operating plan by definition involve stretching the organization to achieve unprecedented levels of accomplishment. As a result, it should not surprise you when even experienced high-performers on your team discover that the skills that have served them well in the past need to be augmented if the new initiative is to be successfully implemented.

There is no one "right way" to conduct the analysis of Step 3. However, if you and the team are disciplined in working through the mental checklist — and do so openly and objectively without putting the initiative owner on the defensive — then you'll be able to assess the true nature of the problem. The real value of Step 3 lies in asking the right questions, in order to uncover the root cause of the problem — instead of proceeding immediately to fixing its current manifestation. For example, failure to hit a sales target may not be a sales problem at all. Instead, it may be that the product given to the sales team is simply not competitive in the market — and you could hire and fire salespeople all day long without addressing the true problem. The best solution may not be the most obvious, and unless the root cause is identified the problem is likely to resurface in another form further down the road.

Of course, the reason to pinpoint where the problem lies is that different problems necessitate different solutions. Step 4 of the follow-through process is to take the necessary corrective actions, the design of which should flow directly from Step 3. In Step 4, as in Step 3, the first key question is whether the issue is structural/external in nature or one of performance.

When the problem is structural or external, then the team should return to the thought process which it employed in developing the operating plan. If a competitor, partner, or group of customers has surprised us, then what new tack can we take to maintain our forward momentum? If an element of the plan is flawed or an assumption unduly optimistic, then what other approach would achieve the same ultimate objective? As we discussed in Chapter 50, if you've built the appropriate margin of error into the plan, then you will have anticipated that there would be problems, even if you couldn't predict their precise nature. Consequently, it should only rarely be necessary to go all the way back to the drawing board and to lower your sights or redefine the strategy. Instead, once the structural or external problem is identified, you should be able to identify alternative paths forward which will achieve the same end result.

• •

> One of the strongest reasons for a disciplined approach to Following Through is to employ the skills of the entire senior team to attack the most important priorities of the company.

• •

When the problem is one of performance, then it is time for you to assume your role as coach. The senior members of your team are accustomed to success, and they are likely to be proud individuals as well. For those reasons, they will often be reluctant to admit that they need help. Yet when they don't ask for assistance even though they are failing to meet their milestones, their initiative is likely to fall further and further behind — unless you take the lead in fulfilling your responsibility as their coach. As you do so, it is critical that you distinguish among the various types of performance problems, and then tailor your advice to the true nature of the problem.

Does the individual need guidance as to how to better manage his time and priorities so that the initiative gets more attention? Is coaching needed as to how more organizational resources can be applied to the effort? Does the individual's skill set need to be augmented, and if so what is the best vehicle for doing so — a training course; an executive coach; or does he need to be teamed with another member of the organization who possesses the requisite skills? Are his skills sufficient, but he needs guidance as to how to get people within his organization to do what *they* must in order to deliver their portion of the initiative?

Although it is important that you supply steady doses of one-on-one coaching to the members of your team, all of the steps in the follow-through process, including Step 4, should be the responsibility of the team as a group. Most of the fixes that are required to get initiatives back on track are team ones, as the initiatives of the operating plan are typically challenging and cross-functional in nature. The primary responsibility lies with the initiative's owner, but when milestones are not being met it is foolish to ask him to solve the problem in isolation without the best thinking, assistance and cooperation of the other members of the team. This in fact is one of the strongest reasons for a disciplined approach to Following Through — to employ the skills of the entire senior team to attack the most important priorities of the company.

Whatever solution is identified to get an initiative back on schedule, it is critical that the team be realistic in applying enough firepower to the problem. In most companies, once milestones are missed it is more likely that over time the performance gap will become wider rather than close. Assurances such as "don't worry, we are on top of it and will fix the problem" are too readily accepted without supporting evidence, and issues are swept under the rug only to become bigger problems at the team's next meeting. Enlightened, disciplined leadership dictates that all members of the team — following your example as CEO — remain appropriately tough and honest in dealing with facts, recognizing the true severity of the barriers to progress, and taking the necessary corrective actions.

Once the team has addressed each initiative where milestones have been missed, the fifth and final step is to bring the overall operating plan up-to-date to reflect any changes that were made. It is a good idea to maintain an up-to-date operating plan at all times to serve as the group's guidepost, and to ensure that no one forgets — as can often be the case — exactly what has been agreed to at each meeting of the team. You should have a simple process in place so that at the conclusion of each meeting the relevant parts of the operating plan are updated. You should then distribute the revised plan to all team members with the adjustments highlighted.

In most cases, the adjustments should be tweaks — relatively minor changes to tasks, perhaps a new action item, or small adjustments to timing. Sometimes targets will need to be refined as well. If in fulfilling your fourth role you developed the operating plan in a disciplined and skilled way, it should be far less common for dramatic changes to the operating plan — or to the underlying strategy — to be necessary. However, when the plan is truly not working, it is the team's responsibility under your leadership to acknowledge that fact as early as possible, and then to adjust the targets, the operating plan or the strategy accordingly. To ensure that the need for a major change is recognized at the earliest possible juncture, each time the team meets to review progress you should conclude by checking that the team remains in agreement that the overall plan is correct and on track. Too many companies and CEOs rely on good intentions to get the company to the next level, when the right prescription is energetic aggressiveness tempered by fact-based honesty and realism.

As we've made clear throughout the last several chapters, the bulk of responsibility for Following Through in all of its aspects lies with the members of your team. Your role as CEO is to institute a high-quality and disciplined follow-through process, and — as lead member of the team — to ask tough questions and supply critical help as needed. By your example you will demonstrate to your organization the critical importance of a culture of follow-through, and through your oversight and leadership you will ensure that such a culture is consistently maintained.

As we stated at the outset of this discussion, the value of Following Through — your fifth role — is to ensure that the carefully laid plans which emanate from roles one through four do in fact come to fruition. Your final role — Communicating — provides the glue that binds the first five roles together, and is the subject of Part IX.

Part IX:
Communicating

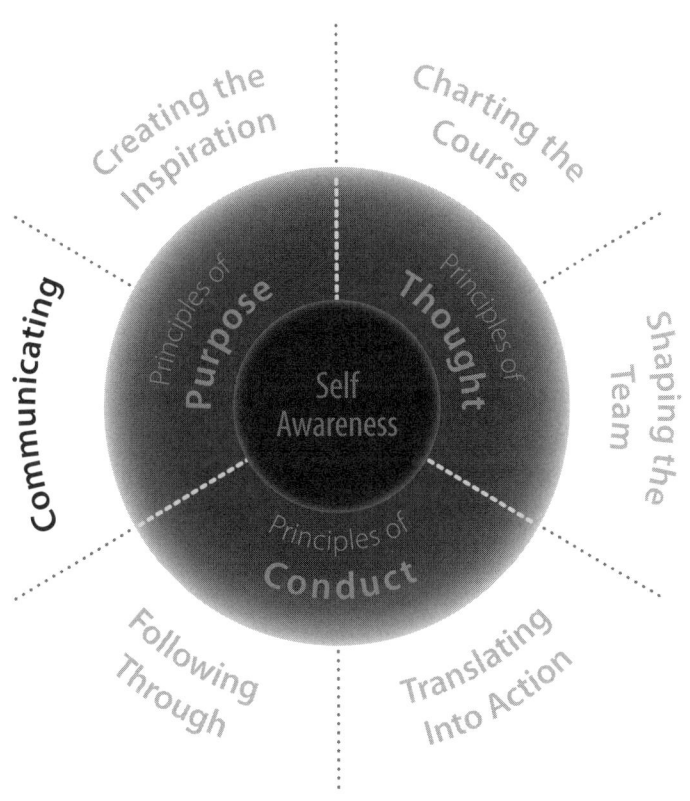

Chapter 52

Squandering the Opportunity

At a pivotal moment in the great 1995 movie <u>An American President</u>, Michael J. Fox (the hotshot political advisor) implores Michael Douglas (the President) to get out of the mental bunker he's been hiding in and give the American people what they crave. The President has been reluctant to respond to the tough and inaccurate attacks of Richard Dreyfus (his sleazy opponent, Bob Rumson), and Fox begs him to trust that the American people can handle the truth, and to go out and give it to them: "Bob Rumson is the only one doing the talking! People want leadership, Mr. President, and in the absence of genuine leadership, they'll listen to anyone who steps up to the microphone. They want leadership. They're so thirsty for it they'll crawl through the desert toward a mirage, and when they discover there's no water, they'll drink the sand."

• •

> The CEO does in fact enjoy celebrity within his company, but it is not because he is the most liked, the highest paid, the most skilled or the most charming.

• •

The people of your organization are similarly thirsty for your leadership. For reasons both practical and psychological, they badly want to be part of a winning enterprise. And they correctly sense that it won't happen unless you step up and make your presence felt in order to unite everyone in the organization in pursuit of your vision.

The CEO does in fact enjoy celebrity within his company, but it is not because he is the most liked, the highest paid, the most skilled, or the most charming — if those were the reasons then it wouldn't be so easy for people to turn their backs on the CEO when he doesn't deliver strong leadership. The reason you are a celebrity is because your people know how much they need you: Unless you reach out to them, help them understand their roles, and get all the parts of the organization working in unison, they know that the company is doomed to mediocrity and will not emerge as a true winner.

You can't lead if you don't connect with your people. And you can't connect if you don't communicate — or if you do so inadequately. We've never encountered a company where people don't crave communication from the CEO, and where a lot of good doesn't happen whenever the CEO communicates openly and honestly. Yet we encounter companies every day where the CEO fails to give this sixth of his roles — Communicating — the priority and careful thought that it deserves. The quality with which you communicate throughout your company is the great multiplier: It will either complete the circle of your vision, strategy, team, operating plan and follow-through, enabling them to be realized as planned, or it will greatly dilute your work on all of those elements and prevent the company from moving beyond its current position.

CEOs who communicate inadequately do so in a variety of ways, and all of those inadequacies are derivative of the personal elements which we explored in the discussion of Self-Awareness in Part III — the CEO's strengths and weaknesses, likes and dislikes, and needs and aspirations. All CEOs understand that communication is important, and all set off to fulfill this role with good intentions. Yet too often CEOs sabotage the effectiveness of their communication by allowing it to be too heavily colored and infiltrated by personal concerns which they've not fully recognized and resolved. Of the six roles, communicating is the most "personality-oriented" as opposed to "intellectual" in nature. It will therefore take particular self-awareness and focus on your part to move beyond an approach to communication that may feel easiest or most comfortable to you, and instead to provide the organization with what it truly needs.

One approach to communication which is of limited effectiveness is that of the CEO as "huckster." This CEO knows that one of his most crucial roles is to inspire the organization, and she sets out to boost spirits and offer encouragement to anyone within earshot. She describes the great future that lies ahead, conjuring up visions of the potential pay-off for all within the organization.

On the surface, there's nothing wrong with any of what we've just described — up to a point. However, the huckster CEO relies on this mode of communication too exclusively, and carries it too far. When roadblocks and disappointments materialize — as will always be the case no matter how successful the company — this CEO sticks too tightly to her stock message. Rather than honestly face up to the severity of the problem and *work with others to solve it*, she presents a cheery "What, me worry?" face to the organization. Her own insecurities prevent her from communicating honestly, as she's afraid that if she admits a serious problem it will reflect on the quality of her leadership. Of course, the exact opposite is true: By *not* acknowledging what is apparent to others, she reduces her credibility as leader.

• •

> In the void that the CEO has created someone less qualified or well-intentioned will step up to the microphone, and the people of the company may be left "drinking sand."

• •

A second variety of poor communicator is the CEO as "manipulator." He is a glad-hander, briefly expressing his interest in some aspect of the work or personal life of each employee he encounters, and offering a few seconds of impassioned and "charismatic" encouragement before quickly moving on. In return for the privilege of being in the CEO's company, he asks the employee to go the extra distance to deliver whatever the CEO needs at that particular moment.

Again, interaction with and concern for your employees is a good thing, and it is part of the equation as you ask them to give their all for the organization. But when the CEO relies on superficial ingratiation as a motivator, it is only a matter of time until he is seen as a phony, and until the reactions he engenders turn from inspiration to resentment. As with the huckster, this CEO underestimates the observation skills and intelligence of his people. They can tell the difference between sincere interest and manipulation — if not at first, then certainly over time as the CEO repeats this pattern of behavior again and again.

A third variety is the CEO as "bully." Lacking the maturity or patience to inspire people the right way, this CEO relies on intimidation — and her power to promote, fire, and pay, which she keeps handy at all times just beneath the surface of her communications — in the attempt to force people to do what she wants. The problem with this approach, even apart from its inherently disrespectful and unpleasant nature, is that it is much easier to successfully intimidate less skilled, less confident and less marketable people than to do so for the strongest and most valuable people in the organization. Over the long haul, intimidators lose their best people while retaining the others.

A fourth form of inadequate communication is exhibited by the CEO as "recluse." This CEO simply doesn't enjoy the sixth of his roles, and as a result he communicates far too little. He may be somewhat quiet or shy in nature, and more inclined to the cerebral parts of the job. He simply does not feel comfortable in the role of communicator. To justify his aversion, he may convince himself that it is a silly waste of time to try to connect with and inspire the unwashed masses, when time could be better spent working on the truly big decisions that cross his desk.

And finally, there is the "avoider." Like Michael Douglas as President, he is afraid to engage and communicate because he does not want to deal with the tough questions that people will ask. Instead, he finds it more expedient to avoid them by keeping to himself. The problem, of course, is that just because he is avoiding them doesn't make them go away. As in the movie, in the void that this CEO has created someone less qualified or well-intentioned will step up to the microphone, and the people of the company may be left "drinking sand."

To some degree we've presented these five fictional CEOs as caricatures, and we certainly don't expect that you will absolutely equate yourself to any one of them. Yet if you are honest in assessing your own approach to communication, then you are likely to recognize elements of one or more of these inadequacies — or of perhaps others — in the way you communicate. *However, your sixth role as Communicator is too powerful a multiplier — either positive or negative — of the first five roles for you to allow these inadequacies to persist.* When you are willing to search inside yourself and exorcise your demons, and to step up and be a strong and positive communicator, then you greatly raise the odds that the company will achieve your vision — and that you will become the CEO you want to be.

Ask yourself what's holding you back. What are you afraid of? Yes, frequent, open and honest communication takes work and involves risk. It is easier to merely decide and delegate, and then to simply assume that the rest will take care of itself. The reality, however, is that the world is not that simple, even if you'd like it to be. Unless you engage this sixth of your roles with deep thought and effort, the rest will *not* take care of itself, and you'll be left at the end of this book at the same place that you started — as a CEO frustrated with his own powerlessness. Communicating is the sixth of your non-negotiable roles, and the one that completes the circle — in ways that we explore in more depth in the following chapter.

Chapter 53

The Rewards of Communication

There are at least five powerful reasons for you to make the investment in frequent and high quality communication to your organization. The thorough reader will notice that all of these reasons hark back to points made in earlier sections of the book, and there is a good explanation for that link: The fundamental role of communication is to reinforce and solidify all that you have done in your first five roles as CEO. We will summarize those reasons here, to make the case all in one place for why it is so important for you to move beyond the inadequacies described in the previous chapter.

The first and most obvious reason for communication is to make sure that *everyone understands the plan*. Remember the old childhood game of "telephone"? The first person whispers a message into a second person's ear, who then whispers it to a third person, and so on down the line. By the time the last person reveals what she has heard, most of the original message has been either lost or garbled. If the content of the message were an action plan which required the cooperation of all of the people in the game, then this group would be in big trouble.

The game of telephone is all too often a metaphor for how communication takes place in corporations. The CEO and her senior team set the company's agenda, but then the word is carried forward only inconsistently. The CEO gives a motivational speech or two. Some members of the team transmit the message thoroughly and accurately to their entire organizations, while others do so less thoroughly or less accurately. People whose jobs are cross-functional in nature or who exist in corners of the organization may never get a full briefing.

Furthermore, as the year progresses and the CEO and her team make changes to the plan, they neglect to continue the communication process and alert the organization to the changes in a systematic way. The net result is that different groups and individuals are operating with different mental blueprints all at the same time. This is an enormous handicap to place on a company while it is stretching itself to reach higher levels of accomplishment and performance.

When you have fulfilled your first five roles as CEO you've completed much of the hard work — but you haven't finished until you've taken the final step of communicating clearly, thoroughly and repetitively to the entire organization, so that all know exactly what is expected of them. Furthermore, you need the message to remain current as changes take place, which requires communication to be a continual and never-ending part of the fabric of the company.

・・・・・・・・・・・・・・・・・・・・・・・・・・・・・・・・・・・

> The enlightened CEO thinks of himself
> first and foremost as a teacher.

・・・・・・・・・・・・・・・・・・・・・・・・・・・・・・・・・・・

Yet merely telling employees what is expected of them is not enough. Not only are people from time to time likely to run into problems in fulfilling the routine aspects of their job, the initiatives included in the operating plan are likely to present particular challenges as the company stretches to conquer new terrain. As we discussed in Part VI (Shaping the Team), one of the most fundamental roles for all managers — including the CEO — is to *teach*. Teaching can't take place without substantive communication, which is why it is the second powerful reason for you to commit to your role as communicator.

The teaching imperative is one of the problems with the profiles of inadequate communication included in the last chapter. If you are a recluse or an avoider, you aren't engaging enough with your people to teach them sufficiently. If you are a huckster, manipulator or bully, then you are communicating with your people, but in terms that are either divorced from reality or focused on superficial transactions rather than serious content. It is always tempting — and saves time in the short-run — to dismiss a subordinate after a brief directive coupled with an implied incentive or threat.

Yet frequently what the subordinate also needs is discussion and *help*: Is there anything ambiguous in the directive which requires clarification? In the various steps required to implement the directive, are there particular components which could provide problems? Is there advice you can provide as to how to surmount them? Or by discussing the potential problems would the two of you recognize trade-offs which would lead you to refine the directive and orient it in a somewhat different direction? By virtue of your vantage point and experience, is there any other coaching you can provide which is likely to improve the end result?

The enlightened CEO thinks of himself first and foremost as a teacher. In all of his interactions, he listens carefully and probes for where and how his coaching could be valuable. And because he appreciates his value as a teacher, he reaches out to the organization to connect with his people as frequently and substantively possible, all the while looking for opportunities to coach — and in doing so to raise the performance of the company.

When the CEO and his team are disciplined in sharing the plan and in teaching, they realize the third reward of communication — *motivating* their people. As we explored in depth in Part VI, the surest way — in fact, the only enduring way — to build loyalty is to respect the intelligence of your people and include them in the most important thought processes of the company.

Try this experiment: Ask a friend whether he likes his job — and then explore the reasons why or why not. If he doesn't raise the point, ask him how much he thinks he's learning on the job. We've asked these questions countless times, and we've found that how much one is learning is a more accurate predictor of when people enjoy and are motivated by their jobs than any other single factor. As CEOs ourselves, among the most gratifying feedback we've ever received are communications from employees telling us they've learned more at our company than in any job they've ever had — and citing that learning as the primary reason they've been willing to give their all in pursuit of the company's aims.

Conversely, CEOs who expect their people to dedicate themselves to the company, while keeping them out of the loop or not making the time to share their experience and perspective, are betting on an imbalanced bargain. Building enthusiasm and dedication across a company of any size is a major challenge, and when you attempt to do so without a commitment to frequent and skilled communication, you are making your job far more difficult than it needs to be.

As Michael J. Fox explained to Michael Douglas, people are rooting fervently for their leaders to be strong. However, they are also acute and accurate observers when their leaders are undistinguished or weak. And that brings us to the fourth reward of communication, which is to foster and maintain your *credibility* as CEO.

• •

By sharing the plan openly with the organization and gauging their reaction, you keep the plan grounded in the real world.

• •

A mixture of good and bad news reverberates every day through the halls of your company. Along with successes, there are inevitable setbacks and challenges, some of them quite serious. Your employees certainly are aware of them, because they are in the trenches and are the ones expected to overcome them.

When you as CEO remain above it all, sequestered or whistling your happy tune as their world grows more and more challenging, you've forfeited your credibility as leader. Your employees need to know and to see that you understand the real world — and not just your vision for a brighter future — or they'll dismiss the latter as fairy-tale fiction. As communicator-in-chief, the enlightened CEO connects with his people by celebrating successes *and* acknowledging problems — with a bias towards the *whole* truth, and towards coaching and assisting others to deal with reality in the best way possible. This is a complex message to convey, and it can't happen unless you are willing to commit yourself fully — in terms of time, energy and intelligent reflection — to the sixth of your roles as CEO.

Finally, the fifth reward of communication derives from its nature as a two-way medium. As you reach out to your people and learn about their progress in their roles, you are likely to learn at least as much as they do. Which aspects of their efforts are going according to plan, and which are not? What unexpected hurdles have been encountered? Are customers behaving as we expected? Are there issues in production, operations or technology which run counter to our initial assumptions? What personnel or process issues have emerged which need to be resolved in order to keep the team operating at maximum efficiency?

Communication serves as a *feedback mechanism and test* of all that you and your team have developed in your first five roles. By sharing the plan openly with the organization and gauging their reaction, and by hearing their experience in implementing it, you keep the plan grounded in the real world. Is the vision still precisely on track, or does it need to be refined in order to keep the company pointed in the right direction and your people inspired? Is our strategy producing the intended competitive advantage, or are real-world results suggesting that a modification to the course is called for? Are the teams throughout the organization operating based on the principles of openness, candor and respect, or are selected interventions required? How should the operating plan be updated and upgraded to reflect the day-to-day experiences of those in the field? Where do we need a more concerted effort to ensure follow-through?

By virtue of this feedback, your sixth role as CEO — Communicating — leads directly back to the first five. Rather than fulfill the six roles sequentially, the enlightened CEO does so simultaneously, forever cycling through the roles so that they mutually reinforce each other. Over time and with practice, the enlightened fulfillment of all six roles can become instinctive, at which point they can merge into a unified mindset for the CEO as he engages with his company every day.

Communication has five extraordinarily valuable rewards: to ensure understanding of the plan; to teach; to motivate; to build credibility; and to feed back and test. Each one of these rewards is so important that by itself it would constitute reason enough for you to invest your time in regular and frequent communication. In combination, the power of these rewards to leverage and drive your company's success is so great as to make "Communicating" a non-negotiable element of enlightened leadership. If you truly are searching for new achievement and satisfaction as CEO, then part of that process must include stretching to be a more purposeful and skilled communicator — so as to realize all of the rewards that come to those who do so.

Chapter 54

Enlightened Communication

As with the rewards identified in the previous chapter, the principles of enlightened communication should be familiar ones to the thorough reader, as we've highlighted them throughout the book. As a result, we'll summarize them relatively succinctly here, so as to have a complete description of enlightened communication all in one place.

The first principle relates to the quantity of communication. As we've described, your effectiveness as CEO will be proportional to the time and energy you and other leaders in the company invest in communication, with that investment measured along two dimensions. For one, your communication should be as pervasive as possible, reaching out to all corners of the organization and to all of your employees. Communication will vary in form and content based on the audience, but all employees need to be informed and inspired, and all will benefit from being included in the process.

In addition, you can't assume that once you've said something to a given audience you've completed the job. Good communication requires frequent repetition, so as to reinforce the message, continue to inspire, and stimulate up-to-date feedback which may be different from that offered the last time the message was delivered. It is virtually impossible to communicate too much, and you should be disciplined in ensuring that you reach out to all audiences on a regular basis.

Beyond the pervasiveness and frequency with which you reach out to the organization, the core principles of enlightened communication are openness and candor. If you invest much time and energy in communication, but spend most of it by simply delivering stock and superficial pep talks or making small talk with employees, then you are wasting your time and significantly diluting your effectiveness as CEO. The real power of communication — including the power to teach and to influence how your people spend their time — comes from delving into the real issues, opportunities and challenges in an honest way with as wide an audience as possible.

As we've reflected, secrecy is over-rated. While there is always selected information which must be kept confidential, many CEOs and managers tend to include far too many items within that veil of secrecy — to the detriment of organizational effectiveness. Your people are smart enough and the rumor mill is strong enough that they will have a general sense of many of the "secrets" anyway. Your choice is to give it to them straight so that you can deliver the message appropriately — or to allow them to fill in the blanks through a process of questionable accuracy, influenced by people whose agenda may not be as well-directed as yours.

• •

> Beyond helping your employees do their job, sharing the underlying reasoning behind your directives in all of your communications is a wonderful discipline to instill on yourself.

• •

Not only is secrecy over-rated, but when extended too broadly, it can be destructive. It impedes teaching, as without the relevant context and information employees will not know how best to direct their efforts. And it is also de-motivational, as no one appreciates being left out of the loop. Conversely, when you share important information openly and candidly you are far more likely to inspire and energize your people in pursuit of the company's objectives.

A related principle — one that is helpful to keep in mind as a guide to help you remain open and candid — is to respect the intelligence of all with whom you communicate. All of us receive a steady flow of communication from a wide variety of sources — politicians soliciting our vote, co-workers seeking our cooperation, and social acquaintances or family members in search of friendship or help, just to name a few. If you were to do a careful analysis of which communications are successful in motivating you towards action, you're likely to find that one of the key delineators is the degree to which the speaker either talked down to you or treated you as an equal. CEOs who remember that their title makes them no better a person than the hourly worker in the call center or assembly line communicate in a way that says, "we're just two people with different jobs and different areas of expertise." These CEOs are more likely to naturally communicate openly and candidly, and in the process, they are also more likely to engender the enthusiasm and loyalty of their employees.

To extract maximum value from your investment in communicating, it is important to share with your audiences the reasoning behind your decisions, and not just the decisions themselves. Because the world is complex and ever-changing, after you've given direction to an audience and then moved on, unexpected variables are likely to surface which raise new questions about their course of action. If your communication is narrowly focused on what to do, then they may not make the right decision as to how to adjust.

On the other hand, when you share the thought process, trade-offs and reasoning behind your directives with your audiences, then you've not only directed them but taught them as well, and as a result they will be better equipped to make good decisions when adjustments become necessary. The more all understand the vision, the strategy, the operating plan and the enlightened team principles that are driving the company, the more effective they can be in doing their part to keep the organization on course to achieve its objectives.

Beyond helping your employees do their job, sharing the underlying reasoning behind your directives in all of your communications is a wonderful discipline to instill on yourself. When you find yourself struggling to explain a decision, or moving quickly past it because you sense that the reasoning won't stand up to close scrutiny, then what *you've* probably learned is that the decision may be suspect and you have more work to do. (Often in these cases, you'll discover that the reason you can't justify the decision to others is because it is grounded in your personal concerns or needs rather than what is truly best for the company.)

Furthermore, when you know that you will have to justify your directives to others, you'll learn to fully check the logic *before* you communicate your decision — as you'll remember how uncomfortable it felt standing in front of an audience with only incomplete or poor reasoning. You'll more reliably ensure that your decisions are correct before you disseminate them — which is another reason why enlightened communication helps produce not only more informed and motivated employees, but also more effective CEOs.

In order to maximize your learning from communication, it needs to be as two-way as possible. In all of your interactions, the more you discipline yourself to listen carefully, the more you will learn. In particular, you should train yourself to probe for not only the obvious message, but also for deeper levels of what is really on the speaker's mind. As CEO you are likely to be an intimidating figure, which will cause employees to test the waters before delivering their true message. When you cut off discussion or respond too quickly, you are likely to lose the truly valuable part of the communication — which may be lurking just beneath the surface.

• •

> Employees need to be full partners in the communications process — trusted not only to hear information, but to understand it in its full complexity, and to feed back their contribution to the decisions faced by the company.

• •

The principles of enlightened communication which we've described — pervasiveness and frequency; openness and candor; respect for employees' intelligence; underlying logic; and communicating in both directions — are all grounded in the overarching principles of *humility* and *trust in your people*. Truly enlightened communicators — those who can go beyond merely giving a snappy speech and instead inspire large numbers of people over sustained periods of time — have found genuine humility. They recognize that in the face of significant challenges and opportunities, they do not have all the answers. They know that no CEO — no matter how talented — has much power to succeed on his own. Instead, he needs the willing, informed and carefully orchestrated cooperation of everyone in the organization, which is only achievable when communication is given the attention it deserves.

Furthermore, these CEOs appreciate that for the whole organization to work together, their people need to be more than mere recipients of information. Instead, they need to be full partners in the communications process — trusted not only to hear information, but to understand it in its full complexity, and to feed back their contribution to the decisions faced by the company.

Finally, it is not possible for you get away with faking this humility and trust for very long. You either genuinely appreciate the value of full communication with your people, or you don't. When you are insincere, it will be readily apparent to others and your attempt to inspire energy, effectiveness and loyalty will be correspondingly diluted.

As a result, the true foundation for the skilled fulfillment of your sixth role as CEO resides all the way back at the core of the enlightenment principles of Part III — self-awareness. When you search inside yourself and reflect honestly about what has kept you from getting to the next level — when you recognize that you can't do it all yourself and that you've not yet captured the full power of the organization — then you will have found genuine humility. And when you do so, you will be ready to trust in the good intentions, skills and power of your people which, under your stewardship, can create a truly stellar company. With a foundation of self-awareness, humility and trust, you will be ready to become a truly enlightened communicator.

Chapter 55

Leveraging Your Board

While the principles of communication which we've described are relevant for a variety of audiences, we'd like to focus a bit longer on additional issues which are specific to your communication with one constituency in particular — your Board of Directors.

Although all public and private-equity-funded companies have functioning Boards, many smaller enterprises do not. Whereas *very* small companies may find it impractical or not economically feasible to form a Board, for companies of any appreciable size the value of a Board will outweigh the cost — *if* you communicate with the Board in an enlightened way. Smaller companies are often better-served by an Advisory Board rather than a formal Board of Directors, as the former can provide many of the same benefits while avoiding the legal requirements and higher costs of the latter — which may prove prohibitive either for the company or for Board members.

Entrepreneurs who are understandably consumed with the challenge of growing their companies may be slow to consider the value of forming a Board. Early in our career as a CEO, we ran a closely-held company with revenue in the tens of millions of dollars, yet with no functioning Board. With twenty-twenty hindsight we recognize the folly of having done so, as many of our most costly mistakes could have been caught in time by a properly functioning Board. If you are running a company without a Board, yet are large enough to afford one, we encourage you to strongly consider putting one in place. Generally, it is not that difficult to find qualified individuals to serve who are also affordable.

Whether you have a Board of Directors or an Advisory Board, your communications should be structured so as to unlock and capture the full potential value of the Board. There are two primary values to be realized. First, the Board should be a check on and contributor to your thinking. A well-constituted Board should have the intellectual capability, the personal disposition and the experience to appropriately question and test your vision, strategy, plan and personnel decisions. They are also likely to bring new ideas to the table which enhance the quality of your most important decisions. By communicating constructively with your Board, you are in effect widening your base of experience, drawing upon additional good minds — rather than just your own and the minds your senior team — as you attack the opportunities and challenges faced by your company.

• •

Nothing is less rewarding for a Board member then to give of her time only to see it employed carelessly and unproductively.

• •

Secondly, a fully engaged Board should be a valuable source of contacts for you and the company. If you have staffed your Board, as you should, with individuals having a variety of backgrounds, then they should be able to make introductions to all sorts of key external constituencies — including potential financing sources, business partners, customers, key hires and suppliers. Once again, the Board serves to widen the circle of contacts beyond yours and those of your internal team.

An interesting trade-off that arises from these two fundamental Board roles relates to the optimal size of the Board. For the Board to truly and consistently enhance the quality of your thinking, Board discussions need to do justice to the subtlety and complexity of key issues, and not just skim the surface. In-depth exploration of valuable perspectives offered by Board members is more likely to occur when the Board is not too large. In our experience, there is a clear and consistent *inverse* relationship between Board size and the quality of Board discussions. Boards with as few as four people (if they are the right people) are in some cases optimal. With as many as six to ten members, well-functioning Boards may still be able to fully explore the views of all members. However, when Board members number a dozen or more, the challenge to avoid meetings which are superficial and disjointed becomes greater.

On the other hand, the second value of a Board is as a source of contacts, and for those purposes, the larger the Board, the better. Over time your company is likely to be able to benefit from a wide diversity of contacts — perhaps a potential business partner in China, someone with an "in" at a key customer prospect, a referral to a financier or headhunter with a particular specialty, or a candidate to be your new CFO. Yet when you minimize the size of your Board, you reduce your odds of striking gold by finding just the right contact.

We have no one-size-fits-all advice for you as to how to resolve this trade-off, other than to suggest that you decide based on the relative importance you place on the two Board roles which we've described. However, we'd like to add one note of caution. Of the two Board values, we have found that CEOs more commonly understand the value of contacts, while at the same time being more likely to structure their Boards and Board communications so as to miss much of the opportunity to enhance their thinking. To the extent possible, we encourage you to limit the size of your Boards to a level that allows for substantive, probing discussions, and which enables Board members to fully contribute to and serve as a check on your most important decisions.

Regardless of the size of your Board, you will maximize its value only if you optimally leverage your time together. In our experience as Board members, we are frequently struck by the poor choices made by CEOs in utilizing scarce and potentially valuable Board member time. Relatively trivial issues which could be dispensed with quickly — or which should never have been included on the Board agenda in the first place — often consume significant chunks of time. At the same time, truly pivotal issues where the Board could make a valuable contribution are either dealt with too quickly or ignored altogether.

When you structure Board time in this way, you not only squander the opportunity to receive potentially valuable advice, you de-motivate your Board as well — because nothing is less rewarding for a Board member then to give of her time only to see it employed carelessly and unproductively. As CEO, it is your job to set the Board's agenda and to ensure that it is focused on the issues of greatest import for the company.

When Board time is mis-allocated in this way, it is not always — or even usually — due to carelessness. Instead, many CEOs endeavor to consume Board time with less critical issues so as distract from items which are more important, but which the CEO is reluctant to subject to Board scrutiny. The issue in question might be one where the CEO simply "wants to do his own thing," or for which he is afraid he has no good answers to what would inevitably be tough questioning by the Board. When a CEO communicates with his Board in this way, there is something fundamentally and seriously wrong at the core.

One possibility is that the CEO senses that he is pursuing the wrong course — one that is unlikely to be successful, or that is based on a personal agenda — and that he therefore must obscure the issue from his Board. Alternatively, if the CEO *is* making the right decision but believes that exposure to the Board would force his hand in the wrong direction, then he has the wrong Board or Board process and needs to do something about it. Whichever of those two possibilities is at work, the CEO and his Board are out of sync and headed for trouble.

In order to stay in sync with your Board, it is your job — as the full-time employee in the relationship — to avoid surprises by keeping Board members current on key performance metrics and issues facing the company. Surprises are avoided when you are honest in forecasting future results — neither making promises you are unlikely to keep nor sandbagging so as to exceed expectations.

Furthermore, a CEO who is a skilled Board communicator is able to anticipate issues of concern to Board members, and initiates discussion of those issues *before* the Board feels a need to do. If either you *or* the Board is consistently blind-sided by what the other has to say, then you and the Board will spend too much time dealing with gaps in communication — rather than working together to attack the opportunities available to the company and to enhance its chances of capturing them. In fact, the steadiness and collaborative quality of your Board communications is likely to be a very reliable indicator of the consistency and quality of the company's results.

Finally, although your Board members are likely to be accomplished and experienced professionals, they still need to be motivated just as your employees do. Furthermore, the key to motivating Board members is the same as for employees. What Board members want is to be trusted, to be fully in the loop, to be respected for the quality of their thinking and not just for their contacts, and to be dealt with openly and candidly. To motivate your Board and produce the most value for your company, you must allow them to be full (if only part-time) partners with you as CEO in the pursuit of the company's vision and objectives — and you must communicate with them in an enlightened way worthy of a full partner.

Chapter 56

Swimming with the Tide

Throughout the entire book, we've argued consistently that the enlightened CEO is one who errs on the side of openness and candor. He promotes transparency throughout the organization, tempered only in limited ways, and only for specific and well-justified reasons. In our view, the case for transparency in communications has always been a powerful one, and as a result it has infused our advice to CEOs as well as the way that we ourselves have functioned as company leaders.

We hope that the many arguments we have made on behalf of transparency throughout the book have swayed you, and have encouraged you to embrace it in your role as CEO. Yet for those of you who still may harbor reservations, we offer one last argument — namely, the predominant communications trend — or rather seismic shift — of our time. It is a force with far-reaching implications not only for business, but for economics, governments and society at large.

We are speaking of course of the explosion of communications technology, and of its implications for information availability. A number of illuminating books have been written on the subject — including Friedman's <u>The World is Flat</u> and Tapscott and Williams' <u>Wikinomics</u>, to name two — and we will not attempt to replicate them here. But one essential point of those books and others is that old business models grounded in hierarchy and the hoarding of information are crumbling — and they are rapidly being replaced by new and extremely powerful models based on transparency and open-source collaboration. As CEO, you can choose the speed with which you adapt to this transformation, but you have no ability to stop it from happening, either in your industry or anywhere else. You can either swim with the tide or try to hold it back, but only the first of those two options will propel you in the direction of your company's objectives.

In the 21st Century, it is simply no longer possible to tightly control most information, even if you wanted to. We recently observed one CEO who ill-advisedly orchestrated a series of internal meetings so as to avoid acknowledging looming bad news which he thought he could keep secret — only to be "outed" and ridiculed for that approach within hours in an anonymous discussion among employees in an online — and very public — chat room. Whether the news is good or bad, the combination of natural human curiosity, the value of information, and the multiple ways in which it can be distributed widely, instantaneously and for free means that we're all operating in a new paradigm. A CEO who remains stuck in an old-world model based on information hoarding truly is swimming against a very powerful tide, and runs a serious risk that he will never make it back to solid ground.

On the other hand, CEOs who embrace the new order of transparency — and who resolve to make it work *for* them — have at their disposal a weapon whose full power we are only beginning to comprehend. For starters, when you share all the knowledge that you possibly can with your employees you maximize their contribution to the company, as they are able to fully leverage their efforts based on the knowledge of others. In fact, companies which base their communications on openness and candor are frequently and pleasantly surprised by their employees — who not only do what is expected of them, but who are stimulated by the shared knowledge to put their creativity to work and to contribute in unexpected ways.

More broadly, enlightened companies are reaching far beyond their own walls to share information openly, and then capturing external contributions that can be brought to bear on behalf of the company. As reported by Huston and Sakkab in the Harvard Business Review, in order to maximize innovation Procter & Gamble has re-structured its research efforts so as to tap the ideas of 200 scientists from *outside* of P&G for every one actually on the company payroll. In doing so, the company has effectively expanded its R&D staff from 7,500 to 1.5 *million* — not by building a bureaucracy, but by sharing information openly and broadly and then working with outside innovators to integrate the best ideas into the company. Enlightened corporations in all industries are applying this model to every conceivable business discipline, from consumer marketing to software development — yet it is clear that for all that we have witnessed so far, it is still just the tip of the iceberg.

Way back in 1597 Francis Bacon reflected that knowledge is power, but the challenge today is how *many* people you can empower with that knowledge. Old school leaders withhold information in an attempt to concentrate power in their own hands and retain an advantage over others. Enlightened CEOs, on the other hand, disseminate knowledge and communicate as widely as possible, in order to empower all within the company, as well as many outside of it — so that they all work together in an informed way in pursuit of the company's vision and objectives.

> CEOs who embrace the new order of transparency —
> and who resolve to make it work for them — have
> at their disposal a weapon whose full power
> we are only beginning to comprehend.

By the way, we are witnessing the same contrast today among governments in various regions of the world — with the same results. Backward-thinking heads of state who insist on keeping large parts of their population uneducated or ill-informed may gain an advantage in keeping themselves in power, but in the process they are relegating their country to the margins of economic and social progress. Again, whether you're running a company or a country, you can choose to swim with or against the tide — but you are powerless to hold it back.

The explosion in the availability and affordability of information means that success today lies not in owning information, but in marshalling it with maximum effectiveness for the benefit of the company. That, in turn, requires the enlightened leadership of the CEO — as he infuses the company's culture and all of its activities with the principle of transparency. The seismic shift in information availability which has exploded all around us is both an argument for enlightened communication and a powerful weapon in its service. As CEO, it is your job to be on the right side of this historic trend, and to put it to optimum use in pursuit of your company's objectives.

Part X:
Your Future as CEO

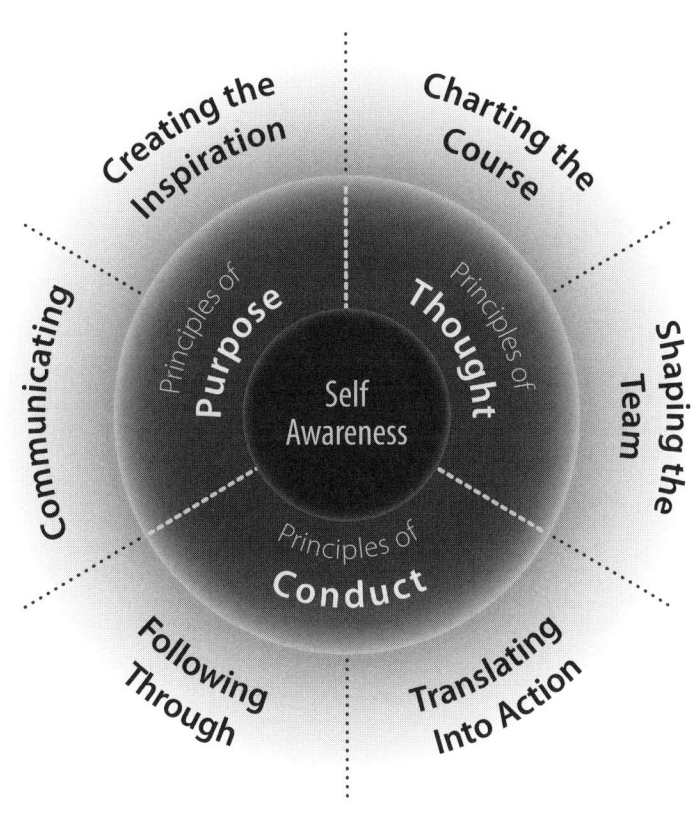

Chapter 57

Your Power … Over You

In the time that it took us to write this book, a dozen high-profile CEOs suffered a very public fall from grace. Some failed to deliver results, others rubbed employees, the Board or investors the wrong way, and still others were guilty of ethical lapses. At the same time, many of our friends who are CEOs of small and mid-sized companies continued to struggle as their companies moved sideways, failing to realize much of the opportunity which the CEO had targeted.

Every day, CEOs of all stripes continue to search for greater satisfaction from their jobs. Typically, they are stimulated by the challenge of the job and enjoy its prestige. Yet CEOs are hard-driving people with very high standards, and relatively few are fully pleased with their own performance. The CEOs we know continue to look for the missing pieces of the puzzle which will enable them to arrive home each night knowing that they have mastered the most difficult job in business — and that they are enjoying themselves in the process.

We have been fascinated by and have reflected on this phenomenon for three decades, as we've worked side by side with hundreds of company leaders. We've also had at our disposal a deep well of experience from our own tenure as CEOs, as we've considered which aspects of the job we ourselves have conducted well or poorly, and why. For sure, some of the obstacles faced by CEOs and their companies have their origins in factors over which CEOs have only limited control — technological upheavals in the marketplace, competitors with entrenched advantages, the scarcity of superb people with which to staff the team, or the inherent challenge of implementing a major new operational or

IT system. Part of the difficulty of the job of CEO is the wide range of issues for which he is responsible, and the very real and sometimes intractable barriers which stand in his way.

Yet the longer we have studied this quandary, the more we have been struck by how much of the solution lies *within* the CEO's control, and how much of the frustration is in fact avoidable. Even better, we've been heartened — elated really — to discover that the solution *is* in fact straightforward and not complex; and even more importantly, it is well within the reach of virtually any CEO — *if* he truly is motivated to do what it takes.

The reason that so much of the frustration is avoidable is because so many of the problems are of the CEO's own making. As we write this, CEOs of companies both large and small continue to dive directly into operational details without first crafting a vision and strategy which charts a realistic course towards true competitive advantage — and without that strategic course, all the operational details amount to nothing more than the spinning of wheels. Other CEOs design powerful strategies, but then neglect the details of operating plans and follow-through — simply because they find them a chore, and not what they like to do. Yet others allow their personal demons and insecurities — and not the company's needs — to be the primary driver behind their team interactions and communications — with the corresponding achievement of massaged insecurities rather than the desired company performance. CEOs reap what they sow, but therein lies the cause for optimism: When you change what you sow, you will change what you reap.

Thankfully, this transformation does not require the magical acquisition of more intellect, or the assimilation of an advanced and complex body of knowledge, or the infusion of a new personality. Rather, you need only embrace a straightforward set of principles, grounded in common sense, and to adhere to them with a discipline which is motivated by the ambition for yourself and your company which you already possess.

For the transformation to take hold, you need to accept that all six of your roles as CEO are in fact non-negotiable, and that each must be fulfilled with a clear-headed focus that will allow the skills of you and your team to be brought to bear. You must inspire with a unique vision; chart a course to competitive advantage; shape an effective and motivated team; translate the strategy into a focused plan of action; follow through with discipline; and communicate broadly with trust and transparency.

It is not overly difficult to fulfill these six roles with excellence, but it is quite easy to screw them up. To get them right, you must imbue all that you do with the tenets of enlightenment: The Principles of Purpose, including the primacy of the company's agenda over your own and acceptance of all of your roles; The Principles of Thought, including openness, the quest for understanding, and objectivity; and The Principles of Conduct, including calm, humility and a sense of equity. These principles collectively serve as your North Star, keeping you focused on what matters most for your company, and on how to carry yourself as CEO so as to inspire and motivate others to achieve the company's objectives.

Yet if you are to keep the principles of enlightenment in sight at all times, you need first to take account of the personal factors that often obscure your view — your own strengths and weaknesses, likes and dislikes, and needs and aspirations. At the core of your six roles lie the principles of enlightenment, and at the core of enlightenment lies an honest self-awareness. For without that self-awareness, you will continually sabotage your pursuit of enlightenment and the skilled fulfillment of the six roles, as your personal demons dilute your efforts and divert them in the wrong direction. Only when you are willing to search inside yourself, to understand your own motivations and to take accurate stock of your current approach to leadership relative to the one we have prescribed, will you have unlocked the final piece of the puzzle and be ready to achieve excellence for both yourself and your company.

In truth, there are some CEOs who we will not be able to reach — much less help — with this book. If you are unwilling to be introspective, then we may have provided a few helpful ideas, but over the long haul nothing fundamental will change and your historical pattern of results will persist. If you are unable to find genuine humility, then it will continue to be all about you, and you will fail to fully galvanize those around you in pursuit of the company's objectives.

And if you're not highly motivated to re-invent yourself as a very different and far more effective CEO, then you'll be scared off by the size of the mental leap which we've prescribed. As a function of the arc and rhythms of our careers — and of our personal lives — there are times when we are ready to make a big leap and times when we are not — but the fact that something caused you to pick up this book and to read it suggests that you may in fact be ready. If so, we hope the book has helped locate for you the higher ground towards which you are ready to leap.

And when you make that leap, the impact will be profound. The journey towards enlightenment is a straightforward one, but it truly will take you to a very different place. Your team, your employees and all of your constituencies will recognize your newfound sense of purpose, direction and self-confidence. They will admire your discipline and principled focus, and over time adopt it as their own. And you yourself will feel like a very different person, as in discovering and embracing enlightenment you will infuse your waking hours with a newfound sense of accomplishment and fulfillment. Yes, if you are to make the principles of this book your own you may need to change markedly as a CEO and as a person — but it may be exactly the change that you have been searching for.

We began this book by acknowledging the powerlessness that is a persistent and central frustration of the job — a frustration that only we CEOs fully understand and appreciate. As CEO, you are likely to have a good idea of where you would like to take your company, but marshalling all of your resources to move as one in the desired direction is a whole different matter. We've argued throughout the book that the true secret to your power lies in your inspiration to and guidance of others — as you teach and empower them to pursue a clearly reasoned path forward, guided by principles of enlightened purpose, thought and conduct. When you have learned and internalized that it is your six roles and the principles of enlightenment that are paramount, and not your personal needs as CEO, then you will have solved the dilemma of powerlessness and will successfully lead your company in the desired direction.

So now the rest is up to you.

Perhaps the principles which we've espoused will fade quickly from your consciousness, crowded out by the crises of the moment, familiar rationalizations or old habits. Or perhaps you will commit to a change that is clearly within your reach, and that will have profound and permanent implications for both your own success and that of your company.

If you do commit to that change, then you will be exercising another power — one which is most within your control, and which will have the greatest impact of all. You will be exercising your power over *yourself* to be the type of CEO you choose to be. For while there are elements of your environment over which you have limited control, you do have the power to lead with the focus and clarity that will optimize the performance of your company relative to whatever the truly uncontrollable variables may be. The most important part of the equation — the one that resides at the heart of all the others — lies directly within your control and reach. It is your power to become an enlightened CEO, and in doing so to unleash the full potential of your company. We'll be rooting for you, and we'll be continuing on our journey as you proceed on yours.

Acknowledgements

The two of us would like to thank three people without whom you would not be reading this book. Paul Favaro produced several of the critical conceptual breakthroughs which caused The Enlightened CEO to take its current form; he is the unnamed "third author" of the book (see the Preface for more details). Beth Eckstein marshaled and managed the resources to get the book produced, and for almost 20 years has been an incredible team member and an extraordinarily devoted friend. Troy Bishop brought his artistic talents to bear to make the book, we hope, easy on the eye. The five of us worked some long hours together, but always with openness, honesty and mutual respect, and we could not have asked for better partners.

This book represents a major stop along a lifelong journey, and each of us would like to further acknowledge some of the people from whom we have learned the most along the way.

Gordon:

I would like to thank all the people with whom I have worked over the years as they provided the feedback that brought reality and practicality to all I read and learned, and which formed the foundation for much of my contribution to this book. Once I learned to be open to it, the greatest lessons and feedback came from the most unexpected places. While I learned from my bosses, peers, and friends, the most sobering (and useful) feedback came from those who worked directly for me and a vast number of others who worked many levels lower in the organization. Those brave souls were always willing to "give it to me straight" and to them I owe a great debt of gratitude for the success I have achieved in my career. Although I am reluctant to single out a few among the legions of people, I must recognize Bill McCausland and Rolando Espinosa who helped shape one of our greatest successes, and in so doing, helped shape me. I also want to thank the most overlooked members of my teams through the years – the many executive assistants who provided unbiased feedback that otherwise never would have reached my ears. Their counsel was invaluable.

It is also important for me to recognize those who are responsible for the foundations of my life, upon which I built my business career. The recently deceased Roger Katz came into my life just seven years ago, but he will be an inspiration for the remainder of it. My late parents, Gordon and Elsie Quick, came from very humble backgrounds, but they gave me not only the opportunity, but the humility which made my successes possible. Working at my father's side from the age of five taught me more about dealing with people than I can begin to express. And last, but certainly not least, is my lifelong partner, confidante, critic and best friend – my wife Jeanelle. Without her encouragement, guidance, and never-ending support I could never have accomplished what I have and enjoyed it so much along the way.

Bob:

I would like to thank all of my professional partners and employees for their insights and contributions, and for their forbearance during my least enlightened years. I can't possibly name them all, but I'd like to single out Michael Kaiser, Lance Pryor and Lisa Hawes for being by my side in the formative years; Ed Boyce, for his outside-the-box thinking and for having the courage (to this day) to always tell me the truth; and Abigail Gorman, for her unparalleled professionalism and integrity, and for being the person I can trust with the things that are most important to me in life. I'd also like to thank all of my clients past and present: I have learned so much from each and every one of you, and you have my utmost admiration and respect.

Joel Kanter and Keith Ghezzi have been rock-solid friends who I know would do anything for me if I asked; and Michael Epperson has been my comrade-in-arms whenever I needed to get away from it all. Alfred Messore has been my mentor for 26 years: It is impossible to express how much he has taught me about professional success, personal happiness and what really matters in this world, and I cannot imagine where I would be without him.

Michael Fifer, Karen Fifer Ferry, Janet Bolen and Dave and Sarah Catron have all been role models, and I carry part of each of you with me every day. Stanley and Therese Fifer provided me with the best education that money can buy when they could barely afford it, showed me what a great marriage is all about, and through their example taught me about love, family, hard work, ethical ambition and the overcoming of adversity. Danny, Becky, Jonathan and Amy Fifer inspire me with their intellectual curiosity, the goodness in their hearts, and their accomplishments and dreams; a day doesn't go by when each one of you doesn't make my heart sing. And Nancy Catron is the love of my life, my best friend and the wind beneath my wings. I wake up every day surrounded by extraordinary family, friends and professional associates, and for that gift you all have my everlasting gratitude.

The Authors

Gordon Quick has served as a senior executive for most of his business career of 30 years. He has been the CEO and COO of both private and public early stage companies, and has also run divisions for a Fortune 500 company. In most cases, he has entered the business when a turnaround was required, and left it after achieving rapid growth. He has also led a very early stage company to just under $100 million in revenue, ultimately resulting in the sale of the business for $800 million. He has taken a private company public and a public company private.

As CEO he has had experience with many different cultures while managing offices all over the world and working with customers on six continents. Gordon has worked in a variety of industries, including software, fixed and wireless telecommunications and transportation/logistics. He has found the principles of successful stewardship of a company to be quite consistent across these various assignments.

Gordon earned undergraduate and graduate degrees in economics, marketing and management, culminating with a Ph.D. from the University of Florida.

After decades of leading businesses and companies, Gordon formed CEO Mentors, LLC. His goal is to share his hard-earned lessons with other CEOs, enabling them to accelerate their learning process and achieve lasting success.

Gordon can be contacted at:

CEO Mentors, LLC
800 South Hanley Road — Suite 5E
St. Louis, MO 63105

www.CEOMentors.com

Gordon@CEOMentors.com

Bob Fifer is President of Fifer Associates, LLC. During the past twenty-eight years, Bob has provided advice to CEOs in the areas of corporate strategy, growth and profit maximization, and operational and human resources excellence. His clients have included a dozen of the Fortune 50 and numerous smaller firms both public and privately-held.

Bob is a counselor to his clients as they manage and motivate their teams, align their organizations, and optimize the functioning of their Boards. He has served as a motivational speaker for hundreds of corporate audiences. He has also been CEO of several of his own companies, including one which he purchased when it had eight employees and sold, 18 years later, as a thriving company with subsidiaries on five continents.

Bob graduated from Harvard College in 1977 with a degree in economics, and from Harvard Business School in 1979. He has authored a variety of books and articles, including the internationally acclaimed *Double Your Profits* in 1993, which became required reading at thousands of companies large and small. Bob is also General Partner of Kaiser Capital Fund, L.P., an investment fund, and has served on a variety of Boards of Directors and Advisory Boards.

Bob can be contacted at:
Fifer Associates, LLC
123 River Park Lane
Great Falls, VA 22066
www.FiferAssociates.com
RFifer@FiferAssociates.com

The authors welcome your feedback.

Ordering The Book

Additional copies of the book may be ordered at:

www.CEOMentors.com

or

www.FiferAssociates.com